From the Press Box

First published in 2013 by
Liberties Press
140 Terenure Road North | Terenure | Dublin 6W
Tel: +353 (1) 405 5701
www.libertiespress.com | info@libertiespress.com

Trade enquiries to Gill & Macmillan Distribution
Hume Avenue | Park West | Dublin 12
T: +353 (1) 500 9534 | F: +353 (1) 500 9595 | E: sales@gillmacmillan.ie

Distributed in the UK by
Turnaround Publisher Services
Unit 3 | Olympia Trading Estate | Coburg Road | London N22 6TZ
T: +44 (0) 20 8829 3000 | E: orders@turnaround-uk.com

Distributed in the United States by
Dufour Editions | PO Box 7 | Chester Springs | Pennsylvania 19425

Copyright © Peter Byrne, 2013
The author asserts his moral rights.

ISBN: 978-1-909718-15-9
2 4 6 8 10 9 7 5 3 1

A CIP record for this title is available from the British Library.

Cover design by Nina Lyons
Internal design by Liberties Press

Front cover images: Arkle (Private Collection), Henry Shefflin (Creative Commons
Library), Packie Bonner, Brian O'Driscoll (Creative Commons Library),
Ron Delany (Private Collection)

Every effort has been made to contact copyright holders and to secure permissions. In
the event of any unintentional omissions, please contact the publisher in writing.

From the Press Box

Seventy Years of
Great Moments in Irish Sport

Peter Byrne

LIB
ERT
IES

– Contents –

– Foreword –
by Sonia O'Sullivan

Many years ago, at a time when I was still only dreaming about making a career for myself in sport, I came across a book written by Peter Byrne called *My Part of the Day*. It was comprised of a long list of great sporting occasions, national as well as international, and it fired me with the thought that if I worked hard enough and got lucky enough I might, just might, get my name into a book like that, one day.

Fast forward thirty years or so and I get a call from Daniel Bolger at Liberties Press, telling me that Peter has written another book along similar lines, my story is in it and would I like to write a preface for it. No second invitation needed and here I am, wide-eyed and as enthusiastic as I was all those years ago, wallowing in the memories of many of the great days in Irish sport.

I'm not old enough to have known or even seen some of the people who feature in this book. But their achievements and the stories of those achievements are told in such a way that I'm transported back through the years to share in the exhilaration of the good days and the heartbreak of those occasions when even the best wasn't good enough.

I've known both in my time in athletics, and browsing through these pages I'm struck by the thought that while much may have changed for competitors and spectators alike in the second half of the twentieth century, the chemistry that went into the mix in the making of sporting idols all those years ago is still largely unchanged in the modern world.

Every generation needs to be inspired by the legacy of the ones that went before and it is in this context that Peter Byrne's recollections from his days in the press boxes of sports stadia around the world, can be inspirational for the children dreaming of one day wearing the green of Ireland in big international events.

As a child, I recall the grownups talking in almost reverential tones of the days that Ronnie Delany won his Olympic 1,500 metres title in 1956. All of thirty years had passed since his wonderful run in the Melbourne Cricket Ground, a place I would later get to know very well, but the way those people spoke, Ronnie's gold medal might well have been won just the day before.

I was well aware of that brilliant achievement growing up but for me, the real role models were people like Frank O'Mara, Marcus O'Sullivan and Eamon Coghlan who were closer to my age group. Marcus and Eamon, of course, were Villanova graduates and when I got the chance of going there on an athletics scholarship, that certainly helped when I first dipped my toe in American collegiate competition.

And then, of course, there was John Treacy, who followed up his two world cross country titles with that magnificent run to take silver in the Olympic marathon championship in Los Angeles. How can you quantify the benefits that flow from achievements like his, in showcasing Ireland and the image of Irish people as a vibrant, upwardly mobile race?

Coming from my background, it is only natural that I should put forward athletics as a sport which has done much to generate good publicity for the country. But I am also conscious of the great public relations work that other sporting associations continue to do in promoting Ireland abroad.

I was just starting out on my international career when Jack Charlton was working his little miracle with the national football team. And travelling to meetings around Europe at that time, I was acutely aware of the favourable impression Irish players were making; and just as important, the manner in which the team's supporters were deporting themselves on their trips abroad.

In more recent times, it is rugby which has captured the imagination of the floating sporting public. And like so many others, I have been lost in admiration for the standards achieved by Munster and Leinster and the manner in which the provincial teams fed into the unforgettable Grand Slam success in 2009.

No less than the GAA, these organisations have done much to keep morale high in a climate of recession and it provides an effective answer to those who would question the merit of government in helping to fund sport, albeit at a lower level, in difficult, challenging times.

Many of the success stories recounted by Peter Byrne in these pages were achieved in equally trying circumstances. In that context, I believe his book has a role to play in reminding us of a glorious past which can help inspire future generations in their attempts to keep the Irish Tricolour flying proudly in stadia around the world. I wish them well in that mission.

Sonia O'Sullivan

– Introduction –

Seated in the body of a conference hall during the annual congress of the International Association of Sports Journalists in Milan many moons ago, I was among old and valued friends. The seating arrangements on such occasions are normally set out in alphabetical order, ordaining that the representatives of Iran, Iraq, Ireland and Israel are accommodated cheek by jowl; and that, as you might suspect, can lead to some unkind if predictable humour.

'I wouldn't want to be sitting in the row behind or in front of you lot', was the usual remark in an era when security was at the top of the agenda for anybody charged with the responsibility of organising an international gathering. 'A lot of fire power in your row,' said one wag. 'But if we're talking sport, I'd want to be with the big hitters – Ireland.'

That got me thinking about our rating in international sport and how much of the world views us as a small country which frequently punches above its weight in major championships around the world.

In a sense, that is the logical product of our great love affair with sport, national and international, which in good times and bad has been a major part of the Irish psyche. Now more than ever, it seems, its value in projecting the image of a nation, defiant and resourceful in a challenging climate of austerity, is more important than ever.

From the relative comfort of the press box, I've been privileged to witness many of the achievements which, in their time, held the country captive. And on those occasions when I wasn't fortunate enough to be present, I couldn't wait to read the accounts of history in the making.

Long years after Ron Delany had confounded the collective wisdom of the world's sporting press at Melbourne in 1956, which of us could fail to be impressed by the exploits of John Treacy, Eamonn Coghlan and, not least, Sonia O'Sullivan in the broad world of international athletics?

The discipline of boxing provided me with an entry to spots writing and because of that, I have always felt a special affinity with this, one of the most demanding of all sports. In line with a pedigree which rates among the best in the roped square, boxers like Barry McGuigan and Steve Collins in the professional game and Michael Carruth, Harry Perry and Katie Taylor among a host of gifted amateurs, did much to keep the Irish flag flying at distant venues in the second half of the twentieth century.

For many people, team sport is where it's at, and recounting the achievements of men like Jack Carey, Liam Brady and John Giles in football and the imperishable genius of men like Jack Kyle and Brian O'Driscoll with a rugby ball in their hands, was a mission undertaken with the enthusiasm of a schoolboy.

For those who complain with some justification that the less popular sports do not receive adequate coverage in the national press, the memories of Stephen Roche's golden year in cycling in 1987, still evoke national pride as do the exploits of Arkle, the remarkable horse who was responsible for a redraft of the parameters of National Hunt horse racing in the 1960s. The passage of time has, in some ways, merely added to the fascination of those successes.

North Dublin was part of another marvellous sporting story in 2007 when players such as Eoin Morgan and John Mooney shared in Ireland's World Cup cricket safari. Even for those with only a limited interest in cricket, Ireland's win over Pakistan and the drama which followed still makes for an absorbing read.

Set among the pantheon of outstanding international performers are the men and women who continue to attract more attention than all others on GAA fields throughout the length and breadth of the country. For the hundreds of thousands who make Gaelic football and hurling the most popular spectator sports, Croke Park in September is a location which will always hold a special fascination.

From Christy Ring and Nick Rackard to modern personalities of the quality of Henry Shefflin and Joe Canning, the battles for hurling's biggest prize on the first Sunday in September are well documented in these pages. And Gaelic football enthusiasts can once more rejoice in the deeds of men like Mick O'Connell, Kevin Heffernan, Mick Higgins and many of those who followed in their footsteps in more modern times.

Reliving the grandeur of those giddy, sunlit days, was for me, a source of deep satisfaction. My earnest wish is that it will be no less enjoyable for you.

Peter Byrne
May 2013

– Chapter 1 –

Date With Destiny

Football – Ireland v England, Dalymount Park, September 1946

On the face of it, there wasn't a lot about the early 1940s to appeal to a boy who prized sport above all else in those dark, deprived days. Across the breadth of Europe and beyond, the most terrible war the world has known was raging with ever increasing consequences for the civil population at large.

Money was scarce, food was rationed severely, oil and fuel supplies dwindled to almost nothing and an acute shortage of newsprint meant that newspapers in neutral Ireland frequently amounted to just four unattractive leaves and sometimes even less.

It doesn't take a great sweep of the imagination to guess that when duty editors came to dividing up those precious column inches, sporting matters came low down the list of priorities. To aggravate those who took exception, there was precious little sport deemed important enough by the editorial authorities in Radio Éireann to warrant coverage on the 'wireless'. In those circumstances, the old crackling BBC *Light Programme* was a godsend and one measure of its influence was that any kid worth his salt could rattle off the names of the eight world champions in boxing, without as much as a moment's hesitation.

I was one of those, and it somehow fostered the ambition that when I 'grew up', I would hopefully get a job writing about sport. It was a notion which, I have to admit, didn't attract any discernible envy from my friends on the road where I lived. But guess what? I was all of nine years of age when, in 1945, I experienced the excitement of seeing my name in print for the first time.

It was the practice at the time, for the two Dublin evening papers, the *Herald* and the *Mail*, to invite readers to submit the names of the League of Ireland representative team they would like to see chosen for the task of taking on the Irish League in the twice yearly games which helped cushion the loss of international fixtures during the war years.

And after delivering my letter personally to the *Herald*'s sports department in Middle Abbey Street, I felt the sheer delight of seeing my team in print the following day. 'Peter Byrne of Glasnevin' it said in bold type before reeling off the names and the clubs of those I had selected. 'Was that your young fellow's letter I saw in the paper the other day?' enquired a colleague of my father. 'Don't know,' he replied. 'Was there anything wrong?' 'No,' came the answer, 'but in selecting his best League of Ireland team, he included eight Bohemians players – would you credit that'. 'Oh, that would be him alright,' said the father. 'He's Bohemians mad. If he paid half as much attention to the school books as he does to football, I'd be happy.'

Growing up on Dublin's north side had a lot to recommend it. Those living on the other side of the Liffey could pop across to Milltown, home to Shamrock Rovers, the most successful of all Irish football clubs or, at a push, divert to Shelbourne Park before Shels abandoned their base to embark on their travels north and south of the river. Most important of all, of course, was the fact that they had Lansdowne Road, the great cathedral of Irish sport, on their doorstep.

Against that, however, we were able to access Croke Park with minimum trouble, particularly on those gloriously sunny afternoons in the long, long ago when the championship season was at its height in late summer and, for all the traffic restrictions of the day, fans arrived in their thousands to pay homage at the shrine of Gaelic Games. And then there was always the option of watching Drumcondra and Bohemians play their home games on alternate Sundays at a time when the FAI Cup and the old League of Ireland championship held a fascination which many in the modern world might find difficult to fathom.

Drums, clad in those blue and gold hoops which became an iconic part of Irish football before their demise in 1972, were at the summit of their powers in the 1940s and '50s when names like Con Martin, Pa Daly, Benny Henderson and Dessie Glynn were an essential part of the Irish sporting lexicon. There was undeniably no love lost between them and their near neighbours from Phibsborough, but for lads of my age group, it was still possible to switch allegiance with an ease that bordered on treasonous.

Ultimately, it was an ill-advised amalgamation with Home Farm that consigned Drums to the scrapheap, but fortunately, Bohemians, the oldest club south of the border, are still alive and occasionally thriving. Many view their momentous decision to espouse professionalism in 1970 as the move which saved the club from extinction, but for the romantics among us, it was the achievements of their amateur players – and two brothers in particular – which gave the club its undying allure.

Kevin O'Flanagan was born in Dublin in 1919, almost three years before his brother Michael saw the light of day. Collectively, they would emerge as probably the two most gifted siblings in the history of Irish sport. What is beyond dispute is that they are the only set of brothers to have represented Ireland in both football and rugby, an astounding achievement which puts them apart from all others in international sport.

More than that, the older brother has all the qualifications needed to meet the criteria for the accolade of the country's outstanding sports person of the twentieth century. Apart from his football and rugby exploits, he was a multiple Irish athletics champion in the sprints and long jump events who would assuredly have earned inclusion in Ireland's Olympic squads but for the intervention of World War II and a six-year suspension of all international sport.

He was also a formidable competitor in amateur golf with Milltown and Portmarnock, and on the rare occasions when a crowded programme permitted it, he wielded a tennis racket with a level of dexterity which suggested that had he applied himself with greater commitment, he might well have challenged the established masters of the discipline in Ireland at the time, Cyril Kemp and Joe Hackett.

As a student at Synge Street CBS, he excelled at Gaelic football and together with his long-time friend, Jack Carey, he was chosen in the Dublin team to play in the minor championship in 1936. All that changed, however, when they were revealed as members of the Home Farm football nursery in Whitehall and the disclosure promptly brought suspension by the GAA. Little more than a year later, the pair made their senior international debuts in a World Cup game against Norway in Oslo.

On the completion of his medical studies at UCD, Kevin moved to London to work as an intern and it was there that he swapped the red and black of Bohemians for the storied red and white of Arsenal – one of the last amateur players to play for the Highbury club. As ever, though, his sporting life remained hectic, and side by side with his football commitments, he managed to fit in the occasional rugby appearance for London Irish, winning his first 'full' rugby cap against Australia in December 1947, as a member of the Exiles club.

If Michael O'Flanagan never quite made as many headlines, he was still regarded by many as the more skilful of the two brothers. Whereas Kevin relied, in the main, on his impressive pace and ability to strike the ball harder than any of his contemporaries, Michael's game was all about ball control and the ability to outwit defenders, in size-14 boots, by sheer skill and courage. And that was equally true of his rugby career, which brought him his only cap against Scotland in 1948 and a special place in history by sharing in Ireland's first-ever Five Nations Grand Slam.

Nor was that his only claim to fame in the 1947/48 season. Just three months before the Scotland rugby game, he made another piece of sporting history by scoring six times in Bohemians' Leinster Senior Cup Final win over St Brendan's, a record which still endures as testimony to the unique qualities which lit up Dalymount Park and many other venues around the country throughout the 1940s and early '50s.

Imagine the drama then, when a unique set of circumstances contrived to put the brothers, who had played together so often for Bohemians, in the Ireland team for the first post-war international at Dalymount since the suspension of international football seven years earlier. England provided the opposition on Monday, 30 September 1946, and that too was laden with significance, marking, as it did, the first time England had put their range of talents on display in the Irish capital since 1912.

Kevin O'Flanagan was named in the original team, even though he was required to work overnight in London, before catching an early morning flight to Dublin to join his international colleagues at the team hotel for a light lunch. At that point, Michael was busy pulling pints for customers in the Confession Box, a small pub he owned on Marlborough Street. Imagine his surprise then when, less than four hours before the 5.30 kick-off at Dalymount, he took a phone call at the premises, inviting him to fill the vacancy caused by the late withdrawal of the selected centre forward, Davy Walsh.

With no help immediately available, there was no alternative but to usher the customers to the door, close the pub, dash home to Terenure to collect his boots and then back to Dalymount for the task of pitting his wits against the legendary England defender, Neil Franklin. It wasn't the kind of preparation he would have wished on the biggest day of his life, but after being left on the bench for the games in Portugal and Spain earlier in the summer, he was up for the challenge.

The prospect of the gifted brothers lining up together for the first time on the national team wasn't the only talking point as a huge crowd converged on the stadium. In goal, for example, the Irish selectors had risked the ire of many of the team's supporters by choosing Tommy Breen, once of Belfast Celtic and Manchester United but now plying his trade with Shamrock Rovers. Back in 1937, Drogheda-born Breen had become something of a hate figure in the south when, at the dictate of Belfast, he pulled out of Ireland's World Cup game against Norway to safeguard his place in the Northern Ireland team. Now, faced with something of a goal-keeping crisis, the selectors conveniently forgot their pledge that he would never again represent the FAI and handed him the yellow sweater.

Then there was Alex Stevenson, a Dublin Protestant who was one of only a handful of southern Irish players to wear the dark blue of Glasgow Rangers. After winning his first cap as a Dolphin player against Holland in 1932, Stevenson's name was conspicuous by its absence from every team sent out by the FAI until the outbreak of war in 1939, during which time he made no fewer than fourteen appearances for Northern Ireland. This was attributed by some to his refusal to play on Sundays but the truth was that Everton, a club which subsequently bent over backwards to placate Dublin, insisted on releasing him only to the Irish Football Association in Belfast. Now the man who the FAI would subsequently appoint as their national coach was back in favour at inside right.

Even without these subplots, all the ingredients were in place for an epic struggle as England, regarded by their supporters as the uncrowned kings of world football, got ready to end their cold war with Dublin after conciliatory talks extending over a period of almost twenty-five years. The reality was, however, that their decision to journey on to Dublin after play-ing in Belfast forty-eight hours earlier had less to do with diplomacy than the need to sample the best of Irish food and living. Wartime rationing was still operational in Britain at the time and the prospect of spending two days in the luxury of Dublin's Gresham Hotel was, it appeared, sufficiently attractive to outweigh all other considerations. Frank Swift, England's legendary goalkeeper, obviously thought so, for in his autobiography published some years later, he recalled the sheer exhilaration of his fellow English players on seeing a mouth-watering four course menu set out before them.

A highly significant occasion was rendered all the more important by the quality of the team England sent out. True, they were playing their second game in forty-eight hours, but such was the facile nature of their crushing 7–2 win over Northern Ireland that they weren't overly burdened by weariness. In the strange practice of the day which allowed the IFA to select players born south of the border, the dark realisation began to dawn on the visitors that they would again be facing two of those who had confronted them in Belfast, Jack Carey and Bill Gorman with a third southern-born player, Tom 'Bud' Aherne, named as a replacement on the FAI's team. It was the first occasion that English officials had experienced at first hand the bizarre realities of the Irish football split and it would play a significant part in the negotiations which rationalised the situation shortly afterwards.

Apart from the legendary Stanley Matthews, England fielded their full array of stars: Laurie Scott and George Hardwick fronted Swift in goal, Billy Wright and Henry Cockburn played on either side of Neil Franklin in the half-back line and the front line was made up of Tom Finney, Raich Carter, Tommy Lawton, Wilf Mannion and Bobby Langton. It was, by any standard, a formidable formation that, in terms of individual skills, far eclipsed many of the selections sent out by the English FA in the years leading up to their World Cup success in 1966.

Having waited so long to see England's national team, a big crowd was not discouraged by the heavy rain which preceded the kick-off, and the visitors would later attribute the pressures occasioned by the famous Dalymount roar as one of the reasons for a performance that fell some way short of the standard they had set in Belfast. After Breen had done well to deflect Carter's shot, the Irish more than held their own in a lively, eventful game with the O'Flanagan brothers, all pace and purpose, occasionally spreading raw panic in the opposing defence.

It was Michael's pass which sent Kevin careering through in a one-on-one with the huge English goalkeeper midway through the first half and when the ball rebounded across the six yards line, Scott was forced to scramble, in-knocking the ball over his own crossbar. That was a let off for the team in white and their relief showed once more when Stevenson's shot struck the crossbar after the interval.

Roared on by the crowd, Ireland spared nothing or nobody in their search for a winner, but in an incident which would be replicated by England at the same venue in 1957, the home team was later made to count the cost of a fateful lapse in concentration. With just seven minutes left, Breen could merely parry Langton's shot and Finney, in his first international appearance, pounced for the only goal of the game.

An historic evening on Liffeyside had been spoiled by just one mistake, but the bigger picture was that Dublin was now firmly re-established as a focal point in international football and open for business on a regular basis with the old enemy.

– Chapter 2 –

New York, New York

Gaelic Football – Cavan v Kerry, Polo Grounds,
New York, September 1947

Looking at the small army of print and electronic journalists who accompany teams on foreign assignments in the modern era, it is easy to forget that that it wasn't always so. The historic happenings in a baseball stadium in New York on 14 September 1947 illustrate the point perfectly.

In a remarkable decision which continued to agitate long after the dust had settled on a day of high drama in the Polo Grounds, home of the legendary New York Giants, the Central Council of the GAA decreed, in its wisdom, to move the final of that year's All-Ireland Football Championship between Cavan and Kerry some 3,000 miles west of its traditional setting in Croke Park.

It was a gamble that surprised some of the association's most influential policy makers, who subsequently contended that the ruling made at the end of the council's meeting was a direct reversal of the opinions expressed by a majority of members at the start of the fateful gathering. And apart from the plethora of logistical problems it occasioned, it gave rise to some difficult decision-making by those who controlled the purse strings of the national newspapers in Ireland.

The *Irish Times* and *Cork Examiner*, for example, decided against the cost of sending journalists on the transatlantic journey, preferring instead to rely on locally based newsmen to cover one of the showpiece events in Irish sport. The *Irish Independent*, on other hand, nominated its sports editor, Mitchel Cogley, to write on the game; and surprisingly, the now defunct *Irish Press* left its specialist GAA reporter, Terry Myles, at home and delegated Anna Kelly, who at that time was in charge of the paper's women's page, to travel and complement the match report of the freelance journalist, Arthur Quinlan.

If their choice of a staff representative in New York was curious, there was no denying the sense of enterprise in the decision of the *Irish Press* management to go for broke in their pictorial coverage of the historic event. Because of the time difference, there was no way that they would be able to get pictures from New York in the conventional manner to appear in the following day's paper. Cue the entrepreneurs at the *IP* offices on Burgh Quay.

They would scoop the opposition big time by utilising the most modern technical development in the newspaper business, the wired photograph. This involved the hush-hush rental of the necessary machine from the Associated Press international agency in New York and, equally important, the hiring of one of their personnel to work it. To the thinly veiled astonishment of the local journalists, it worked and the following morning, the *Irish Press* proudly presented the first ever wired pictures from the other side of the Atlantic. And all this a mere twenty years before the Americans put a man on the moon.

In the heyday of radio, however, it was obvious from a long way back that Michael O'Hehir's commentary would be all-important in quelling the objections of the traditionalists who believed that the authorities were selling out on their heritage by staging the final in New York. The difficulty was that Radio Éireann had never commissioned a transatlantic project to that point and, more importantly, didn't apparently have the means to fund it.

In his book *The Star Spangled Final*, the late Mick Dunne revealed that the financial problem, measured in hundreds rather than thousands of pounds, was eventually referred to the Department of Finance before the requisite funding was provided. But if O'Hehir, just twenty-seven years old, thought that was the end of his problems, he was wrong.

Because of an apparent mix up between the authorities in Radio Éireann and those in the American Telephone and Telegraph Company, it was discovered just twenty-four hours before the match that the necessary lines had not been booked for the commentary. And when hours of frantic negotiations eventually resolved the problem, Radio Éireann bosses, obviously under instructions to cut costs to the minimum, booked only the bare minimum of time for the full commentary.

Just four months earlier, those same radio authorities had been embarrassed on the occasion of Gearóid Ó Colmáin's victory in the European championship heavyweight final at the National Boxing Stadium in Dublin. It was the first time that Ireland had secured the heavyweight title but the occasion was soured somewhat when Radio Éireann terminated Eamon Andrews's commentary and the voices of the singing masses after just a verse of 'Amhran na bhFiann' as Ó Colmáin stood in the middle of the ring with the gold medal hanging from his neck. The nightly news bulletin had to start at 10 PM sharp and despite the joyous celebrations on South Circular Road, no exemptions could be made.

The difficulty in New York was that the elaborate pre-match ceremonies delayed the start and as the excitement built to a crescendo in the dying minutes of the match, O'Hehir noticed that if the American authorities adhered strictly to the original terms of the booking, the telephone line would be cut before the final whistle. And with no producer on hand to make his case, he was left with no option but to plead on air, not just once but three times, for the line to be left open. Fortunately, his entreaties were heard but he left the stadium not knowing whether in fact the listeners back in Ireland had heard his description of the last eventful minutes and, indeed, if the country at large was aware of the result of the game.

The drama in the commentary box in the Polo Grounds was a micro-cosm of the difficulties visited on the GAA's General Secretary, Pádraig Ó Caoimh, after Monsignor Michael Hamilton, a passionate churchman in County Clare and equally articulate in advancing the association's cause, had convinced the sceptics that the decision to bring the final to America was indeed in the best interests of the game on either side of the Atlantic. Among the pluses he mentioned was the assumption that the match would attract a crowd of expatriates in the region of 60,000, but as it transpired this estimate proved wildly optimistic.

More predictable by far was the fact that in the stampede to placate the American lobby headed by John Kerry O'Donnell, few pondered the problem of finding a suitable venue for a contest being billed as the 'World's Greatest Game'. Eventually, the choice fell on the Polo Grounds, a modern stadium in its time which, apart from baseball, had seen some spectacular world championship boxing fights, not least when Joe Louis knocked out the Welshman Billy Conn in thirteen rounds some six years earlier.

The difficulty for the committee overseeing arrangements for the All-Ireland Final was that it was a diamond-shaped field, designed as a baseball arena, and for all the different configurations envisaged by the visitors from Ireland, there was no escaping that fact. Eventually, it was determined to make the best of an impossible situation and go with a pitch which undeniably devalued the occasion. It was just 137 yards long and the width varied from 84 yards at one end to 71 yards at the other. To accentuate the problem, the baseball authorities resisted all attempts to remove the pitcher's mound, measured at some 10 inches high.

In the words of the players, the playing surface was 'as hard as concrete' and, added to the presence of the mound, it made for extremely hazardous conditions. Almost inevitably, perhaps, it would contribute to the injury sustained by the Kerry midfield player Eddie Dowling, which ultimately would have a profound bearing on the outcome.

Not least of the logistical problems faced by Padraig O'Caoimh was that of organising the travel arrangements for the official party of players and officials. Transatlantic air travel was still only in its infancy in the immediate post-war years and no fewer than twenty-five members of the party chose to go by sea, leaving Cobh for New York on the SS *Mauritania* on 2 September for the seven-day voyage. They were already safely in port as the bulk of the travel party, fourteen players from each team as well as officials and the tiny media corps, left Rineanna Airport, later renamed Shannon Airport, at the start of the eventful journey.

None of the air travellers had sat in a plane before and Mitchel Cogley would later recall the consternation and raw fear among the passengers when the pilot left the cockpit to greet his distinguished passengers in mid-flight. 'I looked across the aisle and saw these big, strong men looking absolutely terrified. It didn't do anything to reassure the rest of us,' said the veteran newsman. By no stretch of the imagination could it be called an easy journey for the uninitiated.

'Because of the prevailing winds we had to make an unscheduled stop to take on extra fuel in Santa Maria in the Portuguese Azores,' said Cogley. 'After that, we had short stopovers in Newfoundland and Boston and eventually disembarked in LaGuardia Airport in New York, almost twenty-nine hours after leaving Ireland.' Joe Keohane, a colourful full-back with few equals, was one of five Kerry players who had previously played in New York – they travelled there by ship – in an exhibition game against Mayo before the outbreak of war in 1939. Keohane chose to go by air on this occasion and, as in the case of some of his teammates, there were occasions on the journey when he wished that he hadn't.

Like his teammates Paddy Bawn Brosnan, Bill Casey, Paddy Kennedy and Gega O'Connor, Keohane had a reasonable idea of the strange setting awaiting the players when they set down in the Polo Grounds, but he still professed to being shocked when he saw the state of the playing surface in the stadium. 'There wasn't a blade of grass on it – it was certainly no place to play an All-Ireland Final,' he said. And to exacerbate the problem, New York was hit by a downpour for much of the thirty-six hours preceding the match, making it difficult for players to retain a foothold.

Fortunately, the sun had broken though before the teams set off for the stadium, making it hot and humid inside, but it probably came too late to persuade many intending patrons to watch the match. In the event, 34,941 turned up for the marathon programme, presided over by the mayor of New York, 'Irish' Bill O'Dwyer, which included two local games before the main event. Even as the Cavan and Kerry players flexed muscles in the dressing rooms, however, they received an unexpected visitor in the person of the referee, Martin O'Neill from Wexford.

O'Neill, later to become Secretary of the Leinster Council, was reputed to be one of the best referees of his time, a strict disciplinarian who wasn't afraid to impose his authority. It was this latter quality which probably encouraged the authorities at Croke Park to appoint him, even though he was not overly keen to take on the job which was seen as central to the success of the occasion.

'He came into the room with the air man who had a stern message to impart,' said Joe Keohane, 'and proceeded to lecture us on the significance of the occasion, how we were representing our country abroad and the importance of staying within the rules on all occasions. The underlying message was that he would deal harshly with anything he deemed to be reckless play. But he didn't need to remind us of our responsibilities and the effect was to instil an element of apprehension that ought to be no part of a build up to an All-Ireland Final.'

For Mick Higgins, the main playmaker in a vastly underrated Cavan team, it was a case of home from home. Born in New York but taken by his parents to Ireland as a boy, he was a man who above all others, prospered on the hype and the fears about the pitch in the build up to the game. 'For people in the Cavan camp, it was a chance to seize the moment – and we did.' And the state of the pitch? 'It was manageable and remember – some of the pitches we played on in Ireland at the time weren't too good either.'

Cavan, who required a replay to beat a modest Monaghan team on their way to the final, had good reason to be grateful for the skills and tactical nous that Higgins brought to the team after a positively nightmare start. Even with their charismatic midfielder, Paddy Kennedy, forced by injury to take up an unaccustomed role as a corner forward, Kerry's improvised partnership of Eddie Dowling and Teddy O'Connor dominated in the centre in the early stages and it showed as first Batt Garvey, and then Dowling, crashed home the goals which saw the Munster champions open up an eight-point lead midway through the first half.

Decreeing that drastic situations demand drastic measures of redress, Cavan reshaped their team, withdrawing Higgins and Tony Tighe from the half forward line to take on O'Connor and Dowling in midfield and shunting P. J. Duke, the dashing UCD student, to right half-back to counter the threat presented by Garvey. The switches paid off, but the biggest factor by far in the transformation which followed was the back injury Dowling sustained in a heavy fall on the rocklike surface.

With their power base disrupted, Kerry lost their earlier look of invincibility. Spectacular goals from their impish corner forward Joe Stafford and, almost inevitably, Higgins, hauled Cavan off the floor and back into contention in a game in which Bruddy O'Donnell, on as a replacement for Dowling, could never rediscover the skills which had brought Meath to heel in the semi-final.

In the manner of their making, the Munster men came back to ask searching questions of the opposition after Tim Brosnan had been summoned from the bench to replace O'Donnell, and Gega O'Connor's finely executed point, the first of the second half, brought them level at 2-5 apiece. But the defensive gaps which had earlier threatened to undo Cavan were by now sealed off and with John Joe O'Reilly and Simon Deignan complementing the majestic Duke in the half-back line, the prospect of pulling off an unlikely victory gradually dawned on the rank outsiders.

Peter Donohoe, a barman in Gaffney's famous hostelry in Fairview, just a stone's throw from Croke Park, eventually emerged from the shadow of some of his more illustrious teammates to put Cavan in full control, kicking eight points, most of them from frees, as the watch on Martin O'Neill's wrist ticked towards full time. Nothing if not defiant, Kerry hit them with everything they had in those last, tense minutes but when O'Neill eventually called time, the scoreboard confirmed Cavan as 2-12 to 2-7 winners and the Sam Maguire Cup was on its way to Ulster for only the third occasion.

Twenty-four hours later, American sportswriters were extolling the sportsmanship of the players in this 'remarkable new sport'. The celebrated *New York Times* columnist Arthur Daley was euphoric in writing up Peter Donohoe as the Babe Ruth of Gaelic football, and the highs and lows of an outstanding sporting odyssey were already beginning to pass into history, as victors and vanquished prepared to take their leave of the Big Apple – and the oddest stadium ever to host a major GAA event.

– Chapter 3 –

King Kyle

Rugby – Ireland v Wales, Ravenhill, March 1948

The cost of Adolf Hitler's fixation on waging war on the world in 1939 could be counted in many currencies. No part of life remained untouched as the conflagration raged on for close to six terrible years. For sport in particular and the aspirations of thousands of young men and women to involve themselves at the highest level of their specialist disciplines, the suspension of international competition was, in many cases, ruinous.

Take the case of rugby union football. By the end of the Five Nations Championship in the 1938/39 season, players in the northern hemisphere, no less than their counterparts in the south, were eagerly anticipating the arrival of the roaring forties and, in the case of Ireland, re-applying themselves to the challenge of completing the Grand Slam for the first time. Suddenly, such ambitions were made to look fatuous in the extreme after German troops had marched on Poland. Sport, like so many other normal activities in peace time, was put on hold for the next six years.

One of the consequences was to hone still further the competitive element in domestic rugby, with Old Belvedere's record sequence of seven victories in the Leinster Senior Cup, starting in 1940, setting the standard that ensured there was no shortage of emerging talent by the time peace was restored in 1945 and big time rugby resumed with a series of unofficial international games in 1946.

The immensely gifted Quinn brothers, Kevin, Brendan and Gerry, who had contributed so much to Old Belvedere's dominance in Leinster, played in those unofficial games, but it was another raw talent at the club who would make the more lasting impact. Karl Mullen was a young medical student in Dublin when first summoned to wear the green jersey of Ireland in the fixture against France at Lansdowne Road on 26 January 1946. By the time he took his leave of international rugby in March 1953, he had written his name indelibly into the history of the game.

Aside from captaining Ireland to that coveted Grand Slam, the inspirational hooker led the British and Irish party on their marathon tour of New Zealand in 1950. At the time the Irish team was riding high in the pecking order in the northern hemisphere, not least because of Mullen's motivational qualities and the strengths he brought to an unglamorous position in the middle of the front row. And as it transpired, those qualities more than compensated for his relative immaturity.

Coincidentally, it was another young man with aspirations of a medical career who emerged at approximately the same time to provide the creative nous to complement Karl Mullan's leadership of the pack. Studying at Queen's University Belfast, Jack Kyle was largely responsible for transforming a modest back line into the potent scoring unit that would undo some of the best defences in the championship in what came to be known as the first of the golden eras in Irish rugby.

Judged by the physical makeup of modern rugby international backs, Kyle was a slight but deceptively strong figure, blessed with remarkable vision on the pitch and the kind of acceleration which made those around him look positively pedestrian. Fittingly, the finest fly-half of his generation and, in the opinion of many, one of the greatest of all time, was among the first names down on paper in the selection of the distinguished Lions squad of 1950.

That protracted tour lasted more than three months and Jack recalls the reaction in the Kyle household when he opened the pages of the *Belfast*

Telegraph to discover that he was in the touring party. 'It was only a small story on the sports pages of the *Telegraph* but my father was not impressed. His first question was, "What about your studies – how can you take all that time off without it impacting on your hopes of graduating on schedule?" Fortunately, apprehension soon mellowed into fatherly admiration, and in time Kyle would become an honoured name in the southern hemisphere.

By that stage, he was the finished product but it was somewhat different on the restart of the Five Nations Championship in 1946/47 season. The long duration of Hitler's conflict meant that only a handful of pre-war players featured on the resumption and in the case of Ireland, the indomitable Lansdowne full-back, Con Murphy, was the sole survivor. It all made for a significant exercise in improvisation but the measure of the Irish response was that they fell only at the last obstacle in the Triple Crown race, losing 6–0 to Wales at Swansea.

The critics rated it as an encouraging beginning but they might have been contemplating a rethink before the end of 1947, after the touring Australians had outplayed the men in green as comprehensively as the 16–3 scoreline indicated at Lansdowne Road on 6 December. It scarcely augured well for the start of the championship in the Colombes Stadium in Paris on New Year's Day 1948, one of the few occasions that a championship fixture was played in midweek.

If the awesome power and refined finishing skills which would later identify the French brand of rugby hadn't yet manifested themselves, France still represented a formidable test for any opposition on home terrain. Allied to the comprehensive nature of the collapse against the Wallabies just two weeks earlier, it was an anxious Irish squad that truncated its festive celebrations to embark on the journey to Paris. And that sense of unease was shared by the five Irish team selectors who, conscious of the need to sharpen the competitive element in the team, recalled Barney Mullan and the Dolphin player, Bertie O'Hanlon, to the three quarter line.

Mullan's recall came at the expense of the multi-faceted Kevin O'Flanagan and it served to emphasise Clontarf's acknowledged contribution to the national team. Before Old Belvedere embarked on their long train of success, Clontarf had been the dominant rugby force in Dublin north of the Liffey and among those who contrived to put the club's headquarters at Castle Avenue at the centre of club competition was the celebrated Freddie Moran. Like O'Flanagan, Moran was a national sprint champion and but for the intervention of the war, he would unquestionably have added to his meagre total of eight Irish caps. Now Barney Mullan (no relation of the team captain) was set to enrich the club's history, and in time his place kicking, no less than his innate try-scoring skills, would see Ireland through some treacherous tests.

The most significant change in the pack by far was the introduction of the Dolphin and Munster openside flanker, Jim McCarthy. A player possessed of boundless energy, McCarthy's biggest asset was his ability to complement Kyle on those occasions when the Ulsterman's sense of adventure appeared to surprise his teammates as much as the opposition. Invariably, the red-haired Corkman was at Kyle's shoulder in such situations, and much later Tony O'Reilly would describe him pretty accurately as 'Jack Kyle's outrider'.

Complementing McCarthy in the back row was Bill McKay and packing down immediately behind them were Ernie Keefe, an international amateur boxer when he wasn't playing rugby, and the redoubtable Colum Callan, whose imposing presence on the pitch contrasted starkly with his diffidence off it. In the event, it turned out to be a winning formation with McCarthy and Barney Mullan coming up with the tries that broke the back of France's resistance and with Mullan kicking seven points. Ireland were fully deserving of their 13–6 win.

By most estimates, it was a good day's work and yet, not quite good enough in the eyes of the selectors to warrant an unchanged team for the next assignment, away to England, some six weeks later. Jack Mattsson of

Wanderers was named for his first – and only – cap at full-back, Chris Daly was in the front row in place of another Munster player, Jim Corcoran, Des O'Brien was promoted at number eight and most significant of all, Ernie Strathdee, who had led the team in Paris, was dropped. Instead, it was decided to go with Hugh de Lacy at scrumhalf with the captaincy transferring to Karl Mullen. In the latter instance, it would prove a decision biblical in its wisdom.

The England fixture, then as now, was invested with an importance which put it apart from all others, particularly at Twickenham. But with the new skipper leading by example, the pack provided just enough possession to feed the creative skills of Kyle at number ten. And the Ulsterman was not found wanting, scoring a fine try as well as creating the openings for two others by Des McKee and Bill McKay. Barney Mullan converted one of them and the Irish squeezed home by the narrowest of margins, 11–10.

It was only then that the public at large sensed that this was an Ireland team above the norm, and one of the consequences of the exciting Twickenham triumph was that Karl Mullen's men prepared for the next assignment, against Scotland at Lansdowne Road, in the certain knowledge that victory would assure them of the championship title, irrespective of how they made out against Wales in their final game of the season.

It is a measure of the turmoil caused by the suspension of international sport during the war years and the uncertainty created by that void, that the Irish selectors, like those in each of the other four teams in the competition, chopped and changed the team in bewildering fashion in the hope of putting their strongest formation in the field. That was a product of the times, and in keeping with the trend they duly announced two more changes from the side that had done so well in putting down the best efforts of a strong English combination in London.

One of them was at full-back where Dudley Higgins was recalled in place of Mattsson, and in another remarkable twist in the odyssey of the

O'Flanagan family, Michael was summoned for his first rugby cap in the centre. Ironically, he replaced another versatile performer, Paddy Reid, who in between his rugby commitments with Garryown and Munster had played football for his native Limerick in the League of Ireland.

O'Flanagan, catching the mood of a significant occasion, stretched the Scottish defence with a clever break, but it was fellow Dubliner Barney Mullan who pointed the way to victory with the try that set the game alight early in the second half. It represented another significant achievement by the underrated Clontarf winger but it took an even classier score from Jack Kyle, who left the visiting defence for dead with another thrilling illustration of his skill, vision and pace, to put the seal on victory. For the first time ever, Ireland had won the championship at Lansdowne Road and suddenly, rugby held the attention of the entire nation.

Even though Ireland were now the official champions, one last, difficult obstacle stood between the players and a place among the pantheon of enduring national sporting celebrities. Victory over Wales in their last game would not alone corner the Triple Crown, but secure the biggest prize of all, the Grand Slam which has teased and tormented successive generations of green-shirted warriors. Acclaim on an unprecedented scale awaited the players if they could beat Wales at Ravenhill on 13 March 1948 and Kyle couldn't wait for the big day to arrive.

'Rugby, indeed, sport in general in the immediate post-war era, didn't have the profile it enjoys today but even for the most laidback members of the squad, this game carried a special significance,' recalls Kyle. 'Some of the older officials around the team reminded us that no Ireland team had ever beaten the other four teams in the championship in the same season, and to succeed now would be a huge endorsement for the game here.

'The fact that the game was being played in Belfast gave the northern players an extra incentive. Victory at any championship ground was always sweet, but now with so much depending on the outcome, the sense of occasion was even greater. After the initial shock of losing to Australia the previous December, the team had improved with every game. But Ireland had come up short against Wales many times in the past and we all realised that anything we got out of the game would have to be earned the hard way.'

It was a feeling with which every Irish supporter in a capacity crowd of 33,000 could identify as they awaited the arrival of the teams on the pitch. With players of the quality of Bleddyn Williams, Haydn Tanner and Ken Jones calling the shots, the Welsh attack was acknowledged as the best in the northern hemisphere and in those circumstances, it was imperative that Ireland win the forward battle. And with the front row of Chris Daly, Karl Mullen and Archie McConnell showing the way, they were certainly up for the task.

'Rhys Stephens gave us a few problems in the lineout early on, but once we sorted out the situation we were fine,' said Jimmy Nelson, later to become President of the Irish Rugby Football Union. 'Gradually, we got control up front and with Jack Kyle making the best of the possession that came our way, we did enough to win the game in the second half.'

Kyle, a reassuring presence in the tumult surrounding the game, delivered the long pass that enabled Barney Mullan to go over in the corner for the opening try. But just when the Irish felt that they had drawn the teeth from the visiting challenge, Bleddyn Williams for once found a path through the stout midfield defence provided by Paddy Reid and Des McKee and revealed the class that the home crowd feared, by scampering over near the corner.

That presaged a tense, unyielding battle to play on the nerves still more in the second half but Karl Mullen's half-time talk, remembered by Kyle as inspirational, evoked the requisite response from the pack. Meeting fire with fire, they went back into the lead when Chris Daly, with half a ton of Welsh 'beef' on his back, burrowed his way over the line for the try that would take Ireland to the Promised Land.

Kyle was correctly identified as the hero of the hour, but sensing the historic significance of it all, a section of the crowd made a beeline for Daly, who left the pitch shirtless after having it torn from his back by souvenir hunters. The out-half, as was his wont, made a dignified retreat to the dressing room but, no less than the leadership of Karl Mullen, his had been an enormous contribution to a great season.

Questioned afterwards as to how he celebrated victory, the great man said that in company with some of his northern colleagues, he had repaired to his alma mater to attend a 'hop' in Queen's University. Other, more exuberant members of the team chose a different way to end one of the greatest of all days in the history of Irish rugby.

– Chapter 4 –

The Lonely Outsider

Gaelic Football – Dublin v Cavan, Croke Park, May 1953

Mick Mangan was a man with much to complain about when critics attempted to assess his career in Gaelic football in the 1950s. By common consent, he was a highly capable goalkeeper who would have enriched many a county team in the summer of his years.

The problem was that he was fronted by fourteen exceptionally talented players in the teams sent out by the Marino-based club, St Vincent's. And far from being an asset, that actively militated against his chances of establishing himself as a regular member of the Dublin sides which would change the image of the game in the capital – earning huge sums of money for the purse minders of the GAA in the process.

On the one hand, the opportunities to illustrate his skills were rare enough, given that St Vincent's dominated local opposition to such a degree that rival players rarely got close enough to look into the whites of the keeper's eyes. And then there was the perceived need for the county selectors to be seen as fair to the other metropolitan clubs who trailed in distant pursuit of the perennial champions.

Thus it was, that when Dublin arrived in the final of the 1952/53 National Football League at Croke Park, the selectors deemed it right and proper to award the goalkeeping position in the team to Tony O'Grady of the Air Corps. For Mangan, the consolation was a place on the substitutes' bench alongside his clubmate, Cathal O'Leary.

The assembled wisdom of the men who selected the team decreed that O'Grady should start, not because he was necessarily a better goalkeeper than Mangan, but that his inclusion would be seen as the proof that they were not fixated with placating the vociferous thousands who by now, were aligning themselves with the men from Marino. Club prejudice had ever been the charge levelled against county selectors and in this instance, they wished to be perceived as being as objective as possible in the circumstances.

In a sense, that was a pity, for it's not every year that a club team gets to play against the reigning All-Ireland champions for the second biggest prize in Gaelic football. But with fourteen outfield players from St Vincent's confronting Cavan and two more sitting on the bench, the occasion was still riveting enough to attract 37,800 spectators through the turnstiles – a record for the competition at that point and an enduring source of fascination for those who cherish the parish ethic in sport.

For years, the GAA had sought in vain to loosen the stranglehold which football was exerting on the youth of Dublin. Essentially, Gaelic Games were seen as a rural pursuit, a means of helping the young who flocked to the capital from every part of the country in search of work to settle in an urban environment. In the deprived world of the 1940s and early '50s, when motorised travel was still severely restricted, they provided a home from home for the newly arrived and it saw clubs like Geraldines, Sean McDermotts, Westerns and those catering for specific professions and trades such as Clanna Gael (teachers), Banba (licensed vintners), Kickhams (drapers), Civil Service, Garda and Grocers flourish in local competitions.

In that situation, the emphasis for the local citizenry in the vast majority of the housing estates rising up in the greater Dublin area was on football. And indirectly, that was the reason which prompted Brother Fitzgerald, a Christian Brother teaching at the time in St Joseph's CBS,

Fairview, and his friend Fr William Fitzpatrick, a curate in the parish of Marino, to convene a meeting of interested parents with a view to establishing a GAA club in the parish.

That was the start of St Vincent's and a story which not alone enriched the lives of many Dubliners but also served as a role model for other aspiring champions around the country – a story that would go on to captivate and cajole until time ran out for most of the trendsetters after Dublin's much coveted All-Ireland success in 1958. Their enduring achievement after the initial success in 1949 had been to win the county championship for thirteen of the next fourteen years, the sequence broken only by a celebrated Erin's Hope team, built around two outstanding players, Tom Long (Kerry) and Mattie McDonagh (Galway) in 1956.

For much of the 1950s, sports lovers in the capital were spoilt in the choice on offer in local sport. Individual sports boasted performers of the calibre of Ron Delany, the Olympic 1,500 metres champion in Melbourne and others of the quality of Paul Dolan, Eamon Kinsella and Brendan O'Reilly in athletics, and in amateur boxing, names like Harry Perry, Fred Tiedt, Freddie Gilroy and John Caldwell were frequently splashed across the headlines after the weekly Friday night bill in the National Boxing Stadium.

Aside from St Vincent's in GAA, the great attraction in football at the time was Shamrock Rovers. Even at a club with an unrivalled pedigree, the teams sent out by player-coach Paddy Coad were regarded as extra special, with no fewer than thirteen Milltown players capped by Ireland in the course of the decade. And yet for all the assembled talent dressed in green and white hoops, there were many who contended with some conviction that St Vincent's very often played the better football.

After a brief flirtation with the quick hand pass popularised by Antrim in 1946, the GAA hierarchy effectively rewrote the rules governing the palmed or fisted pass and enforced them to such effect that the ball delivered by the foot quickly took over in the early fifties as the most effective form of passing. And nobody illustrated the art to better effect than St Vincent's players on club or county duty. Their critics were apt to describe it as another form of soccer but surprisingly, perhaps, the counter argument was put forward by some of the biggest pre-war personalities in the game who considered that the controversial toe lift was having the effect of depressing the fluency of the game.

Speaking on one occasion about the manner in which stoppages for free kicks were fragmenting Gaelic football, Paddy Bawn Brosnan, a legendary name in Kerry and all points north and east in the late thirties and forties, described it as a blight on the development of the game. 'There is too much pampering of players by referees,' Brosnan wrote in a national paper. 'The way forward is a combination of the catch and kick game of Kerry and the speed and precision of modern Dublin sides.'

Dublin's was a style which suited the team perfectly. Historically, urban sides always had trouble in matching the physical presence of teams 'up from the country'. In moving the ball quickly with the kicked pass, they now aspired to offset that physical discrepancy and by keeping it low, they hoped to minimise traditional problems in matching the catching skills of Kerry, who had written the template for successful Gaelic football teams for much of the previous fifty years.

The meeting of Kerry and Dublin in the 1955 All-Ireland Final, still regarded as one of the best on record, proved that for all the hype surrounding the Metropolitans' arrival on the scene, fancy footwork still didn't cut the mustard when confronted by strong, finely attuned athletes. But within another three years, their persistence paid off with a first title success in sixteen years over Derry on the biggest day of the GAA's season.

Sadly, Mick Moylan, the biggest man by far in those St Vincent's and Dublin teams, had hung up his boots prematurely because of injuries by the time they reclaimed the Sam Maguire Cup but flanked by Denis Mahony and Mark Wilson in the full-back line, he was very much a part of the team which put the hopes of thousands of Dubliners on the line against Cavan on 24 April 1953. Like Des Ferguson and Norman Allen, Wilson had been an important part of the team beaten by Cork in the All-Ireland Hurling Final the previous year. Now, due to Tim Mahony's misfortune in being hospitalised with appendicitis, he was on course for one of the most important days of his career.

Allen, revelling in the opportunity of displaying his football skills, had Jim Lavin and Nicky Maher on either side of him in the half-back line and in midfield, Jim Crowley was joined by the team captain Maurice Whelan, scarcely tall enough to match the high fielders but in every other sense a formidable competitor who spared nothing or nobody in his pursuit of the game's highest honours.

The half forward line of Des Ferguson and the Freeney brothers, Ollie and Cyril, was in some respects the fulcrum of the team. Ferguson, as we have noted earlier, was a gifted all-rounder. A doughty defender who had outplayed some illustrious names in hurling, his football skills were deployed at the other end of the pitch where skill, married to an intuitive flair for turning up in the right place at the right time, marked him out as a special player.

Cyril Freeney, a stylist beyond all else, was perhaps fortunate to edge Cathal O'Leary for the number twelve jersey but the same could never be said of his elder brother. For many of his generation, Ollie Freeney was the first and possibly the finest centre half forward to redraft the job specifications for men playing on the '40', an innovative personality imbued with the principle that the shortest route to goal wasn't always the best option for playmakers. More than that, he brought a psychological approach to the game which, if it frequently enraged opposing players, was thought to be instrumental in swaying many a match.

Bernie Atkins, at one time on the books of Shelbourne, and Tony Young, a splendid athlete who later abandoned football to concentrate on his hurling career, both fitted snugly into the game plan. But Ollie Freeney notwithstanding, the most charismatic member of the team was undoubtedly Kevin Heffernan at left corner forward.

Heffernan would later emerge as coach of the fabled Dubs teams in the 1970s but at the summit of his playing career, he was to the GAA in Dublin what Christy Ring had been to Cork hurling, a cult figure who commanded a huge following in the capital. He preceded Ollie Freeney as the team's placekicker but it was his ability to spin out of tackles before delivering the trademark drop kick which took the ball beyond the reach of goalkeepers, that endeared him to the masses.

It was a measure of the quality on the team occupying the other dressing room in Croke Park on that memorable afternoon that for all the undoubted quality of the club side from just up the road, Cavan were the overwhelming favourites to succeed Cork as National League champions in 1953. After the storied rivalry of Kerry and Roscommon the previous decade, the men from Breffni were now contesting the top rating in Gaelic football with their neighbours and arch rivals, Meath. And the manner in which they broke Meath in the replayed All-Ireland Final in 1952 suggested that they were in no mood to surrender that exalted position.

Six years earlier, men like Phil 'Gunner' Brady, Simon Deignan, Tony Tighe and Mick Higgins had filled pivotal roles in the making of GAA history, in drafting the blueprint for Cavan's win over Kerry in the Polo Grounds in New York. Now all four were intent on putting down the young pretenders on the way to what they envisaged would be a successful defence of the Sam Maguire Cup the following September.

Brady, the subject of a myriad hard man stories in Gaelic sport, had played in midfield alongside P. J. Duke in New York in 1947 but by now was stationed at full-back. That put him on course for a head-to-head duel with Tony Young, a much younger opponent who was capable of looking after himself in any situation and the neutrals, no less than supporters of either team, could scarcely wait for the action to start.

By contrast, Deignan, who started as a half-back in the Polo Grounds, had been moved in the opposite direction and his placing at right corner forward suggested that the selectors were looking to his vast experience to compensate for a shortage of mobility in the challenge of exploiting perceived weaknesses in the Dubliners' defence.

That was a criticism which could not be levelled at Tighe, by common accord one of the outstanding attackers of his generation. First summoned to wear the county colours as an extraordinarily gifted fifteen-year-old in the team which took part in the 1943 Ulster Minor championship, he was by any standard an excellent forward who wrought havoc with Kerry's defence in the most historic of all the GAA's finals six years earlier. Now, his duel with Mick Moylan promised to be captivating.

And yet, the man who gave Cavan most of their gravitas was a New Yorker. Mick Higgins was only a toddler when he was taken by his parents to Ireland and it would prove the luckiest break in the county's chequered history. Higgins had watched the great John Joe O'Reilly lift the Cup in his native city six years earlier before emulating O'Reilly's big moment in captaining the team to victory in 1952. No less than those gathered around him in the approach to the league final, he now wondered aloud if St Vincent's could transfer their outstanding club form to a higher platform in their quest for the second-biggest prize on offer in inter-county competition.

'Everybody here is aware of what Dublin will bring to the party,' he told a sportswriter on the eve of the game. 'The type of game their forwards play is out of the ordinary and we could be in for a long hard day if they get up a head of steam. We believe they have weaknesses elsewhere but first we must make sure that we deal with the threat of being caught out by the speed of their attacks.'

Normally, in sport, forewarned is forearmed, but not on this occasion. Fuelled by youthful exuberance, Dublin came roaring out of the blocks and before the All-Ireland champions could draw breath, the game had run away from them. Within five minutes, Jim Lavin's long free kick was flicked over Brady's head by Heffernan, and Atkins, getting first run on Jim

McCabe, was in like a flash to shoot past Seamus Morris.

Three minutes later, the Cavan goalkeeper was stooping into his net yet again, this time after Cyril Freeney had put Heffernan in the clear and with the cover scattered, the corner forward fired the shot just inside the base of the upright. The Marino throng on the terraces was on song by now and the melody hadn't yet faded when goal number three arrived.

Ferguson, growing taller on the sheer improbability of it all, had the effrontery to take on three defenders and win in a long solo run that opened up broad avenues to the net that the unfortunate Morris was guarding. And when Ollie Freeney deflected the ball into the path of his younger sibling, the umpire's green flag was being waved yet again.

With just eleven minutes gone, the club team was leading 3-1 to 0-1 and Mick Higgins, for one, knew that the horse had bolted. 'It was a case of our worst fears being realised one after another,' he said later. 'All the things we had promised ourselves in training before the match were somehow forgotten and with the wind in their sails, there was no way we were going to catch them from there. Dublin were simply brilliant that day but then, we didn't play nearly well enough to make it a real test for them.'

To their credit, the champions rediscovered their pride in sufficient quantities to narrow the gap before the half-time break with two points from Brian Gallagher and another from Deignan offering just a flicker of hope for their survival. Already weakened by the withdrawal of Victor Sherlock just before the start, they suffered another setback early in the second half when Pat Carolan departed prematurely with a head injury.

If those twin losses did nothing to help Cavan's cause, they could in no way explain away Dublin's supremacy on the day. Higgins and Tighe, at the front of the champions' attack, were comprehensively contained by Allen and Moylan respectively and with Crowley and Whelan in control in the critical battle for midfield control, Dublin were again dominating the play when a fourth goal materialised in the forty-seventh minute.

Fittingly, it was Heffernan, at the top of his game, who put his name on the score which effectively confirmed the arrival of a new power in the game. Twelve months earlier in the National League 'home' final against Cork, he had been offered the chance of securing a last minute reprieve for his team, only to see his attempt to convert a '50' thwarted by the width of a post.

Now it was vastly different as the arc of Ferguson's cross carried the ball unerringly to his commander-in-chief and the shot was struck with sufficient accuracy to leave the goalkeeper stranded yet again. Dublin's victory on double scores, 4-6 to 0-9, gave them their first league title and a first success in any competition since their All-Ireland football triumph over Galway eleven years earlier.

When Mossy Whelan finally battled his way through the throng to collect the Cup, he was visibly surprised to be handed a second trophy. 'That's for Vincent's being the best ever club team to walk this land,' vouched a jubilant Dub at the entrance to the presentation area.

In the event, it transpired that Whelan was being handed the trophy specially designed and crafted as a centrepiece for the ill-fated Tóstal tourist festival which blossomed briefly in 1953, as an unexpected bonus. But on mature reflection, at a remove of almost sixty years, the aforementioned wag may well have been spot on the money!

– Chapter 5 –

Christy Rings Bell

Hurling – Wexford v Cork, Croke Park, September 1956

Two tales from the myriad which have grown around the legend of the celebrated Cork player Christy Ring illustrate different strands of the character which elevated the Cloyne man to a place above all others in the ancient art of hurling.

The first is built around an incident in a Munster senior championship game against Clare at Thurles in June 1955 when Cork, against all expectations, found themselves toiling against a county which, apart from isolated moments of affluence, was numbered among the supporting cast in the annual drama in the south.

With just minutes to go, Cork were offered the chance of a reprieve as Ring prepared to take a sideline cut some forty yards out on the right. For once however, the great man's skill deserted him and as the ball missed the target by inches, Clare were sufficiently buoyed to qualify for the provincial final for the first time in seventeen years.

Within minutes of returning home to his bed-sitter in Cork later in the evening, Ring knocked on a friend's door and enquired if he was doing anything special. Assured that that he wasn't, the man was then invited to accompany his idol over to the old Cork Athletic grounds where, for the next ninety minutes, late into the summer evening, Ring proceeded to practice the shot which had cost his team victory in Thurles. And just to be doubly sure, Ring, the perfectionist, went through the same routine the following Friday evening, on this occasion with the assistance of his Cork and Glen Rovers teammate, John Lyons.

Then there was the incident which underlined Ring's self-esteem and the confidence which, to his critics, often came across as unbridled arrogance. It was the spring of 1953 and Cork Athletic had just recruited the mature but extravagant skills of Raich Carter to bring the crowds back to Flower Lodge. Carter, an inside forward with mesmeric skills on the ball, first played for England in 1934 and but for the intervention of war would assuredly have won more than thirteen caps.

His arrival on Leeside was the occasion of much rejoicing among Cork Athletic supporters and the national press weren't slow to grasp the significance of the occasion, describing the signing as further evidence of the growth of the game in the south. In the time-honoured tradition of the rivalry between the different codes in Cork, Ring was taunted by one individual with the remark that Carter, an elderly imported Englishman, was now cock of the walk in the city. 'Yerra, would you leave me alone,' came the reply. 'I'd draw a bigger crowd standing in my overalls in Patrick Street than Raich Carter would ever do in Flower Lodge.'

The Rackard dynasty from County Wexford was hewn from a different mine. Not for the boys of Killane, the blinding flashes of brilliance, the eccentricities which derive from something approaching sporting genius. Strength and power, blended with the dextrous stick work which separates the elite from the rest, was the calling card of the brothers who in the space of ten years or so established a whole new tradition for hurling in the south-eastern tip of the country. And together with Christy Ring they scripted much of the drama in a golden era for the game in the 1950s.

Nick Rackard, a big, deep-chested man, was the leader of the pack. In an era when versatility was a lot more common in Gaelic Games than it is now, the cavalier Wexford player captured the sporting headlines on St Patrick's Day 1950 when he represented Leinster in both hurling and football in the double-decker Railway Cup programme at Croke Park. For a county which was the first to win the All-Ireland football championship four consecutive times starting in 1915, he promised briefly to initiate a renaissance in the big ball code before concentrating exclusively on hurling.

That was a fortuitous decision for the game not just on the south-east coast but nationwide. Despite occasional intrusions by Dublin, the Leinster championship was dominated to an unhealthy degree by Kilkenny and the arrival of the purple and gold brigade with their novel, swashbuckling approach, was a prayer answered for the authorities in Croke Park. The elder Rackard contributed substantially to that new style with his trait of tossing the ball forward before powering close in frees to the roof of the net, becoming an indelible image of hurling at the time.

Bobby Rackard, taller, thinner but equally powerful, specialised in stopping goals rather than scoring them. After starting as a half-back, he moved to the full-back line where in company with Nick O'Donnell and Mick O'Hanlon he formed a full-back line which, in a more refined manner, equalled that of Tipperary's famed Hell's Kitchen trio of Mick Byrne, Mick Maher and Kieran Carey. And as the Cork–Wexford plot developed, his duels with Ring became an integral part of the game's folklore.

Then there was Willie Rackard, the youngest member of the trio, whose career would stretch into the 1960s. Like his brothers, he was a tough opponent for any forward but no less than them, his was a scrupulously fair philosophy on how the game should be played. Over time, he matured into probably a better defender than Bobby and at a time when Wexford's profile on the national stage was beginning to dim, he was a steadying influence which delayed the inevitable.

Viewed from any perspective then, the Rackards formed almost half a team in themselves. And apart from other qualities, their enduring legacy was that they introduced a brand new ploy which would enrich hurling long after they had departed into the shadows. The art of reaching high to catch the ball was almost non-existent in earlier generations when 'pulling' on the ball off the ground was sufficiently prevalent to ensure people risked serious injury by attempting to catch it in mid-air.

The boys from Killane would change all that in the course of a couple of eye-catching performances. Making maximum use of their physique, they soon began to undo the opposition with their unequalled aerial ability. And with the other Wexford players following suit, the high-reaching hand soon became a familiar spectacle, even in the most taut, tensely fought championship games around the country.

'We may never have been the classiest hurlers around,' Nick Rackard once observed in retirement, 'but I like to think that we won a few friends by the way we tried to play the game. And when you leave everything you have on the pitch at the end of a match, I believe you have paid your dues, both to your teammates and those who came to watch you.'

Over in Cork, Christy Ring would have subscribed readily to that philosophy. In his early career, he was, indeed, an industrious worker, often ranging far and wide from his allotted position at a time when it wasn't fashionable to do so. Added to his impressive acceleration over ten or fifteen yards, it amounted to a formidable package. By the time he arrived in his thirties, however, he had learned how to manage his energy levels, exploding into games only irregularly in brief but deadly intrusions. And one of his old adversaries would concur that his verbal contributions became equally short and sharp.

Mick Byrne, a valued teammate of Ring's in the blue of Munster but an implacable rival when clad in the blue and gold of Tipperary, was wont to recall one of the many occasions he was tasked with the challenge of containing the maestro. And after shadowing his man effectively for fifty-eight of the sixty minutes, he was entitled to feel that he had done his job well until a momentary lapse of concentration enabled Ring to slip in behind him to produce the match-winning score.

From a Tipperary standpoint, it was an incident with some painful precedents and when the players shook hands after the game, Byrne was gracious enough to congratulate Ring on his achievement with the remark: 'Christy we don't know what to do with you – I think we're going to have to shoot you.' Back like a flash came the rapier remark: 'You might as well – I think you've tried everything else.'

At just 5'8", Ring was still able to boast that he had never encountered a stronger man than himself and added to his relatively low centre of gravity, it made him an extremely difficult opponent to stop when in full stride. Bobby Rackard, big and raw-boned and possessed with the strength that came from his calling as a farmer, got to know that side of the Cloyne man pretty well when they clashed on the biggest stage of the lot – All-Ireland Final day at Croke Park in September 1954.

Wexford, beaten out the gate by Tipperary in 1951 in their first appearance in thirty-three years in an All-Ireland final, absorbed the lessons of that heavy defeat in a hurry – and none more so than the redoubtable Rackard brothers. By the time they overpowered Dublin in the Leinster final three years later and hammered twelve goals past a bewildered Antrim defence in the All-Ireland Semi-Final, they felt they were ready to deal with the best that Cork could offer.

Cork, too, had an emphatic win over Galway in the other semi-final to invest the final with an extra element of appeal for the public. With Ring targeting a record-breaking eighth All-Ireland winners' medal and Wexford on the cusp of greatness, the game attracted a crowd of almost 85,000. They got their money's worth too, for with the Leinster champions matching Cork score for score, it was still all to play for entering the closing stages.

Then Ring, on the burst, took off on a typical run down the middle and delivered the shot just as he was confronted by Bobby Rackard. The ball was deflected wide off the defender's shoulder and as Ring's momentum carried him forward, he clashed so heavily with his opponent that Rackard was forced to retire with a bad shoulder injury. The initial judgement was that the power of the shot had caused the injury but subsequently, Rackard, without a trace of acrimony, acknowledged that the damage was done in the collision with his arch rival.

With the anchor of their defence gone, Wexford eventually capitulated in a dramatic finish when Ring, thriving in the tumult of it all, set up his Glen Rovers clubmate, Johnny Clifford, for the decisive goal. Ring, effusive in his praise for the manner in which the losers had deported themselves, predicted that their hour would come and it duly arrived the following year when Wexford out-hurled Galway to claim hurling's biggest prize for the first time since 1910.

For all Galway's bravery in defeat, it had not been a final to remember for the neutral fan but twelve months later, in September 1956, the public got the decider it coveted when Cork and Wexford survived moments of real fear in their provincial finals against Limerick and Kilkenny respectively, to set up the dream pairing. In Leinster, Wexford had just a solitary point to spare against Kilkenny, but in many respects Cork's 5-5 to 3-5 win over Limerick was even scarier.

Limerick, birthplace of Mick Mackey, another enduring legend of hurling, desperately wanted to avenge themselves on Cork, who had upstaged them at every opportunity since Mackey inspired an historic success in 1940. With just fifteen minutes to go, they were leading by five points and well on the way to doing so until a resurgent Ring began to weave his brand of magic. Described by one contemporary commentator as 'a man hurling in a frenzy', the Cork player proceeded to score three goals and a point in the space of just five minutes. Even by Ring's exalted standards, that was an extravaganza without parallel and it served to intensify the hype in the build up to the big day at Croke Park.

On the first Sunday in September, Cork desperately needed more of that Ring magic. The lessons of the 1954 final, coupled with Wexford's fluent win over Galway twelve months later, told Jim Barry and his fellow backroom workers in the Cork camp that it would take a mighty effort to beat a team they once considered 'too loose' to be regarded as genuine All-

Ireland contenders. And as they toiled under the sheer weight of the champions' early pressure, they may have sensed the worst.

Seamus Hearne and Ned Wheeler were winning most of the 50-50 ball in midfield and with Nick Rackard proving a real handful for John Lyons on the fringe of the square, Wexford were deservedly ahead as the game entered its final stages. Then, in a seminal moment which is still recalled with absolute clarity by most of those who witnessed it, the hand of fate reached out to Christy Ring.

Getting first run on his marker, Bobby Rackard, Ring deserted his allotted place at left corner forward to snaffle the ball just twelve yards out. As he braced himself for the shot and the goal which would have given Cork a one point lead, he appeared to be knocked off balance momentarily by his teammate Paddy Barry before striking the ball. Normally Ring was unstoppable from that distance but in a moment of high inspiration, goalkeeper Art Foley grasped the ball just under the crossbar to demand the admiration of friend and foe alike. And Ring was so impressed by the feat that he forgot his disappointment and ran on in to shake the goalkeeper's hand.

It was a reprieve of monumental proportions for the champions and to rub it in, they immediately swept down the pitch for Nick Rackard to shake the netting for the goal which put the result beyond all doubt. Cork people will forever contend that it was Barry's involuntary brush with Ring, however slight, which deprived the great man of an unprecedented ninth All-Ireland success.

What was not in doubt, however, was the uniqueness of the scenes which followed the final whistle. Without a moment's hesitation, Bobby and Willie Rackard rushed across to hoist perhaps the greatest of all hurlers onto their shoulders in tribute to the man they had just denied. More vividly than words, the spectacle of Ring being borne aloft from the field of battle illustrated the mutual respect of men who, in their prime, captured the imagination of the masses like no others, before or since.

– Chapter 6 –

Scattering the Odds

Athletics – Ron Delany's Olympic 1,500 metres Win,
Melbourne, December 1956

An incident on a lonely college sports ground at the University of California, Berkeley in November 1956 bespoke the meticulous preparation which presaged perhaps the greatest of all Irish sporting triumphs in Melbourne just a couple of weeks later.

Ron Delany was in the final stages of his build up to the Olympic 1,500 metres championship. And for once, Jumbo Elliott, the celebrated coach at Villanova University in Philadelphia, who had masterminded his transition from club athlete to a place among the best four lap runners in the world, was missing. Instead, Brutus Hamilton, another esteemed name in American intercollegiate athletics, was in charge of a session which ended in a rehearsal of the scene that would soon bring so much joy to millions of Irish people at home and abroad.

'We were ambling back to the changing rooms at the end of a long, hard session when Brutus suddenly put a hand on my shoulder and said we'd forgotten something,' recalls Delany. 'We then walked back down the track where he produced a piece of string from his pocket and told me to tie it to two poles on either side of the running surface. I was them instructed to go back and run through the tape with my arms outstretched. At that point he shouted across to me, "Now, I think we've practised everything for Melbourne.'"

Hamilton had always been noted for his attention to detail and in the tall, slim Irishman, his entreaties were falling on fertile ground. And it was this obsession with getting things right which helped transform Delany's sporting ambitions in an era when Ireland was desperately short of role models in the challenge of enhancing the profile of the nation abroad. On his own admission, Ron was less gifted than his older brother, Joe, a prodigious teenage talent who was winning national senior titles while still a pupil at O'Connell School in Dublin.

In long jumping as well as sprinting, Joe Delany was unbeatable in the mood, whereas Ron twice lost out to the Roscrea 440 yards runner Liam Moloney in collegiate competition, first in Leinster and later, the national championship at Tuam in May 1953, just a year before he represented Ireland in the final of the 800 metres championship at Berne. Whereas Joe was never overly committed to training, however, his sibling went to the other extreme and, allied to unshakable self-belief, this would prove crucial in the making of an Olympic champion.

The possibility of Olympic glory was the goal that sustained him in times of stress – never more so than when he was offered a cadetship in the Army in the summer of 1953 and on the advice of his father, Paddy, he accepted. At a time when attractive job opportunities were at a premium, he said yes, only to discover, just weeks into his new calling, that a military career was not for him. In short, Army duty, at least in its early stages, did not offer him the time he needed to pursue his Olympic dreams. After agonising on a decision which, he suspected, would not be popular in the Delany household, he resigned from the Army and, for the first time in his life, found himself at odds with the person whose counsel he valued above all others – his father.

A job as a door-to-door salesman talking up the merits of Electrolux Hoovers, did offer him that opportunity and from his new base in Kilkenny, his career improved sufficiently in 1954 to earn him an 880 yards national record, a place in the finals of the European 800 metres championship in Switzerland and, most prized of all, an athletics scholarship at Villanova and the chance to join one of the most accomplished of all American collegiate teams.

Before Delany set down in Philadelphia, Jumbo Elliott, the Villanova coach, had worked with Irish athletes of the quality of John Joe Barry, Jimmy Reardon and Cuman Clancy. Barry, a middle distance runner of extraordinary natural talent but utterly bereft of discipline, intrigued Elliott as often as he infuriated him. Despite his lack of commitment, Barry was good enough to win a couple of British titles at a time when they carried a lot of prestige and his summer appearance in the meetings promoted by the irrepressible Billy Morton did much to keep track and field in the headlines in the late 1940s, at a stage when there was precious little else happening in the sport.

In terms of attitude, Delany could scarcely have been further removed from Barry. And it took Elliott only a couple of weeks to acknowledge that fact as well as identifying one major fault. As far as his new coach was concerned, the Dubliner was specialising in the wrong event – from that day on, he would be classified as a miler.

'I looked at the kid and knew almost at once that he was built to run the mile,' mused Elliott after his protégé had scooped the biggest prize in Melbourne. 'His 800 metres times told me that he had the required basic speed for the job and despite his sparse frame, I recognised that physically and mentally, he was made for four-lap running.'

Victory over Wes Santes, the top American miler in an indoor meeting in Boston where Santes had set a world record the previous year, confirmed that the graph of Delany's career was rising on schedule but indirectly, the confidence which derived from that victory led him into two ill-fated duels with the great Australian John Landy at the start of the American outdoor season in May 1956. Measured by any yardstick, Landy was a remarkable athlete, a man who, two years earlier, was viewed by

Peter Byrne

much of the world as the one most likely to pip Roger Bannister to the
enduring distinction of being the first to break four minutes for the mile.

History records that it didn't quite work out that way for the tall, elegant Australian, but with the 1956 Olympics looming in his hometown,
fulfilment of a different variety awaited him if he held his form until the
end of the year. It was against that background that Delany, just two
months past his twenty-first birthday, backed his unbridled enthusiasm
against the confidence born of maturity and elected to take on Landy in
the biggest race of the year to that point, at the Coliseum in Los Angeles.

In the event, it proved a gross miscalculation by the Irishman. Wholly
out of character, he threw caution to the wind and bolted into the lead
from the gun. Optimism on that scale was fringed with risk and after running an opening lap of fifty-seven seconds, he was already a spent force at
half way. Landy can only have been surprised by the magnitude of that
gaffe, for some weeks earlier he had mentioned the relatively unproven
Irishman as one of the potential winners in Melbourne. Venturing where
others feared to tread, Delany opted to take on the Australian yet again
just seven days later and this time, suffered an even heavier defeat as he
limped home some seventy-five yards adrift of the winner.

In the space of a week, Delany had been made to absorb two of the
most painful lessons of his young career, but surprisingly the confidence
which had driven him from the first time he set foot in America remained
largely intact. In each instance, he attributed his eclipse to bad decision
making and with the big Melbourne extravaganza now less than six
months away, he vowed to profit from the dearly bought lessons.

And what better place to start than in the Compton Invitation meeting, one of the glamour fixtures on the American calendar. Anybody who
won there had to be taken seriously as a contender for the highest honours,
and while neither Landy nor his compatriot, Jim Bailey, was entered for
the race, it still offered the opportunity of early redemption. In an era
when athletics, even at the highest level, was still an amateur sport, Delany

would recall years later that rehabilitation wasn't the only thing on his mind as he prepared for the race that could wipe the slate clean.

When he arrived at the track, he discovered that his old spikes had packed in and with just ten dollars in his pocket, he was forced to buy replacements on credit from a shoe salesman at the meeting. As it transpired, it proved a lucky purchase, but unimpressed by the drama which would unfold later in the evening, the vendor insisted on recouping the full debt after the meeting.

On this occasion, the man to beat was the powerful Dane, Gunnar Nielsen, who had recently set a new world record for the 1,500 metres and right on cue the race developed into a thrilling head-to-head over the last 200 yards. In the end, Delany nicked it but the biggest thrill of all came some five minutes later when his time was confirmed at 3mins 59.1secs.

He had just become the youngest of the seven athletes who claimed membership of sport's most exclusive club, that of the sub-four minute milers, and among those who tendered their congratulations was John Landy in far-off Melbourne. Boosted still further by a win over Jim Bailey a fortnight later, Delany returned to Dublin with expectations of early selection for Ireland's Olympic team – but he was not to know that others held different views.

Unlike many of their counterparts in more affluent countries, the Olympic Council of Ireland received no state aid in the bleak 1950s and with precious little assistance emanating from the corporate sector, what little funding they got depended mainly on the response to their public appeal. Among other things that precluded long-term planning and, generally, the numerical strength of the Olympic squad was determined a matter of weeks rather than months, before the departure date.

For the discipline of track and field athletics, riven as it was by domestic politics, the lottery of Olympic selection was even more precarious. With the Amateur Athletic Union of Eire locked into a bitter dispute with the ostracised National Athletics and Cycling Association of Ireland, there was little goodwill for the sport or its representatives on the OCI, and for all the merit of his performance at the Compton meeting, Delany was treading dangerous ground.

His case for selection wasn't helped by some deeply disappointing results on his return to his old stomping ground at Lansdowne Road that summer. In spite of his spectacular progress at Villanova and his growing reputation as one of the finest indoor runners of all time, British observers felt that their man, Brian Hewson, was a better bet for the upcoming Olympic 1,500 metres championship. Those claims were given added credence on 25 June 1956, when Hewson prevailed in a thrilling duel down the finishing straight.

It didn't help when Delany was spiked in his next race in Paris in early July and after a dangerously brief four-week rehabilitation, he was rushed, unwisely, into a return meeting with Hewson in Dublin. If the result of their first race was disputed, there was absolutely no argument about the outcome of their second meeting when Delany trailed home almost eighty yards adrift of his arch rival in a time of 4 minutes 20 seconds, his slowest since specialising in the mile event.

That result was interpreted by some as the clap of doom for the Dubliner's chances of even making it to the starting line in Melbourne. Importantly, however, he refused to be either unnerved or discouraged and with Jumbo Elliott unwavering in his assertion that their Olympic preparations were still on schedule, he went back to Villanova determined to show that his misfortunes were merely temporary.

The august members of the Olympic Council were less enthusiastic and as long days of waiting for confirmation of their intentions hardened into weeks and still no indication of a green light for the man based 3,000 miles away, even some of Delany's most committed supporters began to have doubts. As it transpired, it required the casting vote of Lord Killanin, President of the OCI, to ratify his selection, but incredibly, the decision was never communicated to the athlete and it was not until three days before the departure of the squad that Delany knew for certain that he was going to the games.

That, in turn, would spawn another major problem for the athlete. He had discovered on the grapevine that the team would travel from Dublin to New York on the Sunday and journey on from there to California, en route to Australia. He was told that his air ticket, as well as other documentation, would arrive in Villanova on the Friday. But when Saturday morning dawned and there was still no sign of the tickets, the alarm bells were ringing loudly. To make matters worse, the local post office closed for the weekend at noon on Saturday.

There are various theories on how the missing documents were eventually retrieved, but the official line is that the local postmaster agreed to return and open his office temporarily on the Saturday afternoon, enabling Ron to meet up with his teammates. Unfortunately, Brendan O'Reilly, the broadcaster and multiple Irish high jump champion, was not among them. O'Reilly's selection had been conditional on his raising enough money to fund his way to the games, and while his name appeared on the official programme for the high jump preliminaries, he never made it to Australia.

The Irish team eventually arrived in the Olympic village, just three days before the opening ceremony for the games, the last to do so, but out of this chaotic preparation they would eventually emerge as one of the countries with the highest percentage of medals relative to their numerical strength. Little if anything had gone right in the build up to the games and on their arrival, there was a further complication when Christy Murphy, head of the delegation, was taken ill and subsequently detained in hospital for several weeks.

With no other Irish official accredited, team members were effectively left to their own devices and like the other members of the track team, Eamonn Kinsella and Maeve Kyle, Delany had to arrange his own training sessions. Just as crucially, they had to learn how to survive financially, for while their 'keep' was provided by the organisers, they now had no team manager to manage or help finance their leisure time in Melbourne.

In view of the hype triggered by Roger Bannister's sub-four minute mile at Oxford and the increasing frenetic efforts of others to follow him through the barrier, the Olympic 1,500 metres championship in Melbourne was the most talked about race at the distance, before or since. And yet for all the difficulties welling up around him, the Irishman progressed from the preliminaries with little difficulty, finishing third in his heat behind Merv Lincoln of Australia and Ken Wood of Great Britain with fellow sub-four minute man, Laszlo Tabori of Hungary immediately behind him.

Of the five sub-four minute milers lining up in the final two days later – Landy, Hewson, Delany, Tabori and Nielsen – the Irishman was the youngest and least experienced. And yet, Landy was not alone in predicting that the man who ran for Crusaders AC in domestic competition, would probably have a big influence on the race. And the element of intrigue heightened when Delany chose to run at the back of the pack as Murray Halberg of New Zealand and Lincoln took out the early pace.

A mere six yards covered the field at the bell and Delany, running in tenth position at the time, moved out wide to cover the break when it came. Predictably, it was Landy who first struck for home but even as he did so, the Irishman moved into his slipstream and the BBC radio commentator, relating the developing plot of the race to the countless thousands back home, noted that 'Delany of Eire is running well and making up ground on the outside.' Just how well Delany was going is best described by the man himself.

'I knew that if I was to win, I would have to make one and only one decisive move. I restrained myself as long as possible and about 150 yards from the finish, I opened up with everything I had. Within ten yards, I was in the lead and going away from the field. I knew at that point that nobody was going to pass me, for my legs were pumping like pistons. I was of course tired but with the opportunity of a lifetime stretching out ahead of me, I wasn't going to give in to anybody. The Olympic 1,500 metres championship was mine for the taking and my heart swelled with joy as I approached the tape ten feet clear of the rest of the field.'

Ron Delany sank to his knees to say a silent prayer after finishing but was back on his feet by the time the public address announcer proclaimed the news that the Irishman had not only won but established a new Olympic record of 3 minutes 41.2 seconds in the process.

A young man, unfancied even by many of his fellow countrymen, had passed into sporting folklore and in his message of congratulation, Eamon De Valera was moved to compare Delany's win with the exploits of Matt Donovan, the legendary Irish ploughman who was celebrated for his ability to plough a furrow straighter than a straight line. 'Like Matt,' De Valera wrote, 'you have won for the credit of the little village.' Somehow, it seemed to encapsulate the sheer ineptitude of the powerbrokers in the making of the greatest of Ireland's Olympic champions.

– Chapter 7 –

Jack's the Man

Football – Republic of Ireland v England, Dalymount Park, May 1957

Jack Carey, a distinguished manager of the Republic of Ireland team for a period of twelve years, had a simple request when he met with FAI officials to discuss arrangements for the two World Cup preliminary games, home and away, against England in May 1957. The cost amounted to less than £50, but he considered it essential that the association purchase a set of tracksuits for the self-esteem of his players.

'The pride and self respect of our country as well as our players will be on show for millions in the pre-match ceremonies at Wembley Stadium,' he told them. 'And it is important that we present ourselves in the best way possible, in terms of both dress and conduct, on every occasion during our stay in England.'

At a time in the modern era when sportswear manufacturers are falling over themselves in the stampede to equip national sports teams free gratis, it may be difficult to realise that it wasn't always so. Tracksuits for example, were recycled so often that on occasions they became undeniably shabby, never more so than on the occasion of the World Cup game in Finland in 1949.

It was so bad that the cash-strapped FAI officials accompanying the team were forced to buy a replacement set in the course of a shopping expedition to downtown Helsinki. That was an unexpected item of expenditure and to make matters worse, the new gear was impounded by customs and excise personnel on their return to Dublin airport, occasioning an intervention by the political establishment before being released without charge some days later.

That the tracksuit issue should resurface in the approach to the Wembley game was indicative of the gravitas attached to the first ever competitive tie against England. It was only in 1946 that the FA of England agreed to send a team to Dublin after an interval of thirty-four years. That gesture was reciprocated, of course, at Goodison Park three years later when Carey's team, against all the odds, recorded a hugely gratifying 2–0 victory, the first 'foreign' team to beat England on home terrain.

For all its historical value, however, the Goodison game didn't quite compare in significance with either of the matches in 1957. Now it was the prize of World Cup points which would provide the incentive for the men in green and, as the manager was apt to point out at the time, the memory of the little miracle in Liverpool was more likely to motivate England in their search for revenge. And the fact that the Wembley game was being televised by the BBC added to the attraction of the first leg of the tie, if only for viewers on the other side of the Irish Sea.

BBC authorities paid just £1,500 for the exclusive television rights of the game, a tiny figure when set against the mega money now on offer for similar facilities. The fee paid by British Movietone News for the right to show edited highlights of the match in cinemas here and in Britain amounted to just £50. The ancillary fees helped swell gross receipts for the Wembley game to £18,393, of which the FAI's share was £6,883. This represented something of a windfall for an organisation which was forced to survive on slender financial margins in the early post-war years.

It also represented something of a personal triumph for Joe Wickham, the long-serving Secretary of the Association who had stubbornly resisted English pressure for the home association to retain the entire gate in each instance, in the expectation that the Wembley 'gate', based on the superior size and facilities of the stadium, would triple that taken in the return match at Dalymount Park. In deference to London's wishes, however, it was agreed to increase the price of premium stand tickets to 25 shillings for the game in Dublin, a decision which provoked howls of protest from local fans until it was pointed out the corresponding seats at Wembley cost exactly double that figure.

Even with temporary seating, Dalymount held considerably less than 50,000. More tellingly still, it normally offered seated facilities for just 2,200 spectators, a fraction of the number available in London. And it was this consideration which prompted Shelbourne FC, acting independently and to the stated embarrassment of some FAI officials, to write to the Irish Rugby Football Union, enquiring if they would be prepared to make Lansdowne Road available for the occasion.

Thirty years had elapsed since the last time an international football game was played in the rugby stadium and at a stage when there was no obvious empathy between the two associations, the majority feeling was that the request would fall on barren ground. In that assumption, they were proved right, with Bob Fitzgerald, the IRFU Secretary, delivering the curt response that Lansdowne Road was not available to any association for Sunday games.

Not even the spectre of inflated admission charges for the North London arena could diminish the growing enthusiasm of Irish fans who, in that pre-television era, could only read of the diverse skills of players like Stanley Matthews, Billy Wright and Johnny Haynes. Special arrangements were put in place for air and sea excursions to Britain and in the end, more than 3,500 supporters, far and away the biggest support for any Irish team competing abroad to that point, availed of them. Added to the huge expatriate population in and around London, it ensured a substantial Irish presence in the ground on Wednesday, 8 May 1957.

Originally, this was the date suggested by Denmark, the third team in the group, for Ireland's visit to Copenhagen, but when the English FA indicated that they wished to play both legs of the Ireland tie at the end of the season, the Danish assignment was put on hold. That arrangement suited Jack Carey perfectly, for he was wont to bemoan the fact that circumstances normally made it impossible to assemble the national squad for any meaningful length of time.

To that end, he assembled his players at their English base at Weymouth in Surrey on Sunday, 5 May and after the Wembley match, they regrouped at a hotel in Bray where they availed of the local Carlisle Grounds for their daily training sessions until the second leg of the tie eleven days later. A problem common to both managers was the fact that the English FA Cup final between Manchester United and Aston Villa was scheduled for 4 May, the day before the national squads got together and the fear was that if the game was drawn, the replay would clash with the first leg of the World Cup tie.

Matt Busby's Manchester United team contributed four players, Roger Byrne, Duncan Edwards, Tommy Taylor and David Pegg to the England squad as well as Liam Whelan to Ireland. The only Villa player involved was Pat Saward, a valued member of Carey's half-back line. England intimated that in the event of an FA Cup replay being necessary, Maurice Norman (Tottenham), Denis Wilshaw (Wolves), Brian Clough(Sunderland) and Brian Pilkington (Burnley) would be promoted to their squad. Ireland made no provision for the replacement of either Whelan or Saward. As it happened, Aston Villa won 2–1 and Whelan was named as the Man of the Match – an encouraging augury perhaps, for his return to Wembley for the first ever World Cup game to be played there, just four days later.

After expressing a preference for a team of Welsh officials to take charge of both games, the Irish were forced to concede to England's choice of three Scots and by the time Hugh Phillips eventually got the first game under way, a crowd of just over 52,000 was inside stadium. Even for an afternoon fixture in midweek, this was disappointing and with a vociferous Irish presence in the ground, the atmosphere was not wholly different from that on Merseyside seven years earlier when Ireland scripted one of the finest wins in their history.

Alas, there was to be no repeat of those heroics in London. Desperately needing time to settle, a team which included two League of Ireland players, Alan Kelly, the Drumcondra goalkeeper and Gerry Mackey of Shamrock Rovers, was taken off its feet by the sheer pace and intensity of England's early pressure. Crucially, it was Mackey's misfortune to find Tommy Taylor at the top of his form as the tall Manchester United centre forward embarked on the best international performance in his tragically short career.

Inside ten minutes, Taylor had delivered the first of his three goals, taking a pass from Johnny Haynes in full stride and sprinting past Saward before beating Kelly with the angled shot. Just eight minutes later, he struck again, carrying the ball through a broken defence to score from the edge of the penalty area. For an Irish team which had won four of its previous five games – including a 3–0 victory over the reigning World Cup champions, West Germany – it was all too bad to be true, but it got even worse as half-time approached. John Atyeo, a name destined to stick in Irish minds, pounced on Kelly's mistake to score a third and in the fortieth minute, the imperious Taylor completed his hat trick when he soared clear of the defence to head home Tom Finney's corner.

Carey, never the most effusive of men, managed to address his disillusioned players in cool, measured tones during the half-time break, pointing out that those two late scores had totally distorted the half-time scoreline. Whether it was this reasoned approach or England taking their foot off the pedal which made the difference remains a matter of conjecture, but the game was transformed in the second half when the Irish team dominated territorially.

Much of the inspiration stemmed from Joe Haverty's skill on the left wing and predictably, it was the artistry of the Arsenal player which set up a goal for Dermot Curtis in the fifty-sixth minute. It ought to have provided the springboard for a spirited fight back, but with Arthur Fitzsimons and Peter Farrell missing good chances and the crossbar denying Liam Whelan, that was as good as it got for the visitors. Then, in the last minute of normal team, Atyeo struck again and a 5–1 scoreline represented Ireland's heaviest defeat in four years.

For the thousands of Irish supporters in the stadium, it was a chastening reminder of the length of the road still to be travelled if their team was to reach the promised land. Yet, the more discerning of them would have drawn comfort from the manager's post-match comments after the initial flood of disappointment had subsided and his mind turned to the challenge of getting even with the team that had just imparted such a painful lesson.

'Look back on the game and you will see that two of England's goals came in the minutes just before half-time and another when we were expecting the full time whistle,' he told his players. 'All those goals were due to low levels of concentration on our part and if we repeat them, we'll be punished again in Dublin. But in spite of losing by four goals here, I believe we can regain our respect at Dalymount Park.'

That represented a brave statement of intent in the light of Ireland's total eclipse in the first half and Carey was only too aware of the wages of the defeat in the context of qualifying for the World Cup finals in Sweden the following year. It meant that England now merely had to take a point from the second-leg match to book their Scandinavian passage. Ireland, on the other hand, had to win at Dalymount and then beat Denmark in Copenhagen to earn a play-off with England for group honours.

Having analysed the Wembley performance in some detail, the manager realised that to have any chance of turning the table, he needed to stiffen his defence. Out went the two locally based players, Kelly and Mackey, as well as the exposed Everton right-back, Don Donovan.

Controversially, the axe also fell on Peter Farrell, a splendid competitor in his twenty-eight earlier appearances in the national team but now utterly unable to restrict the threat posed by Johnny Haynes. Like Donovan and Mackey, he would never again wear the Ireland shirt.

Kelly, replaced by the veteran Tommy Goodwin in goal, would have to wait five long years before getting the chance to redeem his international career. Also back in favour was Ronnie Nolan, one of the great utility men at Shamrock Rovers and a superb box-to-box player whose performance against Haynes would be key to the drama about to unfold at Dalymount.

Yet, the most significant selection by far was that of Charlie Hurley, a strapping nineteen-year-old centre half from Millwall FC, who was born in Cork but taken to London by his family as an infant. In his first season at the Den, Hurley had been chosen to play for London in the old Inter-City competition. Now, after being forced to delay his Ireland debut by seven months because of an injury sustained while he was doing his military service in Britain, he was ready to handle the biggest challenge of his young life by putting the shackles on Tommy Taylor.

'Before coming over to Dublin for the game,' Hurley recalled, 'my father gave me a few words of advice. He warned me never to let Taylor out of my sights, to go everywhere he went and if it meant accompanying him to the toilet, so be it. I think Tommy got the message early on and I was on my way in international football.'

Following the demotion of Farrell, Noel Cantwell was appointed to captain the team for the first time and no less than the other big men in the home defence, Hurley and Saward, he would reach out for the acclaim of the crowd on a day when a record 47,600 crammed into the old stadium to provide the perfect backdrop for the occasion. And they had to wait just a mere three minutes before getting the opportunity to vent their joy in a vast explosion of sound. Hurley and Haverty combined to put Arthur Fitzsimons clear down the left flank and the deep cross was converted into a golden goal by Alf Ringstead.

For Ringstead, son of a jockey at the Curragh, it was far and away the most important of the seven goals he scored in twenty Ireland appearances. And it set the mood for a vibrant, noisy day when every Irish pass was cheered to the echo and Tommy Goodwin, a hero at Goodison Park in 1949, rolled back the years to demand the admiration of friend and foe once more.

Four times, Goodwin stood between England and certain goals after Taylor (twice), Atyeo and Haynes, had got in behind the last Irish defender – and on the one occasion he was beaten, Seamus Dunne recovered to clear the ball off the line. Soon afterwards, the visitors enjoyed a similar reprieve in the seventy-fifth minute with Billy Wright smothering Haverty's shot as it sped towards an otherwise unprotected net. Still, as the first of three minutes' additional time were being played, that seemed irrelevant with Ireland protecting their lead admirably and looking forward to the likelihood of a third meeting with England to determine Word Cup qualification.

Then, with the home crowd clamouring for Hugh Phillips to blow for full time, came the goal which fell like a clap of doom on the stadium. It all looked so innocuous when Haverty lost possession up at the School end of the ground but almost quicker than it takes to relate, Jeff Hall fed Tom Finney down the right wing and as Saward and Cantwell backed off the wily Preston winger, he delivered the cross which Atyeo headed home for an equaliser that England never deserved.

Whereas Ireland's goal had provoked scenes of ecstasy, Atyeo's effort was received with eerie silence, so much so that radio commentator Phil Greene was moved to tell his audience that, 'The pained silence here at Dalymount can be heard all the way back to Nelson's Pillar.'

For the second time in twelve days, John Atyeo of Bristol City had broken Irish hearts with his finely honed opportunism and the Republic of Ireland team was out of contention for a place in the World Cup finals. Ironically, Atyeo would never again play for England and for the remainder of his working life earned his living as a schoolteacher. But long after his star had faded, his name would remain synonymous with one of the great anticlimaxes in Irish sport.

– Chapter 8 –

The Longest Run

Rugby – Ireland v Australia, Lansdowne Road, January 1958

As athletes go, Noel Henderson was never likely to be recalled as the quickest around. A tall, heavily built man, his forte was an ability to break tackles on a rugby field and create the spaces which enabled other, more nimble players around him to carry the ball across the try line.

Yet the record book shows that when the chips were down, Henderson was capable of weaving his own particular brand of excellence, as evidenced by some crucial tries at different stages of his international career and, not least, his ability to take on the role of emergency goal kicker with gratifying success.

For those of us old enough to remember it, however, it was a try fashioned by power, pride and an indomitable sense of purpose, which will identify his most important contribution to Irish rugby on a day when he reached out for the acclaim of sports enthusiasts across the island. For some, it will be recalled as the longest fifty yards run in history, but for all the hyperbole, the fact is that it was Noel Henderson who wrote himself into the annals of sporting history with the score that enabled Ireland to beat Australia on Saturday, 18 January 1958, the first time they had overcome an overseas touring team.

The term 'Grand Slam', as applied to the Five Nations rugby championship, hadn't yet been coined in the immediate post-war years. The big prize for the northern hemisphere nations was to finish at the top of the championship table and while extra significance attached to the victories of those doing so with maximum points, that, essentially, was the icing on the cake.

For those old-timers whose interest in the championship preceded the arrival of France, the honour of winning the Triple Crown was almost as alluring. Here the scalp of England was the one most prized by Irish supporters but it was diminished undeniably if, per chance, the men in green slipped up against either Wales or Scotland or, perish the thought, by both in the same season.

Then there was the challenge of lowering the colours of a southern hemisphere team on tour in Britain or Ireland. By definition these opportunities arose only infrequently at a time when the world looked a lot bigger than it does now, and the luxury of long-distance travel in the name of sport was given only to a few. When they did materialise, it was at once a privilege and a profound challenge to engage and overcome teams from the Southern Hemisphere.

The first touring team to visit these shores was garbed in the all black strip of New Zealand in 1905. That resulted in a 15–0 defeat for the Irish and that outcome was to be repeated in four subsequent meetings of the countries prior to 1958. The match series against South Africa, initiated at Ravenhill on 26 November 1906, followed a similar pattern and it wasn't until the sixth meeting at Lansdowne Road on 6 April 1965, that Ireland broke the sequence by a slender 9–8 margin.

Although Ireland had played against a team representing New South Wales, losing 5–3 in the process, at Lansdowne Road in 1927, it wasn't until 1947 that the full Australian test side put their resources on display in Dublin. It would be another eleven years before they returned and by that stage, the peerless Jack Kyle was the sole survivor from the team which fell to a 16–3 defeat.

Noel Henderson, then completing his second level education in

Belfast, followed the diminishing fortunes of the Irish team by means of Ronnie Thornton's commentary on Radio Éireann in 1947, but within another two years he had joined Kyle, later to become his brother-in-law, on the Ireland team. For player and country alike, it would prove a happy partnership.

From the team which had completed the championship and Triple Crown double with four straight wins the previous year, the Irish selectors were forced to make two significant changes when they set out to consolidate that success in 1949. Paddy Reid, a useful football and hockey player to go with his prowess on a rugby pitch, had gone to England to join the noted Rugby League club Huddersfield and he was joined there by Chris Daly, who in his last appearance in a green shirt had entered the hallowed halls of folklore by producing the winning try against Wales at Ravenhill.

Their replacements were interesting. Tom Clifford, a manual worker with Limerick Corporation, was awarded Daly's place as loosehead prop while the vacancy in the centre was filled by Fr Tom Gavin, an England-based priest who played for London Irish. Gavin was the only Roman Catholic priest to play rugby for Ireland but it was his misfortune to be introduced to a misfiring backline for the opening championship game against France at Lansdowne Road.

Three penalty goals from George Norton was all that Ireland could muster in response to France's total of two tries, two conversions and two penalty goals and after another muted performance in the win over England, a good man of the cloth paid with his place when the selectors met to name the team for the next game against Scotland. In a sense, it was rough justice on the newcomer who never regained his place in the national team, but if that decision was questionable at the time, there was certainly no doubting the quality of the youngster who replaced him.

Henderson had been the outstanding player of his era in schools competition in Ulster and showed sufficient improvement in his first year at Queen's University to warrant a brave decision by the national selectors for the Scottish assignment. He would justify that leap of faith by slotting seamlessly into the three quarter line and on the back of some brilliant tries by Jim McCarthy, Ireland won their last two games to retain the championship and secure the Triple Crown for a second consecutive year.

It is a measure of the impact Henderson made that, in spite of Wales sweeping the boards in 1950, he was one of eight Irish players selected in the Lions squad which Karl Mullen captained in the first post-war tour of New Zealand in 1950. The All Blacks won three of the four test matches with the other one drawn, but the experience gained on that marathon of endurance would serve the Queens player well on his journey to the pinnacle of international approval.

With George Norton forced to call time on his short but highly successful international career in 1951, Henderson was one of several placekickers used by Ireland during their international campaign that year. But while the championship was won for the third time in four years, they could only draw 3–3 with Wales after spurning at least three feasible penalty chances and the Triple Crown eluded them.

As it transpired, that was as good as it got for the first Golden Generation of Irish rugby players and the loss, at varying intervals, of players like Bill McKay, Des O'Brien and Jim McCarthy deprived the team of the back row skills which in other times had commanded the respect of all opposition. Jack Kyle survived until 1958, however, and as long as he remained as the playmaker, Henderson's development and the emerging talents of Tony O'Reilly, Cecil Pedlow and more latterly, Niall Brophy, were enhanced accordingly.

Yet, with the impending visit of Australia acting as the prelude to the 1957/58 championship, the national team was far from settled as preparations were put in place for the first game against an overseas touring team since New Zealand's 14–3 win at Lansdowne Road four years earlier. Despite all the uncertainty, few were prepared for the radical team nominated by the selectors, who included Dudley Higgins, a member of the historic 1948 squad. In all, it included six new caps, but seldom has an influx of new talent had such a significant impact on Irish rugby.

Three of the newcomers, Ronnie Dawson, Bill Mulcahy and Noel Murphy, would go on to captain the international team and it is a measure of Dawson's leadership qualities that within eighteen months of making his international debut, he was the popular choice to lead the British and Irish Lions on their tour of New Zealand and Australia.

In time, he would emerge as a highly influential legislator whose ability at this level was quickly recognised by counties in the southern hemisphere and in this role, his contribution to the evolution of international rugby was immense. The other newcomers, Jim Donaldson, Jim Stevenson and David Hewitt, were from Ulster with Hewitt following in the footprints of his father, Tom, capped ten times by Ireland in the 1920s.

By any standard, it was a highly improvised selection with that superb international competitor, Ronnie Kavanagh, flanked by Murphy and Donaldson in the back row. Kavanagh, a competitive amateur boxer and swimmer before concentrating on rugby, had made his first international appearance against France in 1953 at a time when the national team was undergoing some profound changes in personnel.

In time, he grew into the best number eight in the northern hemisphere, helping to bridge the gap between the loss of outstanding forwards such as McCarthy, Des O'Brien and McKay and the emergence of the new back rowers who would serve the team well through the 1960s and beyond. He remembers the mood well as they prepared for the arrival of the formidable Wallabies.

'Televised sport was still only a remote possibility at that time and in the context of sport, the world wasn't as small as it is today. It meant that that the aura surrounding teams coming here from the southern hemisphere was even greater and it was manifested in the growing hype in the weeks and days leading up to the game at Lansdowne Road.

'In the sense that we had met Australia only once previously, there were a lot of questions which needed answers and the fact that we were going into the game with six uncapped players merely heightened the uncertainty of it all. But Jack Kyle and Noel Henderson were still there to oversee things behind the scrum and while the new-look pack had to be taken on trust, I believe all of us were acutely aware of the need to work for each other and keep it going for the full eighty minutes.'

For Australia, the first unpleasant surprise of the day was discovering that the weather in Dublin had turned foul in the extreme on the morning of the game with a strong, bitterly cold crosswind aggravating the problems occasioned by earlier rain. That must have been a shock to the system for the tourists, for if numbed fingers were causing the Irish players to fumble passes, one could only guess at the inner feelings of the visitors and their hankering for the warm, sunny climes they had left behind.

To make things worse, they lost the toss for the choice of ends and found themselves playing into the teeth of the elements in the opening half. And yet for all their early woes, they jumped into a twelfth-minute lead which may have surprised even the most optimistic of their number. Hewitt's immaturity showed when he missed a tackle on his opposite centre, Shane White, and Kyle was marginally too late to prevent Ken Phelps exacting maximum retribution in the corner.

Potentially, that was a mortal blow for the home team and while Cecil Pedlow's penalty, over off an upright, had Ireland level at 3–3 at the interval, the manner in which the Australian forwards dominated the Irish pack and its four newcomers in the opening forty minutes boded ill for the home team.

Ironically, as so often happens on these occasions, it was an unsavoury incident precipitated by a couple of Australian forwards within three minutes of the resumption, which spurred the Irish players and the 50,000 spectators to even greater endeavours. Murphy, invariably at the heart of the action, was on the receiving end of a stray boot to trigger the first incident and later, the crowd was incensed when Paddy O'Donoghue, the durable Bective Rangers prop, was knocked backwards by a punch. The effect in each instance was to galvanise the crowd as well as breaking the momentum of the tourists after Summons, their nimble out-half, had transfixed friend and foe alike with some delightful footwork to score their second try far out.

For the second time in the game, the Irish newcomers were facing a huge test of character and for one player in particular, the response would launch him on a path to a place among the great Irish locks. Revelling in the physicality of it all, Mulcahy was frequently inspirational and with the front row of Gordon Wood, Dawson and O'Donoghue grinding down the opposition, Ireland gradually turned the screw in the last ten minutes.

On the back of that ascendancy, the Irish attack finally hit their stride and when Kyle released Tony O'Reilly on the burst, an attack that traversed the width of the park and back again, looked certain to yield a thrilling try until Andy Mulligan was eventually hauled down just yards short of the line. From a position in which they looked likely to see out the game safely, the tourists were suddenly rattled and when Dawson and Wood combined to smother Terry Curley's attempted clearance, Dawson was first to react with the touchdown that levelled the scores.

Worryingly, Henderson's attempt to put Ireland in the lead with the conversion wobbled in the wind before hitting a post and going dead. But far from disillusioning the crowd, that exasperating miss merely had the effect of raising the decibel of the noise in the stands and on the terraces. Not for years had the weather-scarred Lansdowne Road stadium witnessed anything like it and as the excitement increased, so Ireland intensified their search for a winner from the drop out.

Given their relatively low level of expectation entering the game, the Irish players might have been excused had they settled for an honourable draw at that point. Instead, they sensed the long arm of opportunity reaching out to them and directly from the restart they set about the tourists' defence once again. On this occasion, their initial surge was contained and when the ball emerged on the Australian side from a ruck on the Irish ten yards line, the crowd held its breadth once more.

Suspense gave way to exhilaration, however, when a looped pass from Summons to Phelps was intercepted by Hewitt, who waited until confronted by Curley, the last Australian defender, before unleashing Henderson on his long run into history. The Ulster man had all of fifty yards to cover when he set off for the line and while he had a good start on the pursuit, the anguished looks on the faces of the multitudes in the stadium told of a neck or nothing race for glory.

As he neared the Promised Land, Henderson could almost feel the hot breath on his neck from Summons immediately behind him, but we knew for certain that he had made it when he finally launched himself into the dive that took him over the line. Various witticisms have been invoked to convey the tension and ultimately the joy of it all, but as Henderson, utterly drained, looked up to accept the congratulations of his colleagues, we knew even then that the scenes we were witnessing would be told and retold for generations still unborn.

'The rest of us were strung out in the distance as we watched Noel curve his way to the line but those of us who had played with him in other big games knew that once he got to within touching distance of the whitewash, nothing or nobody was going to stop him,' recalled Ronnie Kavanagh. 'And it couldn't have happened for a better person, for in every aspect of his approach to sport, Noel Henderson was indeed a gentleman.'

Moments of tension still remained after that dramatic score but Jack Kyle twice kept his cool to mark the ball under towering Garryowens from Summons and the explosion of noise which greeted the final whistle captured the gravitas of it all. Back in the dressing room, Noel Henderson sucked on his pipe before delivering himself of his verdict on an historic performance. 'It's a great day to be Irish and even better to think of what it will mean for Irish rugby in the years ahead,' he said.

We were not to know it then, but Jack Kyle would make just one more appearance in the green before terminating a career without parallel at that point, and he would be followed into retirement by his brother-in-law just a year later. Between them, they had done much to brighten the lives of many thousands of their fellow countrymen.

– Chapter 9 –

Lion of Munich

Football – Northern Ireland's World Cup Odyssey, Sweden, June 1958

There was something about Harry Gregg that put him apart from the pack. Tall and strong, forthright in what he said, fearless in what he faced, he was a man who commanded attention on a football field and the respect, non-sporting people afford footballers only grudgingly, off it.

Like all goalkeepers, he was given to the odd eccentric decision but once he was on his game and fully focussed, he was the kind of man everybody wanted in his team. And in a time of urgent need, his tightly cut red hair was a sight to reassure those who claimed kinship.

That is why the name of Harry Gregg will forever remain an integral part of the story of how the exceptional Manchester United team of the late 1950s came to grief on a snow-covered runway at Munich in February 1958. And how the pain of one of the most tragic of all sporting disasters was lightened, if only marginally, by the towering courage of the man from Coleraine, County Derry.

He did not attempt to hide the apprehension he shared with everybody else on the doomed Elizabethan airliner as it taxied to the end of the runway for a third attempt to get airborne. Or the sense of numbed disbelief among the survivors as the plane crashed headlong into a disused building on the periphery of the airfield after another failed liftoff.

Gregg was one of the fortunate ones to be catapulted to safety as the plane broke in two before being engulfed in flames. The natural instinct was to run and distance himself as far as possible from the expected explosion as the fire reached towards the fuel tanks. Then, through the cries of anguish, he detected the sound of an infant crying, the same infant he had seen being taken aboard by her mother only minutes earlier.

Without a second thought, he stumbled back on to the stricken aircraft, picking his way in the stygian darkness through the dead and the dying until he found the child and then, miraculously, carried her from the carnage to safety. Spontaneity is often the father of monumental heroism and the passage of time has merely served to magnify the bravery of the man who numbered many of his teammates among the twenty-three people who perished in that terrible accident.

From a modest start to his football career with his local club, Coleraine, Gregg grew to a position where, at the pinnacle of his powers, he rated among the best keepers in the world. From Coleraine he journeyed to Doncaster Rovers, then under the management of Peter Doherty, where he joined Dubliners Kit and Jimmy Lawlor in a team which, although fated to trade in the lower divisions, played with a vision and verve which suggested that in time, they could be contenders for a place in the old English First Division championship.

That never happened for the club, but ultimately Doncaster's progress provided Gregg with the chance of enlisting in the Manchester United squad which Matt Busby envisaged would take the game in Britain on to a different level. In time, Busby's hopes were on the threshold of fulfilment, only to be ruined in the short term by the Munich disaster. By that stage, however, Gregg had already made the transition to international football as a key segment of the grandiose plans which Peter Doherty, an iconic name in football on either side of the Irish Sea, devised for Northern Ireland.

He was still in the embryonic stages of his career when Doherty took his courage in his hands and called him up for the game against Wales at

Wrexham in 1954. Norman Uprichard was his first choice goalkeeper at the time but when the Swindon player became unavailable, the manager had no reservations in going with his own club man. It would be another two years before Gregg got the chance to establish himself in the side, and he recalls the match with England at Windsor Park on 7 May 1956 as a turning point in his career.

'It was one thing playing against Wales in Wrexham but a meeting with England was something else,' he said. 'Not only were the influential English sportswriters covering the game but all the First Division managers were clued in as well. And for me, it attracted attention for all the right reasons.'

Playing directly in front of him that day was Jackie Blanchflower, his clubmate at Old Trafford, who would later be forced to abandon what promised to be an outstanding career because of the injuries he sustained in the Munich disaster. Operating alongside his elder brother, Danny, in the half-back line, Jackie Blanchflower was quite superb in the manner in which he restricted Tommy Taylor's input for England and it meant that Jimmy McIlroy's goal was good enough to earn the home team an unlikely 1–1 draw.

That confirmed Northern Ireland's progress under Doherty and it fostered hope that even in a World Cup qualifying group which included Italy and Portugal, they could make it to the finals in Sweden in the summer of 1958. Compared to the Republic of Ireland, who had been involved in the World Cup since 1934, the competition was relatively new to the IFA. In common with the other British Associations, they boycotted the tournament until 1950 and, as such, they were an unknown quantity to the great majority of European football nations, not to mention those further afield.

Doherty and his equally astute team captain Danny Blanchflower determined that far from being a burden, this was an advantage which could be exploited to telling effect. In short, Northern Ireland did not figure on the roadmap of European football and while players like Jimmy McIlroy, Peter McParland and the Blanchflower brothers had their admirers outside Britain, few were aware of the manner in which the Northern Ireland squad had been honed into a hard, competitive unit.

The opening qualifying game ordained that they travel to Portugal for a 10.30 PM appointment in Lisbon's Stadium of Light, a difficult assignment that would test the character of Doherty's emerging players. The Portuguese were not yet at the level which earned them so much respect in the 1960s, but on their home patch they would still ask pertinent questions of the Irish. So it proved, but Billy Bingham's goal earned the visitors a gratifying 1–1 draw in a game which finished long past midnight.

If that test was tough, the one which followed would be more difficult still. A mature Italian team in Rome in late April would tax them mentally and physically as never before, the more so since Doherty was forced to go without McParland (Aston Villa) and Jackie Blanchflower (Manchester United). With these clubs due to meet in the FA Cup Final at Wembley shortly afterwards, there was never much chance of either player being cleared to make the journey to the Eternal City. In those circumstances, a 1–0 defeat for the visitors was not nearly as comprehensive or disillusioning as the management team had feared.

The return leg of the Portugal tie was scheduled for Windsor Park just six days later and with McParland and Blanchflower still out of bounds, it was scarcely surprising that the team was unchanged. Whereas the Rome assignment had been an exercise in containment, the emphasis was now on pressurising Portugal from the kick off, and it proved a winning formula. Establishing early control in midfield, they won with Billy Simpson, Jimmy McIlroy and Tommy Casey plundering the goals which opened up a whole new vista in the group.

Now everything depended on the return meeting with Italy in Belfast in December. A point from that game would suffice to qualify the Italians for the Swedish extravaganza, but taken in conjunction with the draw they salvaged in Portugal, victory would propel Northern Ireland into the World Cup Finals. That represented a glittering prospect for everybody in Northern Ireland and before they got to their day of destiny, they received a tremendous boost along the way.

England's national team and the results they achieved in the broad world of international football was the barometer by which Ireland teams, north and south, measured their progress. A good result against the English was interpreted as approximating to an honours standard in academic terms and that was why the Republic's team derived so much satisfaction from their brave but ultimately unrewarded stand against Walter Winterbottom's team at Dalymount in May 1957.

And it was England who would provide Peter Doherty and Danny Blanchflower with the opportunity of fine tuning their preparations for that heavyweight collision with Italy by hosting a British championship game at Wembley on 6 November 1957. For all the motivation which flowed from playing England, they had never beaten them on English terrain, with a 2–2 draw at Goodison Park in 1947 far and away their best result in the recent past. And that was achieved only with the assistance of six southern-born players.

It's a long road that has no turning, however, and that theme provided the eloquent Irish management partnership with all the material they needed as they addressed their troops before walking onto the Wembley pitch to be introduced to the Duke of Gloucester, Patron of the FA of England, at the start of the pre-match ceremonies. 'Peter Doherty could be inspirational when he spoke before big games and never more so than in the build up to the 1957 match at Wembley,' Danny Blanchflower recalled. 'He convinced us that man for man, we were as good as England. I don't know whether in his heart of hearts he believed it, but it certainly worked for us that day.'

In other years, they might have baulked at the prospect of putting the squeeze on the Busby Babes who provided the backbone of the English team, but not this time. A sequence of outstanding saves by Gregg was clearly uplifting for the players in front of him and with McIlroy, Sammy McCrory and Simpson hitting the target, they achieved an historic 3–2 success in front of tens of thousands of shell-shocked England supporters. Ironically, McCrory would never again play for Northern Ireland, but for the remainder of the team, the victory put added pep in their stride for the crucial World Cup appointment looming up ahead. And right on cue, that newly acquired self-belief propelled them to a 2–1 win over Italy in January 1958 and a first-ever appearance in the World Cup Finals in Sweden.

For Gregg, the immediate payoff was a move to Manchester United and the opportunity to take his club career on to a new level. Matt Busby liked what he saw of Gregg in the Wembley rollercoaster and he knew for certain that his expensive investment was gilt-edged after his new arrival had dislodged Norman Uprichard as Doherty's top goalkeeper in the approach to the global showpiece in Scandinavia in the summer.

Before they got there, Irish Football Association officials were required to circumvent their embargo on Sunday football. Their programme in Sweden included Sunday fixtures, prompting some critics to ask why they entered the competition in the first instance. Ultimately, the progressive element in the association had their way, the Sabbath ban was repealed temporarily and a potential landmine was avoided. It was as a direct consequence of this that the rule was eventually changed to permit Sunday games 'outside Northern Ireland'.

Although Gregg had emerged from the horror of the Munich crash physically unscarred, there was still a mental issue to be addressed in terms of flying and he was one of those who made the journey to Sweden by boat. There was one other, even crueller legacy from the disaster, however, with Jackie Blanchflower being forced to withdraw from the squad because of the injuries he sustained in Germany. Crucially, it meant that Northern Ireland travelled with only seventeen players.

West Germany, the reigning World Cup champions, Argentina and Czechoslovakia joined Northern Ireland in Group One and the Irish were the choice of almost everybody to finish at the foot of the group table. But if this dark thought ever crossed the minds of those in charge of the squad, it certainly never showed, either in training or in game time.

Ironically, the match arrangements ordained that Doherty's team open their programme on a Sunday with Czechoslovakia providing the opposition at Halmstad. Peter Doherty would later recall that the theme of the sermon at the local church that morning was 'Faith Moveth Mountains', and it certainly worked for the men in green, for against all the odds Wilbur Cush's goal gave them a 1–0 success. Their next outing against Argentina was less satisfactory with the South Americans winning 3–1, but their third match against the powerful West Germans would soon re-establish morale.

Once more, they found inspiration in a Sunday setting, this time in Malmo. At times, it looked like a rerun of the Aloma but with Gregg pulling off one flamboyant save after another, the Irish team stood tall and two goals from Peter McParland had them 2–1 in front with just seven minutes to go. Then Uwe Seeler salvaged German pride with an equaliser, and coupled with Czechoslovakia's surprising 6–1 dismissal of Argentina, it contrived a situation in which Northern Ireland would now take on the Czechs for a second time, in a play-off to determine the second qualifiers from the group, just forty-eight hours later.

Gregg's heroics, which would later see him named as the best goalkeeper in the World Cup Finals, came at a cost however and a badly swollen ankle meant that he had to be replaced by Norman Uprichard for the play-off. As it happened, Uprichard would himself figure in an injury drama not dissimilar to that which put his friend and arch rival out of the match. The Portsmouth player twisted an ankle within ten minutes of the kick-off and then, even more alarmingly, he sustained a bad injury when, in scrambling across his line to save, he crashed into an upright.

It was subsequently discovered that he had broken a bone in his hand, but with no replacement available, he had to soldier on. Bertie Peacock was another serious casualty in the second half but in spite of all the problems welling up around them, Peter McParland linked with Wilbur Cush to equalise Nihan's lead goal for the Czechs and force the game into extra time. During the break, Doherty resisted Uprichard's pleas to be moved outfield because of the pain in his hand, but then, with both teams almost out on their feet, the irrepressible McParland put his name on another goal, his fifth in the finals, to break the opposition in a mini war of attrition.

Northern Ireland, the least fancied of the sixteen finalists, had made it into the quarter-finals of the most important football competition in four years. From a position in which they scarcely merited a mention in the international press in the build up to the finals, they now found themselves at the centre of the media's attention as other, apparently stronger teams headed home. Four games in the space of eleven days had eaten into the reserves of a squad which started out under-strength, and with additional injuries now adding to Doherty's troubles, the outlook was worrying in the extreme for the management team.

Peacock's injury would keep him out for the next three months and once the full extent of Uprichard's injury became apparent, there was no question of him facing France for a place in the semi-finals. Gregg, still under treatment for his damaged ankle, would normally have sat out the game, but in the prevailing circumstances, the manager had no option but to press him into emergency service.

It was an impossible gamble which could never pay dividends and within fifteen minutes of the kick-off, the talented French team, and Just Fontaine in particular, had uncovered the gaps which would end Northern Ireland's brave adventure. A nasty gash in Tommy Casey's leg merely accentuated Doherty's injury troubles and in the end France ran out convincing 4–0 winners.

Sadly, there were no more goodies left in Peter Doherty's sack of dreams but even as they took their leave of Scandinavia, the legend of Sweden '58 had already begun to form. And for Harry Gregg, the man who, perhaps above all others, epitomised the courage and commitment of that team, the journey had one last bonus.

Conscious of his dark ordeal some five months earlier, he decided to return home by air in the company of veteran team selector Sammy Walker, some twenty-four hours before the departure of the main group. It was his first flight since the Munich disaster and, as such, played a big role in his rehabilitation. He was already safely home when he learned that the plane carrying the bulk of the Northern Ireland party developed engine trouble on takeoff from Bromma International airport in Stockholm and was forced to circle the airport for an hour to burn surplus fuel, before making a safe emergency landing.

– Chapter 10 –

Upside Down

Gaelic Football – Down v Kerry, Croke Park, September 1960

Mick O'Connell knew precisely what was required of Kerry if they were to retain one of the most coveted trophies in Irish sport when he left his home on Valencia Island and journeyed to Dublin for an appointment with destiny on Sunday, 25 September 1960.

Down, the team which critics contended was on the verge of changing the course of Gaelic football history with qualities of power, pace and panache rarely witnessed in the code, were about to put that high rating on the line in an All-Ireland final like no other. And O'Connell, already the biggest name in the sport after just a couple of seasons in the senior grade, was acutely aware of the latent threat they presented.

'We played them in the National League earlier in the year and saw enough that day to know that this was indeed, a very good Down team,' he said. 'They were young, fit and exceptionally talented. Most important of all, perhaps, they were driven by a sense of purpose which demanded admiration from every side they met in the league.'

In September 1959, O'Connell had captained Kerry to an impressive win in the final over Galway before establishing an uncontested first by omitting to take the Sam Maguire Cup with him when he closed the door on the Croke Park dressing room and headed home in the gathering gloom. Far from meriting a reprimand, the incident merely served to heighten the aura of mystique surrounding the man whom the majority of Gaelic enthusiasts acclaim as the greatest player of them all.

Tall and splendidly proportioned, he was a player, one sensed, who could have made up into a splendid number eight in Ireland's rugby team or a centre forward to be feared in the national football side. Instead, he chose to channel all his skills into Gaelic and in the process provided the template for the many thousands who would follow him into the code. A master of the kick pass, his fielding was acknowledged as being on a par with that of Paddy Kennedy, the renowned midfielder of earlier Kerry teams.

And yet, his most valuable asset was an ability to find space in even the most claustrophobic situations, before delivering the accurate pass at pace to the inside forwards. It was that kind of service which allowed players like Tom Long, Paudie Sheehy and Tadgh Lyne to undermine Galway in the 1959 final and it now represented Down's biggest worry as they plotted their strategy for the biggest day in the county's history.

Unlike Mick O'Connell, Kevin Mussen, a product of the noted St Colman's football nursery in Newry, was relatively unknown south of the border. True, he had been part of the Ulster team which defeated Munster in the Railway Cup Final in 1956 – one of only two Down players in the side – but with Cavan, Tyrone and Derry the dominant forces in Ulster, he got little exposure in the southern press in the intervening years.

Removed from the power base of Down football in the south of the county, Mussen needed all his qualities of leadership to retain the team captaincy ahead of another of the county's iconic personalities, James McCartan. Such was his influence in the half-back line, however, that he was quickly recognised as the player to take the team towards the alluring goal of a first provincial title as a stepping stone to success on the biggest stage of all in the GAA's priority list, Croke Park on the last Sunday in September.

It would require players of exceptional vision and commitment to remove one of the enduring impediments to the association's hopes of establishing the six north-eastern counties as major players in Gaelic Games. Having proved his motivational qualities in his college days, the Newcastle-based school teacher was accorded due respect when, in the days leading up the All-Ireland Final, he told journalists, 'The only thing which will prevent us taking "Sam" across the border is the customs barrier.'

The history of teams aspiring to be the first to achieve that distinction was scarcely encouraging. Antrim had twice been beaten in the final, first by Cork in 1911 and then by Louth a year later. And the Glensmen came up short again in 1946 when, after interrupting Cavan's long sequence of provincial successes, Kevin Armstrong's team, espousing a new style of hand pass, lost out to the eventual champions Kerry at the semi-final stage.

It was Armagh's turn to feel the pain in 1953, when not even the presence of outstanding players like John McKnight, Mal McEvoy and Bill McCorry could rescue them from a 0-13 to 1-9 defeat by Kerry. And for all the midfield might of Jim McKeever, Derry fared no better in going down to a six points defeat at the hands of Kevin Heffernan's Dublin side in 1958.

It was against this background that Kevin Mussen and his teammates jutted jaws and looked the reigning champions in the eye in 1960. Earlier in the year, they had announced their arrival as big-time players by dismissing Cavan 0-12 to 0-9 in the National League Final, a significant result against a team which for so long had set the standard for all others in Ulster. More than that, they had beaten Kerry along the way and it was, perhaps, the memory of that achievement that provided the greatest source of encouragement when they lowered Cavan's colours for a second time to claim their first provincial title some three months later.

Central to that success was the contribution of the half-back line in which Mussen was joined by Dan McCartan, younger of the two gifted brothers, and Kevin O'Neill. Joe Lennon, a physical instructor at

Gormanston College, and the underrated Jarlath Carey, provided the midfield axis which enabled Sean O'Neill, Paddy Doherty and, of course, James McCartan, to blend with Tony Hadden, Patsy O'Hagan and Brian Morgan in one of the most stylish of all attacks.

And yet, for all that latent power, they almost came to grief in their semi-final meeting with the Leinster champions, Offaly. Matching the Ulstermen's brand of high octane football with traditional qualities of strength down the spine of the team and the accuracy of Tom Cullen, Peter Daly and Mick Casey up front, Offaly considered themselves unlucky in having to settle for a draw in the first game and then came agonisingly close to putting Down away in the replay before losing 1-7 to 1-5.

That was something of a reality check for Down but Kerry, for their part, were also less than imposing in seeing off Galway on a scoreline of 1-8 to 0-8 in the other semi-final. Twelve months earlier, they had won pulling up against a Galway side containing the last survivors from their successful 1956 squad and the first of the emerging players who would establish the westerners as the team of the 1960s. For all that latent talent, however, Galway were not expected to finish so close to Kerry and, inevitably, it spawned stories that all was not well in the southern camp.

With Niall Sheehy and Kevin Coffey again manning the central positions, the defence which had stood tall in the face of late Galway pressure in 1959 was still intact. Mick O'Connell now had a new partner in Jerdie O'Connor in midfield and with Seamus Murphy joining Tom Long and Paudie Sheehy in the half forward line, they held all the advantages in experience if not in motivation.

Predictably, Down's arrival in the final was the occasion of a vast outpouring of pride within the county. From early morning, the Belfast to Dublin road was one enormous procession of cars. Even those with no access to motorised transport were on the move with hundreds converging on the capital on bicycles. 'Older people still talk about the travelling support we had that day,' recalls team trainer Barney Carr. 'Nowadays, many appear to take it for granted that there will be a northern team playing in Croke Park on football final day.

'It was a lot different in those days, however, and just as Armagh and Derry had done before us, we were making a bit of history by getting to the final. It showed in the sheer joy of the supporters entering Croke Park in red and black colours hours before the throw in and if we needed any reminding of how much victory would mean to Down people everywhere, the evidence was there to be seen as our coach arrived at the stadium.'

In the event, the attendance was returned as 87,768, the biggest on record at the time. And it is a measure of the Ulstermen's contribution to the drama which subsequently unfolded that more than 90,000 turned up to watch them play Offaly in the final the following year. A new dimension had been added to the championship by people from the six counties and the GAA authorities could boast that for all the reservations harboured about their ability to bring Gaelic Games to people in the major urban areas, they had found new terrain for exploitation in the north-east of the island.

Still, not everybody in Dublin was aware of the new celebrities in their midst when the men from the north established their match day base in the Maples Hotel on Iona Road in Glasnevin. Anxious to relieve the growing tension before setting out on the short journey to Croke Park, several members of the squad took to the road outside to play what Dubliners would call 'Combo' with a bouncing ball.

Alarmed at this spectacle, local residents rang the Gardaí to report that a group of adults were involved in some form of sport outside their homes with a consequent risk for passersby, not to mention their property. A Garda arrived in due course and no less than the residents, he was intrigued but not outwardly enthused by what he saw. Unaware of the importance of the participants, he was already reaching for his notebook when an official emerged from the hotel to acquaint him of the identities of the people involved. In cricket parlance, play was suspended immediately, but the incident, later recalled with some amusement, served the purpose of breaking the growing tension in the camp.

Nor was that the only topic of conversation in the Maples Hotel before the game. When it came to organising a pre-match meal for the party, a couple of players occasioned surprise by ordering steaks. This drove a coach and fours through conventional thinking but the Down management team explained it away by saying that this was standard practice for the people in question and they saw no valid reason why they should change on the biggest day of their careers.

If the players had overindulged at the table, it certainly didn't show in the early stages. Playing into the Canal goal, they moved the ball at pace and fears that they would toil in the face of Kerry's renowned aerial power were not substantiated. On occasions, Mick O'Connell, with sporadic assistance from those around him, fielded majestically but in between, finely taken points from Tony Hadden (twice), Sean O'Neill, Joe Lennon, Paddy Doherty and James McCartan had Down in front 0-6 to 0-2 at the end of the first quarter.

That wasn't in the script prepared by most neutral critics but in the manner of their calling, Kerry were not prepared to roll over. Some of the stories emanating from the south in the days leading up to the game suggested that key players were carrying injuries and in the case of John Dowling, the sense of foreboding was indeed valid. Dowling, a key personality in their All-Ireland wins of 1955 and '59, limped into the game with what appeared to be a damaged ankle and after struggling to make an impact, he was replaced.

That was a significant blow to Kerry's hopes of keeping their dominion intact. But if Dowling struggled, there was no doubting O'Connell's influence. Valued too was the contribution of Mick O'Dwyer in his customary position at left half-back and from this base, the Munster men contrived a recovery of impressive proportions to trim the deficit to just two points, 0-7 to 0-5 at the break. Those who had watched Kerry build their empire over the years spoke of their uncanny ability to escape the consequences of poor starts by lulling opponents into a false sense of security before striking quickly and decisively in the second half.

Thus, when O'Connell and Seamus Murphy swung over long range points to level the scores within five minutes of the restart, the knowing ones nodded sagely. This was where tradition and the accumulated knowledge garnered in the march to nineteen All-Ireland title successes would kick in and the precocious upstarts from north of the border brought to heel in a manner which fitted history.

It was then, however, we discovered that this northern uprising was built on more than words and pious hope. Before the final, the Down management had enlisted the assistance of Peter McDermott, the distinguished Meath forward who had shared in his county's All-Ireland triumphs of 1949 and 1954, as part of their back-up team. In between those victories, he had refereed the 1953 final between Kerry and Armagh, so when it came to talking about the pressures of final day, the Navan man was an authority. McDermott warned that in almost every final, there was a crisis point for one or both teams and that the roles of victors and vanquished would be defined by the manner in which players responded in such situations.

Perhaps it was those words which inspired the purple patch and the scores that heralded the birth of a new superpower in Gaelic football approaching the three-quarter mark. Pointedly, Down won the kick-out following Murphy's equaliser and play was concentrated in the half of the pitch defended by Kerry when James McCartan, roaming some fifty yards out towards the right wing, dropped a towering kick into the square. Normally, speculative scoring attempts like this were food and drink to Kerry goalkeeper, Johnny Culloty. But with no opposing player within ten yards of him, he inexplicably lost concentration on this occasion and the ball slipped from his grasp to cross the line.

That was the most expensive error in the colourful career of the man who started out in the Kerry team as a corner forward and finished as the outstanding goalkeeper of his generation. In quicker than it tells to relate, the Kingdom's anticipated recovery was aborted and Down, borne on tidal waves of noise, ensured there would be no second chance of redemption for the green and gold.

The stadium was still seething with excitement when the Ulstermen struck again. This time it was Sean O'Neill, boring in on Culloty's goal, who did the damage. O'Neill was eventually hauled down inside the square and the referee had no hesitation in awarding the inevitable penalty. A penalty wasn't the easiest kick to take in an era when the ball was placed on the fourteen yards line, but with the expertise of a player who had enjoyed a reasonably successful football career in England and Northern Ireland, Paddy Doherty drove it precisely beyond the reach of the goal-keeper

In a matter of minutes, the barricades which for almost eighty years had stood between teams from the six counties and Gaelic football's supreme accolade were torn aside and after points had been traded in the closing minutes, a mighty roar rent the air as Kevin Mussen lifted the Sam Maguire Cup on a scoreline of 2-10 to 0-8.

Following their win over Cavan in the National League Final earlier in the year, the two major trophies in the sport now rested in the Mourne county and among other things it caused Maurice Hayes, a former senator and long-serving official on the Down County Board, to recall an incident at the Mussen family home in Hilltown. The local postman, a stout member of the Royal Irish Special Constabulary, became aware of the National League Final against Cavan only days before the match and, totally out of character, it caught his imagination.

'I hear Down are playing Cavan in the Cup Final on Sunday?' he enquired of Kevin's mother. Then, when he returned to the house to deliver the post on the Monday, he asked about the result. On being invited in to inspect the trophy, he took it in his broad hands and proclaimed, 'Isn't it great to take it from that southern crowd.' Now, one could only guess at his inner thoughts after the aristocracy of the south had again been laid low.

– Chapter 11 –

Wages of Defeat

Hurling – Tipperary v Dublin, September 1961

Controversy and Des Ferguson were strange bed fellows. For fifteen years, Ferguson wore the sky blue of Dublin with distinction in hurling and Gaelic football, playing in the 1952 and 1961 All-Ireland hurling finals in addition to three appearances, two of them victorious, in the football decider.

Equally significant for his small army of fans was the fact that he was an integral part of the St Vincent's teams which dominated club competitions in Dublin in a manner which put them apart from all others, not least in their achievement of providing a new power base for club hurling in an erstwhile barren area for the game, on Dublin's north side in the 1950s.

Beneath the shadow of the Croke Park stands, a new power was emerging to make the traditionalists sit up and take notice, and the measure of the ability of the men in the blue hooped jerseys is that soon they were in a position to match the Cork hurling champions, Glen Rovers, in challenge games that attracted attendances of 40,000 plus to Croke Park on Friday evenings in high summer.

Dublin had never seen anything like it and Ferguson's blond head epitomised the glamour of it all. And yet for many, the success he achieved and the sack of trophies he acquired along the way was secondary to his exceptional discipline in even the most stressful situations. The fact that he never once fell foul of referees in a protracted career is for many the finest accolade for a man with few equals in his time.

How ironic, then, that his name is linked to one of the enduring controversies in GAA history, one which not merely affected the outcome of an All-Ireland Final but accentuated a problem which is still ongoing over a bridge of more than fifty years. Above all else, victory for Dublin over Tipperary in the 1961 All-Ireland Hurling Final was seen as crucial to the GAA's hopes of finally establishing the game on a sound basis in the capital.

It failed to materialise largely because of a free conceded by Ferguson just minutes from the end and is still remembered by Dubliners as a bad call by Limerick referee Gerry Fitzgerald. After Tipperary had lifted a long siege on their net, the right back was adjudged to have picked the ball off the ground and Jimmy Doyle pointed the free which gave the Munster champions a tense 0-16 to 1-12 win.

That was the last occasion the Metropolitans made it into an All-Ireland Final and Ferguson, seldom one to raise his head above the parapet in the recurring criticism which referees in all codes are made to suffer in silence, is adamant that Fitzgerald got it wrong. 'The ball was certainly off the ground when I picked it up – the game was at such a crucial point that I would never have done so had I been in any doubt about the validity of what I was doing.' Just as definitively, the Tipperary players closest to the incident contended – and in some instances continue do so – that the man known to the Gaelic world by his nickname of 'Snitchie' did, in fact, foul the ball in one of the undying talking points of hurling.

That ball hopping incident apart, there was a dimension to the 1961 final which merited the attention of the authorities in Croke Park. For years, they had sought to break the stranglehold of football in the capital by nurturing a love of Gaelic Games among the youth. To succeed, they needed the co-operation of the teaching professions, particularly at the first level of education, and with many teachers in the city emanating from rural backgrounds, that responsibility was in many instances assumed with a zeal that at times bordered on missionary.

That gave rise to a phenomenon in Dublin known as Christian Brothers hurling. It lacked the intuitive flair of players from traditional hurling areas such as Kilkenny, Tipperary or Cork, but it contrived a situation in which players, born and reared in the city, had aspirations of competing at the top level with a reasonable degree of expectancy.

The last Metropolitan team to lift the Liam McCarthy Cup in 1938 contained just one native Dubliner, Jim Byrne. The teams beaten by Cork in the All-Ireland Finals of 1941 and 1942 were likewise dominated by provincial men based in Dublin and it is interesting to note that two of the players involved, Jim Donegan and Mick Butler, would later return to Kilkenny and render them splendid service in the process.

It was largely because of this provincial presence that the achievements of Dublin hurling teams overshadowed those of their contemporaries in the football sides, but with the advent of players like Kevin Matthews, Joe Butler and the Donnelly brothers, Paddy and Liam, things were changing when they lost out to Waterford in the 1948 final. Defeat, this time to Cork, was again the lot of the Dubliners in 1952, but with the emergence of the St Vincent's trio, Des Ferguson, Norman Allen and Mark Wilson, the outline of a successful 'natives only' policy was already in focus.

A similar policy was in vogue for the big ball code and central to the success of both was the emergence of St Vincent's as the most powerful club in the country. As we have seen, their influence on Dublin's National Football League success in 1953 was profound and men from Marino again dominated the county team in the finals of 1955 and '58 when Dublin finally ended their sixteen-year wait for success.

Another major contributory factor was the success enjoyed by Dublin teams in colleges competition. The teams that won the All-Ireland minor hurling and football titles in 1954 were built on the talented O'Connell

Schools squad which only narrowly missed out on the Leinster Colleges double in the same year. Later came the St Josephs, Fairview teams which produced the inimitable Foley brothers, Lar and Des, on a conveyor belt of significant inter-county players.

The measure of the transition from relying on provincial players to backbone Dublin hurling teams was graphically illustrated in the composition of the team which played in the 1961 final. Whereas the successful team of twenty-three years earlier had contained just one fully qualified Dubliner, full forward Paddy Croke was the only non-native hurler in the side that faced Tipperary.

Like the legendary Jim Prior who captained the team in 1952, Croke was born in Tipperary and actually played alongside Tony Wall and Bill Moloughney in the Tipperary minor team beaten by Kilkenny in the 1950 final. Now Wall and Moloughney were part of the Tipp squad which stood between the adopted Dubliner and his great ambition of winning the top prize in the game.

Whereas Dublin were striving to end a long vigil for success when they reported to Croke Park on 3 September 1961, Tipperary had recorded the last of their seventeen successes in the championship as recently as 1958. Yet, for all their impressive pedigree, they were still some way short of the standard set by hurlers of the quality of Pat Stakelum and the Doyles, John and Tommy, in their golden years in the late 1940s and early '50s.

If their recent record in the championship was sketchy, there was certainly nothing wrong with their form in the National League in the approach to the 1961 championship. In May of that year, they beat Waterford on a score of 6-6 to 4-9 to take the title for a third consecutive win and they built on it when recording a wholly comprehensive 3-6 to 0-7 victory over Cork in the Munster final some two months later. The merit of that performance resided mainly in an outstanding display by a half-back line in which Tony Wall was flanked by Michael Burns and the ageless John Doyle, with the uncanny accuracy of Jimmy Doyle in attack.

Any win over their arch rivals Cork was prized in Tipperary and for all the protestations to the contrary, it may have coloured their attitude initially in the approach to the game against Dublin. That soon changed, however, after it emerged that Wall and Jimmy Doyle had both picked up injuries in training and were struggling to make the deadline for the final.

Wall, an army officer, had proved himself a worthy successor to Pat Stakelum in the pivotal position in defence, a fine striker of the ball whose positional sense was such that he was rarely removed from the action when danger threatened. Jimmy Doyle, by contrast, depended on pace and accuracy for his contribution to the team but no less than Wall, his was a presence that the league champions could ill afford to lose. As it transpired, both made the starting line up with varying degrees of success in the drama that ensued.

A curious feature of the Dublin team which had dismissed Wexford on a score of 7-5 to 4-8 in the Leinster final, was that it contained three sets of brothers. Bernard Boothman who had captained the successful minor team in 1954, was joined by his younger brother Achill in attack and the Fergusons, Des and Liam, formed the right flank of the defence. But in the Foleys, from farming stock in north County Dublin, the Metropolitans possessed players whose physical power was matched only by their competitive instincts.

Lar Foley who, aside from Gaelic Games, was a skilled practitioner in clay pigeon shooting, was once described by the legendary Kerry footballer Paddy Bawn Brosnan as the only Gaelic footballer of his generation who compared favourably with those who had gone before. From one renowned competitor to another, that was a telling tribute, but while his football career would ultimately prove more successful, he made no secret of the fact that hurling was his first love.

Yet it was Des, the younger of the pair by two years, who would emerge as the more influential. It is a measure of his ability as a hurler that on the strength of an outstanding career as a minor player, he was selected for

Leinster before he made his senior debut for Dublin. Unlike Lar, he missed out on Dublin's 1958 football success but enjoyed sweet compensation by captaining the Metropolitans to victory over Galway in the final five years later.

Jimmy Gray, later to become an influential administrator, was the Dublin goalkeeper who, in common with his teammates, was left to bemoan an agonising one-point defeat by Kilkenny in the Leinster final of 1959. Another survivor from that team was the man directly in front of him, Noel Drumgoole, while Mick Bohan, equally proficient in football and hurling, played at centre half forward, alongside his Sc Ui Chonaill teammate, Larry Shannon.

Together with the Boothman brothers and Fran Whelan, Bohan was a significant contributor to Dublin's win over Tipperary in the 1954 All-Ireland Minor Hurling Final but remarkably, the two outstanding members of that team, Vinny Bell and Aidan Kavanagh, failed to make the grade in senior hurling subsequently. After a brief spell in the Dublin senior team, Bell was soon lost to hurling while Kavanagh, another gifted dual performer, had to settle for the consolation prize of a short career with Meath's hurlers before retiring from sport.

An attendance measured at 67,836 saw Tipperary make the better start. Determined to justify their role as favourites, they were three points ahead before Dublin settled and Des Foley began to dominate the battle for midfield control. Points from Billy Jackson and Larry Shannon provided the reassuring evidence that the Leinster champions weren't there merely to make up the numbers and soon, Tipperary began to lose their earlier aura of invincibility. And the spectacle of Wall struggling to stay with the pace did nothing to reassure their supporters.

Yet with Dublin conceding frees under pressure and Jimmy Doyle as economical as ever in exacting retribution, Tipperary, for all their unexpected problems, were still in front, 0-10 to 0-6 at the interval. That was a tribute not merely to Doyle's resource under pressure but to the persistence of a dogged defence which, despite Wall's fitness troubles, still ensured that any scores Dublin got, were earned the hard way.

From the Leinster men's viewpoint, the first half had testified to the development of Des Foley as one of the top midfielders in the country. Although he was just a couple of years out of minor ranks, Foley was quite outstanding, out-hurling older, more mature players in a manner which suggested that in spite of all the doubts voiced by the critics, it was still possible for gifted athletes to combine hurling with Gaelic football at the highest level.

Less satisfactory was the contribution of Foley's midfield partner, Fran Whelan. Regarded as one of the more accomplished members of the squad, Whelan never reproduced anything like his best form during the opening thirty minutes, but fortunately for the Metropolitans, his contribution improved thereafter and it was key to a much sharper team performance when the game eventually took flame after the interval.

Central to many of the pre-match forecasts was the fear that an early goal for Tipperary would drain the final of its competitive element and turn hurling's biggest attraction into a massive mismatch. But in spite of the broad seam of experience running down the spine of the team and the accuracy under pressure of Jimmy Doyle and Donie Nealon, the Munster champions never seriously threatened to disturb the netting behind Jimmy Gray.

It wasn't until the thirty-seventh minute that the green flag was eventually raised – and to the consternation of the Munster men, it fluttered in the wind to signal a goal for the outsiders. Christy Hayes, running Des Foley a close second for the accolade of Dublin's outstanding performer at centre half-back, found Shannon with a long clearance and when the ball was transferred quickly to Jackson, the defence buckled with disturbing ease.

Jackson, a goalkeeper turned corner forward, suddenly wheeled away from the Tipperary captain, Matt Hassett, and needed only a moment's concentration before driving the sliothar beyond the reach of Dennis O'Brien and into the far corner of the net. Essentially, it was a score fashioned out of nothing, but the effect was to lift Dublin's morale and at the same time implant the seeds of self-doubt in the opposition.

For all their apparent advantages going into the match, Tipperary were floundering and Achill Boothman's equalising point was followed by two more to put the home team within sight of victory with just twelve minutes to go. It was then that the Tipperary management team made their master move, withdrawing Liam Devaney from the front line to replace the struggling Wall at the heart of their defence.

With Devaney sealing many of the gaps exposed down the middle at the height of Dublin's supremacy, the balance of the game swung back in Tipperary's favour and three-point frees from the ever-reliable Doyle had the favourites back in front again. That was followed by another of the game's startling twists when, following a scuffle in the goalmouth, Lar Foley and Tom Ryan of Killenaule (on as a replacement in the Tipperary full forward line), were given their marching orders.

Undeniably, the bigger loss was Dublin's, for the elder Foley brother, hard and rugged, was frequently inspirational as he emerged from a thicket of players to make long, telling clearances. The Metropolitans were still only in the process of reorganising their defence when Des Ferguson, stationed immediately behind his brother Liam on the right flank of the defence, was on the wrong end of a refereeing decision which would endure long after other aspects of the match had faded into oblivion.

The ball was on the twenty-one-yards line and the home defence under intense pressure when the older man nipped between Nealon and Tom Moloughney to make what appeared to be an important interception. Even as he prepared to make the relieving clearance, however, the referee's whistle sounded and the finger pointing in the direction of the Dublin posts confirmed Ferguson's worst fears.

The Dubliner was still arguing his case that he had secured the ball legitimately as Doyle bent his back before striking the ensuing free over the bar to stretch the lead to two points with just a couple of minutes left in the match. Almost immediately Achill Boothman struck his fifth point to reduce the game to the minimum and set his team up for one last, thrilling assault on the Tipperary goal.

Jackson, reaching out for the gratitude of the Blues' supporters for a second time, hit the side netting with a stinging drive and Dublin knew for certain that the game and the glory had slipped from their grasp when Shannon got his angles marginally wrong and his forty-yards free, from a difficult angle out on the left, missed the target by inches. Theirs had been a brave stand against the odds but in the end, a doubtful refereeing call had cost them the replay that their tenacity deserved. And fifty years on, the GAA is still counting the cost of that failure as Dublin awaits the seventh All-Ireland success which would testify to their rebirth as a major hurling power.

– Chapter 12 –

Against the Odds

Football – League of Ireland v English Football League, October 1963

Before his untimely death in 1993, Ronnie Whelan Snr was apt to recall that growing up in Cabra on Dublin's north side, he was never regarded as the best player, even on his own street. Given that another sporting family of the same name lived on the other end of St Attracta's road, that wasn't altogether surprising to those who supervised the local playground, surely the most productive of all nurseries in the development of future Ireland international players.

The eldest member of the other Whelan household, Christy, went on to become a fine League of Ireland player in spells with Bohemians, Drumcondra and Transport. John, the youngest of three brothers, represented Drumcondra with distinction for a number of years but it was the lad in between who captured the imagination of the scouts who trawled Cabra on a regular basis in search of still more football nuggets.

Liam Whelan was the rarest of football's pearls, a superb player on the ball whose mazy dribbling skills and ability to open up defences was still on an upward curve when the carnage of the Munich air disaster robbed Manchester United, and the wider world of sport, of one of the more obvious talents in a distinguished generation of footballers.

Having regard to this calibre of competition on his doorstep, it wasn't altogether surprising then that Ronnie Whelan should suffer in the comparison. And yet for much of the period that followed, it was the lesser-known of the two families which would dominate the football headlines.

Ronnie Whelan Snr knew little of the professional comforts enjoyed by his namesake, Liam. As a part-timer with St Patrick's Athletic, he often recalled that on those occasions when he was required to work the night shift at the Unidare factory in Finglas, he would cycle the seven miles from there to Richmond Park to train on his own for a couple of hours the following morning.

'It wasn't the ideal preparation for senior football but I quickly realised that if I wanted to stay in the game, I would have to make sacrifices,' he later recalled. 'At times, I wondered if it was worth the effort but then I would think of the extras that my football money bought and trained even harder because of it.'

Some twenty-five years after Ronnie's time in the sun, his son would light up the firmament of club and international football. Ronnie Jnr never had to endure the hardships of life as a part-timer after a gifted apprenticeship with Home Farm had opened the way to a hugely successful career at Liverpool and no fewer than fifty-three Ireland caps in an era of unmistakable riches for the national team.

At a time when Blackburn hotshot Andy McEvoy was holding down the number eight shirt almost by right, in Ireland's team, Ronnie Snr won just two international caps. The first materialised in a scoreless European championship draw with Austria in Vienna in September 1963, the second as a fifth-minute replacement for Joe Haverty in the 3–1 defeat by England at Dalymount Park some eight months later.

But sandwiched between those two high-profile games was a fixture against the English Football League which would ensure a place in local sporting folklore for the tall man from Cabra. With the notable exceptions of that friendly game at Dalymount Park in 1946 and the World Cup match in 1957, England hadn't played a senior international fixture in Dublin since 1912.

In the pre-television era, that had the effect of promoting a climate of mystique about the teams sent out by the English FA. And it was primarily responsible for elevating inter-league fixtures involving the 'home' leagues to a status which ensured that they were viewed as only marginally less important than full international games.

Thus it was that, over a bridge of twenty-five years, the older football followers could still reel off the names of the eleven green-shirted heroes who on St Patrick's Day in 1939 stood sporting logic on its head when Paddy Bradshaw's goal secured a fabled 2–1 win over the Scottish League at Dalymount. The scale of that achievement became even greater on the resumption of the inter-league series after World War II and the occasional 'moral victory' – a euphemism for defeats of less than three goals – became the norm in meetings with the English league.

The exceptionally talented teams which Paddy Coad coached for Shamrock Rovers in the 1950s ensured a couple of highly encouraging home results for the League of Ireland in that decade, notably in 1956 when a side containing seven Milltown players salvaged an exciting 3–3 draw. Three years later, there was another glimmer of hope after a brave rearguard fight had enabled the home team to salvage a scoreless draw in Dublin in September 1959. Normal business was resumed just a year later, however, with a team representative of the best talent in the country sinking to a 4–0 defeat that reflected the chasm in class between the resources available to the visitors and their ambitious hosts.

It didn't auger well for the fixture at Dalymount on 2 October 1963, the more so since the English FA had recently embarked on the most concentrated team-building programme in their chequered history. At that point they were less than three years away from hosting the World Cup and Alf Ramsey was charged with the task of assembling a team that would do justice to the occasion.

Ramsey, a meticulous man whose air of arrogance in public concealed an intuitive knowledge of the game, was already well into his rebuilding programme when he addressed the task of naming the league team to play in Dublin. And unknowingly to the majority of the crowd which converged on the Phibsborough venue that evening, it contained several of the players who would go on to secure the Jules Rimet Trophy at Wembley.

Among them was Bobby Moore, one of the enduring 'greats' of the English game who embodied Ramsey's concept of the total team player. A wing half by training and inclination, he now found himself converted into a centre-back in Ramsey's groundbreaking 4-4-2 formation which rewrote the rules for the modern game with the exclusion of specialist wingers. Ramsey was quick to acknowledge Moore's quality of leadership by awarding him the team captaincy, and while Jack Charlton hadn't as yet forced himself into the manager's plans, he emerged in time as the man who would complement the West Ham player at the heart of England's defence.

Moore was accompanied to Dublin by two of his Upton Park teammates, Martin Peters and Johnny Byrne, who would experience contrasting fortunes when the World Cup rolled around. In 1963, Peters was still only at the fringe of Ramsey's plans before developing into a key component in the team that downed West Germany in the World Cup Final.

The graph of Byrne's career was markedly different. When he set down in Dublin in 1963, he was a regular member of England's team with every indication that he would play a significant part in their World Cup odyssey. But just a year later, his career veered off course dramatically and the man whose family originally came from Dublin, found himself upstaged by Peters by the summer of 1966.

Two other players in the side which faced the League of Ireland, Ray Wilson and Roger Hunt, would also figure in England's World Cup plans and when you counted in the other members of that multi-honoured inter-league team, Tony Waiters, Jimmy Amfield, Gordon Milne, Ian

Callaghan, Jimmy Melia and Mike O'Grady, it amounted to a massive test for the Irish part-timers. In total, the visiting team which took the field boasted no fewer than 353 caps, a statistic designed to unnerve all but the most intrepid supporters of the home team.

'Standing in the dressing room waiting to go out, was like making ready for a visit to the dentist,' Peter Fitzgerald told a local journalist. 'We knew that we in for a hard time but if we held our nerve, we would be all the better for the experience when it was over. But deep down, I think every one of us, even the older players, was apprehensive about the result.'

Fitzgerald, a member of the renowned Waterford footballing family, could be pardoned if he considered himself something of an outsider in the home team that evening. All ten of his teammates were attached to Dublin clubs, a fact which reflected the affluence of clubs like Shamrock Rovers and Shelbourne at a time when the good times hadn't yet arrived at Kilcohan Park.

Eamonn Darcy had taken over the goalkeeper's sweater from another colourful personality, Kevin Blount, and immediately in front of him was a formidable back three formation of John Keogh, Freddie Strahan and Willie Browne. Keogh, seldom less than resourceful in Rovers' remarkable sequence of FAI Cup successes in that period, would later go on to be capped by Ireland, an honour which was replicated by the other two.

Browne, a true Corinthian when the term was sadly becoming redundant in sport, was in fact, the last amateur to attain full international status with Ireland. An accomplished tennis player when he wasn't involved in football, Browne's take on training didn't always conform to the norm. But come match day, the quality of his performance was as constant as the arrival of the dawn.

Although the longevity of Ronnie Nolan's remarkable playing career would extend for another seven years, his best years were already judged to be behind him and in that situation, the team selectors saw fit to promote Shelbourne's Paddy Roberts, a hotel waiter by trade but no slouch when it came to shackling his immediate opponent that evening, Jimmy Melia of Liverpool.

Of Johnny Fullam, charged with the task of 'sweeping' behind Strahan, it can be said with some certainty that he spurned the chance of a big career in England for the comforts of home. Back in the 1960s, Preston North End hadn't yet slipped into the decline which made a mockery of their old Proud Preston tag, but in spite of the entreaties of their then manager, Cliff Britton, Johnny came marching home to enrich local football in general and Shamrock Rovers in particular.

In addition to Fitzgerald and Whelan, the responsibility of hunting down goals against the mature English League defence devolved on the Shamrock Rovers trio of Jackie Mooney, Eddie Bailham and Tony O'Connell. Mooney is remembered most for his aerial ability, a superb header of the ball even in the most pressurised set piece situations. Bailham, by contrast, built a successful club career on his capacity to score from long range, thanks to the shooting power which, even at an early age, had stamped him as a fine player in the making.

O'Connell, one of the few players with Kerry roots to make it into Ireland's football team, was the only forward to survive from the team which had crashed to an embarrassing 3–1 defeat at home to the Irish League the previous March. Now confronted by the England captain Jimmy Armfield, he faced a huge test of character which, by common consent, would have a crucial bearing on the home team's hopes of fashioning the best inter-league result in Dublin since that defeat of the Scottish League almost twenty-five years earlier.

With the exception of Ronnie Whelan, the team met up and trained together for the first time the evening before the game. Whelan was working the night shift at the Unidare factory that week and it was only after much cajoling that he talked his charge hand into giving him time off to play at Dalymount.

For all the disappointment of earlier games in the series, another huge crowd turned up to welcome the arrival on the pitch of Armfield and his men. Paramount to the Irish team's survival was the need to stay disciplined in the face of early England pressure and in that aspect their game plan was spot on.

Rolling forward with obvious intent, the visitors opened at a pace which suggested that they were not in the mood to trifle with opposition, described in the British press on the morning of the game as 'willing but likely to be found wanting in skill'. Milne's weighty tackle on Mooney was conclusive evidence of their intention to avoid the stigma of becoming the first English team to lose in seventeen meetings with the League of Ireland.

In that scenario, Darcy needed to be vigilant when getting down quickly to hold a firmly struck shot by Hunt. And when the fair-haired Liverpool player unleashed another daisy cutter shortly afterwards, the goalkeeper was relieved to watch the ball speed past the outside of the upright. That was a jolt to the senses and so too was the sight of Byrne ghosting away from Strahan before firing narrowly over the top.

The pace of the English attack was such that, out wide, Keogh and Browne had to call on all their guile and experience to cut down space and deal with the threat presented by Callaghan and O'Grady. In sharp contrast, the English goalkeeper, Waiters, was little more than an interested onlooker in the opening fifteen minutes as the visitors' relentless pressure condensed the game to the confines of the Irish penalty area.

The suspicion was that something had to give – and it did, with the timepieces showing that the game had just passed the twenty minute mark. For the second time in the game, Byrne got way from his marker and when he was still in the process of taking the ball around Darcy, the goalkeeper was forced to extend his arm to bring down the West Ham player.

John 'Pip' Meighan, the Dublin referee in charge of the game, had no hesitation in pointing to the penalty spot and despite the protestations of the crowd, he remained unmoved as Byrne prepared to exact revenge. Even as the visitors got ready to celebrate, however, Darcy dived to his right to knock the ball against the butt of an upright and then hugged the rebound to his chest with the crowd roaring their appreciation.

That was a moment to stoke the fires of ambition in every Irish player but before they could capitalise on the reprieve, the English team had broken the stalemate. In view of what had gone before, nobody could protest that the goal had come out of turn. But the sense of disappointment was everywhere in evidence as Hunt outflanked the defence down the right flank before delivering the cross with sufficient precision to make Byrne's short-range header a mere formality, with just twenty-four minutes on the clock.

Minutes later, Hunt's header from a cross by Callaghan extracted another good save from Darcy as the visitors went in search of the second goal which might have broken the Irish spirit and when the goalkeeper parried another genuine scoring effort approaching half-time, Browne was forced to scamper to complete the clearance.

Not even the most avid Irish supporter could question the 1–0 scoreline in the visitors' favour as the teams reappeared for the second half, but despite the one-way traffic which characterised play in the first half, hope still lingered that, with luck, the men in green could yet haul themselves back into contention. To achieve it, they needed an early break and it almost materialised in the fifty-sixth minute when O'Connell quickly took Robert's free kick under control before smacking the ball against an upright.

That miss had the effect of heightening the Irishmen's intensity and as confidence grew, so the visiting defence came under concerted pressure for the first time in the game. Whelan had a shot smothered by Armfield and then, as the screw turned, came an equaliser that rocked the stadium. Moore's headed clearance following O'Connell's corner kick travelled only as far as Bailham lurking just outside the penalty area and the shot, struck with venomous power, flew into the top corner of the net.

Suddenly, joyously, the game was transformed. A thirty-yards free kick from Roberts crashed against the underside of the crossbar, only for Whelan to head the rebound directly into the arms of Waiters, and then Armfield was visibly relieved to block O'Connell's shot after the winger had won possession from Moore.

The crowd could scarcely believe the drama unfolding in front of them and from a position in which the margin of the English team's win had earlier been the only point at issue, the long arm of opportunity was now seen to be reaching out to their opponents. Fitzgerald and Mooney combined to throw the visiting defence into something approaching panic with a swift break down the right soon afterwards and then, for the second time in the game, Dalymount erupted with just eleven minutes to go.

Fullam, growing in authority with each passing minute, tapped an indirect free kick to Bailham and when the latter's pass arrived at Whelan's feet just yards out, the finish was inch-perfect. After his long periods of inactivity in the opening half, Waiters found himself retrieving the ball from his net for a second time and as the scorer raced to accept the acclaim of the masses, history was in the making.

True, it required another agile save by Darcy to prevent Hunt snatching an equaliser as the crowd held its collective breath in the dying minutes of an historic game, but with 'Pip' Meighan in no mood to stretch their nerves to breaking point in added time, the end came just in time to provoke some of the most remarkable celebrations the old stadium had witnessed in years.

The unsung heroes of the League of Ireland were at last able to claim a victory over the English aristocrats and Ronnie Whelan could recount with some veracity that the most important goal of his career had rescued him from the anger of the crowd. 'I knew I should have done better when Paddy Roberts's free kick came back off the crossbar but all was forgotten with that winning goal,' he said.

Some twenty-five years later, he would have the pleasure of watching his son, Ronnie Jnr, fill a leading role in Ireland's defeat of England in the 1988 European championship in Stuttgart to ensure that the Whelan clan from Finglas would always hold painful memories for those English supporters who believed that victory over the Irish was no more than the fulfilment of their destiny.

By the time the Dalymount game ended, even the man responsible for arranging the work roster in the Unidare factory had probably grown to appreciate the importance of it all. The morning after the most significant inter-league game ever played in Ireland, the papers were full of praise for the Irish victory and the manner in which Whelan had recovered from his earlier gaffe to secure the historic win.

With his name splashed across the headlines, he was now viewed as one of the country's favourite sons and when he reported for work the following evening to be told that the departmental manager wanted to see him, his mates were teasing him about the likelihood of receiving a bonus or perhaps even a promotion for the media profile he had earned for his employers.

Imagine his pained surprise then, when the man brandishing the sports pages of the *Irish Press* on the other side of the desk informed him that he did not, in fact, have permission to play in the game and if he absented himself from work in similar circumstances in the future, he would be dismissed on the spot. There are indeed times in life when one just cannot win!

- Chapter 13 -

All Hail Arkle

Horse Racing – Cheltenham Gold Cup, March 1964

There is something about the Irish which makes us uncommonly suscepti-
ble to the thrill of horse racing. True, the English and the French have their
own special affinity with four-legged friends, not to mention the
Americans or even Australians and their fixation with the splendid edifices
of the sport in Kentucky and Flemington.

Yet you merely have to look at the excitement on the faces of Irish pun-
ters at racecourses such as Cheltenham and Liverpool on good days and
bad, to realise that when it comes to horse racing and National Hunt meetings in particular, we are indeed a rare breed. For as long as racing has infat-
uated the masses, Ireland has enjoyed a truly global reputation for the
quality of its bloodstock industry. And just as constant is the esteem in
which the truly great animals are held.

From Golden Miller to Dawn Run in National Hunt races and
Nyjinski through to See The Stars on the flat, there has always been a special place for equine heroes in the pantheon of Irish sport's super stars.
Debate on the subject and those qualified to be classified as such can be a
source of endless enjoyment, but of one thing there is near unanimity. For
all the varied qualities of racehorses through the ages, there has never been
a better animal over fences than Arkle.

No less than Tom Dreaper, the trainer, and jockey Pat Taaffe, Arkle was rarely out of the sporting headlines in the 1960s, an enduring source of pride and entertainment for his myriad of supporters and acknowledged as such in song and story for much of the last fifty years. Yet, he might never have blossomed but for the astute judgement of the man who for so long was fondly known as the 'Guv'nor of Greenogue'.

Tom Dreaper was a person who fitted easily into the landscape of north County Dublin. A stocky man who rarely appeared in public without his familiar soft hat, his was an authoritative voice in an area with a rich tradition in horses and horsemen. But it was an ability to interact with all strands of society which made his establishment, located just off the North Road between Finglas and Ashbourne, one of the most efficient in the business.

'He had this marvellous ability to make everybody in the stable feel as important as the next person,' said one former stable employee. 'It was a happy yard to work in and, of course, it was that much happier because of all the winners he sent out.' Before Vincent O'Brien emerged to put down new benchmarks in National Hunt racing, Dreaper was viewed as an icon in Britain and Ireland, sending out animals of the stature of Prince Regent, Shagreen and Sunria to dominate steeplechasing at home and abroad.

But there were some people close to him who maintained that, much as he liked horses, he loved cattle even more. That may or not be valid, but significantly, cattle were always a part of the lands adjoining the stables at a time when the presence of Arkle attracted a constant stream of admirers to Kilsallaghan. Pat Taaffe was from the opposite end of the county but as he was wont to remind his friends, when he went looking for a wife, he didn't wander far from his workplace, meeting and marrying a member of the famous Nugent family, another household name in racing, based just down the road at the Ward.

Pat, too, was steeped in racing tradition. His trainer father, Tom Taaffe, was a contemporary and, on race days, a sharp rival of Tom Dreaper while brothers, Willie and Tom, better known as Tos, were also successful riders. Tos, in fact, rode for Vincent O'Brien when the latter was still involved in

National Hunt and later went on to become an accomplished trainer in his own right.

On his own admission, Pat Taaffe was never the most stylish of jockeys. In his autobiography, Terry Biddlecombe, the best National Hunt jockey in Britain in his prime, related how 'Pat's arms and legs were all over the place in riding out a tight finish, so much so that we Brits nicknamed him "The Indian". But as a horseman he was in a class of his own. And it made him the perfect partner for Arkle.' In that assessment, Biddlecombe was articulating the thoughts of many, for Pat, who was hunting at the age of six and a point to point winner at sixteen, was reputed to know horses better than any of his contemporaries.

The other important person in the Arkle success story was Anne Duchess of Westminster, an enthusiastic supporter of National Hunt racing and a loyal patron of the Dreaper establishment. The Duchess bought the horse as an unraced three-year-old at Goff's Horse Show Sale in Ballsbridge in 1960 and named him after a mountain on one of her Scottish estates.

Arkle was bred by Mrs Mary Baker of Malahide and foaled at Ballymacoll Stud in County Meath. Her dam was a modest chaser named Bright Cherry and coincidentally, Pat Taaffe's first professional ride for Dreaper in 1950 was on Bright Cherry. Dreaper never forgot the horse and when Arkle came up for sale, his advice to the Duchess was, 'Buy him if you like but his dam never stayed more than two and a half miles.' In the event, the Duchess liked him enough to pay 1,150 guineas and had him broken in on her estate before sending him to be trained by the Master of Kilsallaghan.

Arkle was almost five when he had his first outing at the old racecourse in Mullingar in 1961, finishing third in a modest bumper and he struggled again in his next race, in which he placed fourth in another bumper in the Christmas meeting at Leopardstown. That wasn't the stuff of a great horse in the making, but Dreaper liked the scope of the animal and soon afterwards informed the Duchess that, with luck, Arkle might in time mature into a Cheltenham Gold Cup horse.

For all the maestro's intuitive skills, however, there were enough flaws in the performance of the potential champion in those two races to warrant serious concern. But wholly in character, his judgement was proven to be spot on the money. Starting with a runaway success in a three mile novice hurdle at Navan, he amassed a total of seven victories in 1962, securing the Powers Gold Cup at Fairyhouse and the Broadway Chase at Cheltenham in a manner which stamped him as the best novice in Britain or Ireland.

That view, it has to be said, was not shared by the legendary English trainer, Fulke Walwyn who, no less than Dreaper, was an honours graduate in steeplechasing. Walwyn had won the 1962 staging of the Cheltenham Gold Cup when Mandarin held off a strong finish by the Dreaper runner, Fortria, to finish two lengths to the good with Duke of York back in third place. In style and substance, that triumph was good enough to suggest that the winner could keep the trophy for at least another two years but tellingly, Walwyn believed that he had an even better Gold Cup contender in his yard by the start of the 1962/63 season.

Like so many of the outstanding 'chasers in Britain, Mill House was foaled in Ireland and directly after his introduction to racing, he was acclaimed as an outstanding talent. Before being purchased by Walwyn, the horse had been broken in by Pat Taaffe and he was so impressed by the power of the engine beneath him that he was moved to write to his great friend, Willie Robinson, Walwyn's first string jockey, emphasising the merit of the yard's new arrival.

By contrast, Arkle was a little bit backward at that stage of his career but once he began to motor, Taaffe was soon putting pen to paper again for his old mate from Summerhill in County Meath. 'Mill House is still a great horse,' he told Robinson, 'but we've got one here who is going to be even better.' One can only imagine Walwyn's indignation when shown the letter and it would have given him additional ammunition as he prepared for the first meeting of the horses in the Hennessy Gold Cup at Newbury in November 1963.

Everybody in racing was aware of the significance of the duel – and it ended in shock for the Arkle team. Giving away lumps of weight to all his rivals, the flying Mill House beat Happy Spring, receiving 25lbs, by a staggering eight lengths with Arkle, 5lbs better off in the weights than the English champion, a further three-quarters of a length away in third place. It was a victory conclusive enough to preclude any valid excuses until the Dreaper camp came up with one of their own.

An even bigger crowd than usual turned up at Newbury that day in expectation of an absorbing battle and Taaffe confessed that Arkle, an intelligent, alert horse, had become distracted when he noticed the large crowd of spectators gathered at the third last fence. Taaffe reacted as most of his fellow jockeys would, by giving his horse a sharp reminder with the whip to get his focus right again. Startled by this, Arkle lost his stride momentarily, sprawled on landing and was always struggling subsequently.

Taaffe admitted afterwards that he had erred in his reaction, vowing, 'From here on in, I'm going to let Arkle do the jumping.' Not everybody accepted the plausibility of that excuse, however, and when the horses met again the 1964 Gold Cup at Cheltenham, Mill House started at 8/13 with Arkle at 7/4. It is a measure of the esteem in which the pair were held that only two other horses, King's Nephew and Pas de Seul, went to post.

The effect was to concentrate the attention of the packed stands even more intensely on what was certain to be a tactical struggle between the champions of Ireland and Britain. Mill House, a superbly proportioned horse, had galloped all over the opposition at Newbury. In view of the spectacular success of that assignment, there was never a doubt that he would again attempt to make it all from the front in spite of Cheltenham's reputation as a course which was more demanding that any other in this part of the world.

His Achilles heel, however, was an inability to quicken in the closing stages, a weakness which had never really been put to the test in the Hennessy Cup. To exploit it, however, Arkle needed to be within striking distance at every stage of the race and avoid a repetition of the small but hugely expensive jumping error which had cost him so dearly four months earlier.

Taaffe's suspicion that the apparently invincible favourite could be vulnerable under pressure was confirmed for him by British jockey, Dave Dick. With a candour bordering on treason in this England–Ireland duel, Dick assured him that Mill House, for all his galloping power, was lacking genuine acceleration and if Arkle took him on from the third last jump, he would prevail. The plan seemed almost too simplistic to be viable, but it worked.

Measuring his jumps perfectly, the favourite was two lengths clear at the third last but anxious Irish eyes couldn't fail to be reassured by the spectacle of Arkle cantering behind him. Then, as they approached the next fence, Taaffe went for broke and in a matter of strides, the epic battle of Cheltenham was won and lost. Arkle, finding the extra turn of foot that Walwyn had secretly feared, was up and away from the fence in the style of the great horse he undoubtedly was and, barring the unthinkable, on his way to victory

The crowd held its collective breath as they raced into the last with everything on the line, but as they soared over the timber, it was Arkle who now looked unbeatable. Prospering in the tumult, he lengthened his stride to break the resolve of the partnership now receding into the distance and to the delight of his supporters, came powering up the hill to win by five lengths with Pas de Seul strung out with the washing in third place.

Even by Cheltenham standards, the welcome he got as he made his way to the winners' enclosure was enormous. Superlatives were the order of the day, none more so than those of Pat Taaffe. 'There's nothing to equal him,' said the successful jockey after dismounting. 'He's a Rolls Royce of a horse, a horse in a million.' Fulke Walwyn was vastly disappointed but still gracious in defeat. 'I couldn't believe my eyes when it all began to unravel for us,' he said. 'I genuinely believed that Mill House was the best in the land but not any longer. I am shocked.'

From that day, the legend of Arkle would grow far beyond the shores of Ireland. Dubliners found a new destination for exploration on Sunday afternoons at Kilsallaghan, where children in particular delighted in watching the horse play with a well-worn tennis ball in his stable. And the Guinness group, impressed by newspaper reports that the equine king liked his bran mashed with some of the dark stuff, provided it free gratis for the rest of his career.

Fresh from his Cheltenham success, Arkle won the Irish Grand National at Fairyhouse with 12st on his back the following month and in the autumn of 1964 he reaffirmed his superiority over Mill House in the Hennessy Cup at Newbury when, under top weight of 12st 7lbs, he finished ten lengths clear. The heart of the great horse from Walwyn's yard had been broken by his defeat at Cheltenham but just a week after stunning the crowds at Newbury, Arkle was himself foiled by the handicapper when, carrying 12st 10lbs, he lost by a short head and a length by Flying Wild (receiving 32lbs) and Buona Notte (receiving 26lbs).

Not since the great Golden Miller some thirty years earlier had any horse carried such huge lumps of weight so bravely and so successfully as the Kilsallaghan equine machine. Like the 'Miller, Arkle won the Cheltenham Gold Cup three times, beating Dormant by a staggering thirty lengths in the last of them, the Leopardstown Chase three times, as well as breathtaking wins in all the major sponsored 'chases over three miles.

Before he headed to Kempton Park in search of a second success in the King George VI 'chase on 27 December 1966, only six horses had finished in front of Arkle in his twenty-six 'chases. The previous month he had been touched off by the grey Stalbridge Columnist in a thrilling finish to the Hennessy Gold Cup, a race in which he was conceding 2.5st to the winner, but Tom Dreaper was adamant that the pride and joy of his life was in 'tip-top form' as he prepared for the last challenge in a remarkable year.

The portents were not encouraging in as much as bad weather caused the meeting to be postponed for twenty-four hours, but out on the track all was well with the champion as he bowled along just off the lead. Despite hitting the fourteenth fence, he overtook Dormant in cruise control between the last two fences on his way, it seemed, to yet another flamboyant win. But then, dramatically, he began to struggle up the finishing stretch and as he slowed to almost a standstill, Dormant, in receipt of 21lbs, got back up to beat him on the line.

Clearly, something was wrong and sadly, the worst fears were confirmed by the subsequent veterinary reports which showed that he had broken a pedal bone in his off-fore. On just three sound legs he had come close to winning one of Britain's showpiece 'chases but the decision to detain him in England bespoke the gravity of his injury. After Terry Wogan, the BBC Radio presenter, had chosen Tom Jones's rendition of the 'Green, Green Grass of Home' to assuage the anxiety of the horse's legions of admirers, Arkle was eventually returned to his base in north County Dublin. But in spite of being made sound, he never raced again and when arthritis eventually set in, he was put down on 31 May 1970.

In his thirty-five starts over six seasons, Arkle won twenty-seven times but that statistic will never convey the full measure of his greatness. More relevant by far was the style in which he won them and the fact that in his last nineteen races he never carried less than 12st. Even the most insensitive of the hard-headed handicappers could only stand and applaud as they watched the making of a large chunk of National Hunt history in those sunlit days of long, long ago.

– Chapter 14 –

Showdown in Paris

Football – Spain v Republic of Ireland, November 1965

From the moment the draw for the preliminaries of the 1966 World Cup decreed that the Republic of Ireland should play Spain and Syria for the right to participate in the finals of the championship in England the following year, there was an unmistakable sense of foreboding in the headquarters of the Football Association of Ireland.

The knowledge that that we would have to meet Spain was daunting in a technical sense but logistically, it was a dream come true. A year earlier, the FAI had organised a charter flight, a first ever for the association, for a European championship qualifying game in Seville and the decision was vindicated by players and supporters alike. Just three months later, the Spaniards were celebrating success in the championship after outplaying the Soviet Union 2–1 in the final, but in spite of the apparent discrepancy in class between the teams, the prospect of taking on the reigning European champions did not unduly alarm manager Jack Carey.

An assignment in Syria was, however, a whole lot different. At the time, it was not unprecedented for countries in the Middle East to be grouped with those of Europe for the purpose of World Cup qualification. But any tie involving Syria was, almost by definition, fraught with anxiety. Even then it was regarded as one of the most troubled regions in the world, with a permanent United Nations peacekeeping force deployed there.

In short, a journey to Damascus was something to be avoided if at all possible and the expectation of problems in the making was everywhere in evidence as the FAI weighed the advantage of being included in a three-team group against the dark possibilities of journeying into an area of armed conflict.

At the time, Joe Wickham, the FAI Secretary, was taking advice from Irish members of the UN force serving in the area and the word coming back was that the security situation in Syria was, in fact, deteriorating. The sad irony was that Wickham's son Terry, an Irish army commandant who represented the army on the FAI's Senior Council, was himself killed as a member of that UN force, just a couple of years later, after being caught in an ambush.

At different times, Syria were reported to be on the verge of withdrawing from the competition but after the FAI was assured that the tie would indeed go ahead, they risked the wrath of all the League of Ireland clubs by postponing the FAI Cup games scheduled for 14 February 1965 to accommodate the first leg of the World Cup tie. Then, just weeks before the Syrians were due in Ireland, they notified FIFA that they were withdrawing from the competition.

Confirmation of that decision was received with some relief in Dublin and after Joe Wickham had acted quickly to arrange a replacement non-competitive fixture for the date vacated by the Syrians, Carey and his players were ready to contemplate the prospect of taking on Spain, home and away, for the alluring prize of a first appearance in the World Cup Finals.

Judged on the evidence of the European championship games the previous year, the threat presented by Spain could scarcely be overstated. The team Carey assembled in Seville was representative of the cream of Irish talent with the exception of the injured Manchester United full-back, Tony Dunne. Yet, after Andy McEvoy equalised an early goal for the home team, Spain simply overran the men in green with Amancio and Marcelino each hitting the target twice.

It wasn't a lot better for the Irish in the return match at Dalymount Park. On this occasion, it was Zaballa who did the damage with a brace of goals to secure a 7–1 aggregate win on their way to the European title, their biggest success to that point, just three months later. And still, for all the damning evidence of those statistics, Ireland could console themselves with the thought that, on rare occasions, they had indeed, delivered on Spanish terrain.

There was, for example, that storied occasion in Barcelona in 1931 when, on their first appearance in Spain, they attracted a crowd of 100,000 to the Montjuïc Stadium, forerunner of the stadium on the same site for the 1992 Olympic Games. On that occasion, a young Shamrock Rovers player answering to the name of Paddy Moore celebrated his first cap by producing a brilliant goal to secure a 1–1 draw.

It was far and away the biggest crowd to watch an Ireland game in the period between the Great Wars, and the FAI was so delighted with its share of the gate receipts that they awarded the players a £5 bonus. The exception was Bohemians half-back Sean Byrne who, as the only amateur in the side, was instead handed a £5 voucher for jewellery. When he requested that it be replaced with a clothing voucher, he was dismissed with some indignation and never again selected for the national team.

Then there was the game in Madrid in 1946 when Ireland resumed their international programme after the guns had finally fallen silent at the end of World War II and the FAI embarked on a tour of the Iberian Peninsula. The first match ended in a 3–1 defeat by Portugal at Lisbon but with Con Martin taking over as an emergency goalkeeper from Ned Courtney, they shocked Spain just a week later with Josiah Sloan obtaining the only goal of a tense struggle in the Bernabeau stadium.

It was memories such as those which now sustained Jack Carey, who played in the 1946 fixture and then captained the side which beat Spain at Dalymount Park some nine months later. The Spaniards, it has to be said, had established themselves as one of the great powers of international football in the intervening years, not least because they could call on the great majority of the Real Madrid team which dominated the early years of the old European Cup championship.

Given the dimensions of Spain's historic success in the European championship just eleven months earlier, their first competitive appearance since that magical evening in Madrid, a midweek game at Dalymount Park on 5 May 1965 attracted a good deal of international attention. Carey interpreted that as an encouraging omen after the low-key 2–0 defeat by Belgium in a warm-up game at the same venue two months earlier.

The big pre-match talking point for Irish supporters was the first appearance in a green shirt of Shay Brennan, a revered name at Manchester United in the rebuilding of the squad from the ruins of the Munich air disaster. Brennan had been a member of England's preliminary squad of forty for the 1962 World Cup Finals but failed to make the travelling squad to Chile. Now, with the introduction of FIFA's new eligibility rules enabling players to represent the country of their ancestors, he jumped at the chance of playing for Ireland.

The initial approach came from Matt Busby, Manchester United's venerable manager, who contacted the FAI to notify them of the player's Irish qualifications and his desire to fulfil a long-held ambition. Brennan still needed a clearance from the English FA but when Alf Ramsey informed the FAI that he had no plans to select Brennan, a new page of Irish football history was about to be written.

Other topics of conversation were the selection of the Manchester United goalkeeper Pat Dunne for his first international appearance and the choice of his Old Trafford clubmate, Noel Cantwell, at centre forward. Jackie Mooney of Shamrock Rovers had worn the number nine shirt in each of the two preceding Ireland games but scarcely did enough in either match to warrant retention.

In that situation, the team selectors, acting at Carey's behest, decided that a bigger, more experienced player was needed to lead the attack, inviting speculation that they would renew the experiment of playing Charlie Hurley, the powerful Sunderland centre-half, out of position. In a similar quandary the previous year, they had gambled on Hurley for the meeting with Norway in Oslo and the big man came up trumps by hitting two of the goals in a 4–1 win.

The fact that Shay Brennan and Tony Dunne were now automatic choices at full-back suggested that Cantwell would get the nod at centre half in an all-Manchester defence but typically, Carey was not in the mood to be swayed by public opinion. Hurley, he decided, would anchor the defence with Cantwell leading the hunt for goals and that judgement was wholly vindicated when, after playing with discipline in the face of some sustained Spanish pressure, Ireland broke the deadlock in the sixty-third minute.

Frank O'Neill, on his way to becoming the most capped League of Ireland player in history, arced a free kick from a narrow angle on the right into the six-yards area, and with one eye on the in-rushing Cantwell, the Spanish goalkeeper Iribar lost track of the ball and succeeded only in knocking it into his own net. It wasn't the prettiest of goals but it was important enough for the convivial Irish captain to claim it.

'I feel that Iribar was otherwise occupied as the ball floated in and I'll claim any credit that's going,' he told the press corps, tongue in cheek after the game. 'Spain currently claim to be the best team in Europe and to get this win was sweet beyond words. At worst the tie will now go to a third game but with luck, we can win it in two when we go to Spain in October.'

Those were sentiments with which Jack Carey could readily identify. Even then, there were indications that he was finding it increasingly difficult to marry his Ireland team duties with the day to day responsibilities of club management in England. And he possibly saw in the draw for the qualifying process for the 1966 World Cup, an ideal opportunity of leaving on a high note.

'I was fortunate enough to play in a World Cup game on my first appearance for Ireland in 1937,' he wrote, 'but to have the chance of coaching the national teams in the finals of the competition in England next summer, would surpass anything I've known in football.

'Spain are not European champions for nothing and playing in front of their own supporters, they will be even more dangerous when we go there in the new season. I thought we defended with great discipline at Dalymount Park and if we can repeat that in the second game, we will have a real chance of going to the finals.'

Carey was not to know at that stage that fate would intervene in the approach to the return match, and for all his enthusiasm about Brennan's international debut and the contributions of his Old Trafford colleagues, Tony and Pat Dunne, the manager didn't need telling that it was Charlie Hurley's domination of his penalty area which really scuttled Spain.

In the eight years since making that sensational first appearance for Ireland in the return World Cup meeting with England in 1957, Hurley had established himself as one of the outstanding central defenders in European football, a rating which was duly vindicated in the manner in which he dominated Marcellino at the front of the Spanish attack in Dublin. And it was the memory of that imperious performance which made the news of an injury he picked up in a club game for Sunderland all the more serious in the run up to the return fixture.

If Ireland were to survive the minefield of Seville on 27 October 1965, it was essential that Hurley report for the task of marshalling the defensive screen in front of Pat Dunne. But the word in Sunderland was that he would not alone miss the second instalment of the tie but also the third game if a play-off became necessary to determine the qualifiers from the group.

Back in Dublin, that prognosis came as a big shock. Carey desperately needed Hurley's proven composure if they were to stand defiant in the face of the expected Spanish onslaught and in his absence the manager was now noticeably less bullish in his pre-match statements. Among other things, it meant that Noel Cantwell would have to be withdrawn from the attack to play at centre half with the uncapped Shelbourne player, Eric Barber, promoted to fill the vacancy at centre forward.

The manager's sense of impending disappointment was, it seemed, shared by Joe Wickham, for during the traditional pre-match lunch, he discussed the practicalities of finding the most suitable venue for a third game if a play-off became necessary. It would prove the start of a long negotiating process which consumed many column inches in the sporting press over the following two weeks.

If Carey had good reason to lament the absence of his stricken player in Sunderland, he could still console himself in the knowledge that in Andy McEvoy he had a potential match winner in attack. Together with the celebrated Jimmy Greaves, McEvoy was the hottest shot in English club football in the first half of the 1960s and while he wasn't at his best in the first Spanish game, he still represented one of Ireland's bigger assets on the day.

Far from being overwhelmed by the pace and weight of Spain's early onslaught, the men in green defended well before stunning the crowd by going on the offensive. And they looked to have made the perfect start when Frank O'Neill rolled a free kick to Mick McGrath at the edge of the penalty area and the Blackburn man fired his shot into the roof of the net in the nineteenth minute. Even as the Irish celebrated, however, the referee ruled that O'Neill had taken the free too quickly and disallowed the score.

Refusing to be demoralised by that controversial decision, however, Ireland broke through again just seven minutes later – and this time it counted. John Giles crossed accurately from the left and McEvoy, expansive in his better moments, drove the ball at speed past Betancort in the Spanish goal. It ought to have been the signal for another evening of carnival among Irish supporters, but on this occasion the Spanish were not in the mood to be bullied.

Juan Mario Pereda, one of the players brought into a revised Spanish attack, changed the course of the game by scoring twice in a five minute

spell immediately before the break, the second of them ironically following a free kick which the Irish protested had been taken too quickly. Pereda
completed his hat trick within eighteen minutes of the restart and when
Lepetra added a fourth, Ireland were looking at a 4–1 defeat which did not
reflect the trend of the game.

Unhappily from an Irish perspective, they were now faced with the
doomsday scenario of a play-off and the challenge of finding a suitable
venue for the fixture. Spain favoured Lisbon and then, even more naively,
suggested the Irish party might stay over and agree to a play-off in Seville
two days later, thereby reducing travel expenses.

The FAI suggested Wembley Stadium in London, more in hope than
in confidence and as such, can scarcely have been surprised when the
Spanish Federation said no. Paris was the Spaniard's next choice with the
FAI nominating Amsterdam, a city which had brought them some success
in the past. It was at that point that FIFA got involved and instructed the
two federations to agree on a venue within forty-eight hours, or else they
would impose one on them. Soon afterwards a friend of Wickham's in
FIFA phoned Dublin to inform him that FIFA had, in fact, settled on
Paris in the event of the national federations not being able to reach an
agreement.

'Of course, I realised that Paris, with its easy access for Spanish supporters, was a bleak prospect for us,' Wickham told me later. 'But faced
with the certainty of being directed to play there, I immediately contacted
the Spanish Federation before they learned of the situation and told them
that we were prepared to accept Paris if allowed to retain the gate. In the
event, we collected a sum which approximated to the profits we would
normally make from international games over a period of two years.'

The consequences of that decision were everywhere in evidence for the
Irish players as the team coach neared the old Colombes stadium on match
day. All the approach roads were thronged by Spanish fans and with the
official attendance returned at just under 36,000, there was possibly no

more than a couple of hundred Irish supporters and a similar number of curious Parisians in the crowd. It was a home game in everything but name for Spain but in spite of the naked partisanship of the crowd, the Irish team stood up admirably to the ordeal.

With the exception of isolated scoring attempts by McEvoy and Giles, the traffic was nearly all one way and yet McEvoy might well have opened the scoring when his shot beat goalkeeper Betancort, only to strike a defender chasing back and go out for a fruitless corner. An Irish defence weakened by Hurley's ongoing absence was depleted still further when Theo Foleo had to go off for a time with an injury, but they still managed to hold out until a freak goal, eleven minutes from the end, decided the match in Spain's favour. Pereda's cross from the right was completely missed by Suarez but the effect was to wrong foot both Cantwell and Mick Meagan immediately behind him. The ball ran through to the unmarked Ufarte who, to the delight of the Spaniards flooding the stadium, dispatched it to the net. Ireland's World Cup dreams were shattered and for all the mountainous commitment, it would be another thirty-five years before they reached the Promised Land and World Cup qualification in Italy.

– Chapter 15 –

Classical Comeback

Rugby – England v Ireland, February 1972

Kevin Flynn wasn't exactly a spent force in rugby when a friend, barely able to contain his excitement over the message he was about to convey, phoned to tell him that he was in the Ireland team to face France at the start of their Five Nations championship programme in the old Colombes Stadium in Paris on 29 January 1972.

At that point, he was still a key member of Wanderers team and playing well enough to fill the number thirteen shirt for Leinster in one of their better seasons in the interprovincial championship. Yet, for all his imposing pedigree in the game, it was almost six years since he was last requested to present himself for duty in the green shirt. And the element of surprise in his selection was such that it dominated every newspaper account when the team was announced some twelve days before the action started in Paris.

It is true that the popular Dubliner, weeks away from his thirty-third birthday, had just come off the back of a splendid run by Leinster which saw them claim the interprovincial title by beating Ulster 12–10, Munster 9–0 and Connacht by a surprisingly close 12–6 margin. Yet, given the quality of some of the other players in contention for the outside centre position, few were prepared for the decision which saw the name of M. K. Flynn appear in the French match programme.

It represented a vast leap of faith by the selection committee in an era in which courage was often a distant second to conservatism, but when the year had run its course and momentous events had already been consigned to history, the Big Five could reflect that theirs had been a judgement bordering on Solomon-like.

Posterity recalls the 1971/72 season as one of heartbreak for Irish rugby with the joy of away victories over France and England utterly diluted by the controversial refusal of Scotland and Wales to fulfil their scheduled fixtures at Lansdowne Road because of what they termed the 'civil disturbances' in Dublin and its environs. That refusal probably cost Ireland the Five Nations grand slam, leaving young and old alike to bemoan the heavy hand of fate at a time when so much else was going wrong in the country.

Yet, all were agreed that even in its truncated state the championship had produced moments of enduring grandeur for those who ventured to Colombes and Twickenham as well as the millions watching on television. And central to it all was the sleight of hand and breadth of vision which put the man from Terenure in a class apart from so many others at the start of 1972.

Kevin Flynn was always destined to leave his imprint on the game after a glittering schools career at Terenure College had confirmed him as one of the golden talents of his generation. It made for a situation in which every senior club in Dublin was monitoring his progress, but eventually he opted to join Ronnie Dawson, another gifted young player, at Wanderers. At that point, one of the most successful clubs in the capital was at the summit of its powers and the newcomer's arrival was interpreted as another move designed to consolidate that affluence.

Dawson, later to captain Ireland and the Lions, made his first international appearance in the historic victory over Australia at Lansdowne Road in 1958 and that would have encouraged Flynn in his ambition to follow the front row player on to the biggest stage of all. The achievement of Niall Brophy, the gifted Blackrock student, in shortcutting his apprenticeship on his way to a place in the national team would also inspire him.

Brophy, a useful sprinter with UCD and Crusaders AC when he took his annual summer break from rugby, had long been seen as an Ireland winger in the making. Flynn, a couple of years behind him in schools rugby, was also perceived as an embryonic international player and in this instance, it was his nimble footwork and assured handling skills which stamped him as a special prospect in his teenage years.

Eventually he too joined the elite international club, linking up with Brophy and Dawson in the team which took on the champions elect, France, at Lansdowne Road on 19 April 1959. With victories over Scotland and Wales and an honourable draw with England to their credit, the French were entitled to view their visit to Lansdowne Road as an ideal opportunity to showcase their impressive talent against an Ireland side which had come up short in their meetings with both England and Wales.

Even with home advantage, it was scarcely the ideal scenario for any teenager hoping to make a spectacular entrance to international rugby but, nothing if not ambitious, Flynn did just that with the thrilling break through the centre of the French defence to put Brophy over for the opening try of the game. It got even better when Mick English and David Hewitt each potted shots at the French posts and the newcomer's career in the big time was off to the perfect start with a 9–5 win over the startled champions.

For much of the next seven years, Flynn's name was closely interwoven with the fortunes of the national team and never more so than on a marvellous day for the Irish at Twickenham in February 1964 when he twice crossed England's line in addition to having a hand in the flamboyant try which enabled Pat Casey to apply the gloss to a wholly unexpected 18–5 win over the most implacable of their rivals.

Yet by 1966, at a stage in his career when he ought to have been tormenting defenders even more, he was beginning to lose his way at the top level. The thrilling breaks, which had had been so often a feature of his early years in the national team, were becoming fewer and while he remained central to Leinster's domestic campaign, he drifted out of the plans of the national team selectors.

It was against that bleak background that he embarked on the 1971/72 season, uncertain of his future at the top level but determined to make it difficult for the national selectors in their fixation to look elsewhere for an outside centre. It helped that Leinster had hit one of their better patches in the opening months of their campaign but it was still a major talking point when the selection committee, comprised of Ronnie Dawson, Michael Carroll, Noel Henderson, John Hewitt and David Gleeson, decreed it was high time that his velvet skills were restored to the three-quarter line.

So it was that when the team was eventually made public and the Big Five decided to venture to Paris on a wing and a prayer in the last week of January 1972, the omissions of the previous six years were conveniently forgotten and Flynn reached out to grab the opportunities offered by what would surely prove a short but fitting finale to his career in international rugby.

In the 1960s, when Ireland's rugby team didn't always perform to a level commensurate with the sum of its component parts, the big match preparations were occasionally called into question. Then, in 1971, the incumbent president of the IRFU, Dom Dineen, and team captain, Tom Kiernan, saw fit to introduce a new, more intensive build up to the international championship which began like so many others for the Irish, with a visit to Colombes and another collision with the dreaded heavyweights of the northern hemisphere.

In Ray McLoughlin, a superb competitor in any setting, they had a leader of the pack, who physically and psychologically compared favourably with the best in the game. McLoughlin believed implicitly in the principle that a good preparation is half the battle and in Kiernan returning to lead the team at full-back after a protracted injury, he had the perfect ally. Kiernan was looking at winning his forty-ninth cap in Paris, and with Willie John McBride and Ken Kennedy joining McLoughlin in the battle for forward superiority, the visitors certainly did not lack experience in that area.

Mike Gibson, a name to illuminate any team sheet, joined in a midfield partnership which oozed creative craft but against that, it has to be recorded that Ireland took five uncapped players to Paris. Tom Grace and Wallace McMaster were on the wings, Johnny Moloney was promoted at scrumhalf with Con Feighery of Lansdowne and Dungannon's Stewart McKinney gaining inclusion in the pack. It was, by any standard, a bold statement of intent in a stadium where they hadn't won in twenty years, and central to the master plan for survival was their capacity to strike early.

For days, Kiernan had preached the virtues of a bright start but even he must have been agreeably surprised when his team surged into the lead in just eight minutes. After Barry McGann had been stopped on the line, the ball was quickly recycled and when Denis Hickie fed Moloney, the young scrumhalf feinted to go wide. Instead, he spotted the tiniest of gaps in the line and before the French could get to grips with him, he wriggled through it for the most audacious of tries.

After waiting so long for something to cheer in Paris, the tiny band of Irish supporters in the ground could scarcely believe the evidence of their eyes as the visitors continued to dominate up front, and they knew for certain that something special was on the way when the indomitable McLoughlin breached the home defence yet again just a minute before half-time. On this occasion, Hickie combined with McKinney to upend Olivier Saisset inside the French 25 and after grabbing the loose ball, the burly prop scattered defenders in all directions in his charge to the line.

For good measure, Kiernan kicked two penalties and it was not until the sixth minute of injury time that Jean Paul Lux got in for the consolation try, converted by Pierre Villepreux, which distorted the 14–9 scoreline. That was a point emphasised in Paul McWeeney's match report in the *Irish Times* as the veteran writer reflected on the fact that he was the sole surviving Irishman in the press box from the group which had 'covered' Ireland's last success in the stadium in 1952.

It was a rare moment of joy for the country at large as the civil unrest in the north descended to a new low with the killing by British paratroopers of fourteen innocent people who had had taken part in a protest march in Derry. By way of mistaken retaliation, a mob then proceeded to burn down the British embassy in Dublin and another low in relationships between the two governments soon raised doubt about the feasibility of going ahead with the Ireland–England game at Twickenham a fortnight later.

As it transpired, the possibility of postponing the game was never discussed by the English Rugby Union and with Ireland only too willing to make the journey in the wake of the win in Paris, it was soon confirmed that the match would go ahead as scheduled. Even before they set out for London, however, officials of the IRFU saw fit to consult their counterparts in Edinburgh about the Scots' scheduled visit to Dublin on 26 February and were assured that in spite of the deteriorating security situation in Ireland, they had no undue worries about making the trip.

That was a cause of some relief and as Ireland set down in London on the eve of the game with an unchanged team, the mood of the players was one of rising hope. On each of their three most recent visits to Twickenham, they had been undone late in the game with Bob Hiller's siege-gun kicking putting them to the sword on each occasion and, worryingly from an Irish perspective, the elegant full-back was still laying claim to the number fifteen shirt in the home dressing room.

Having finally exorcised the ghosts of Paris, Tom Kiernan was not going to be unnerved by any English side even at Twickenham, and as he made ready to celebrate his fiftieth Ireland appearance in the grand manner, he echoed the thoughts of many of the team supporters travelling to

London when he told a local journalist on his arrival in the capital that he believed this Irish team was on a par with that which had dismantled England at the same venue in 1964.

That was the kind of message that the hosts didn't want to hear and it possibly gave them an added source of motivation in the first half when, playing with the advantage of the wind in their backs, they led 9–3 at the break. In fact, the gap could have been greater but after landing a penalty and then adding the extra points to a try by Beese, Hiller missed two kickable penalties to the astonishment of home supporters and the thinly veiled relief of those in the opposite camp.

That was a significant deviation from the norm and it fostered the hope that with the elements now assisting them, the Irish could prosper in the second half. So it proved with the pack recovering from the travail of the first half in which Andy Ripley and Chris Ralston monopolised the lineout to grind their rivals into submission. Liberated from the defensive roles imposed on them during the opening forty minutes, the Irish backs were now asking all the pertinent questions of their markers and when Barry McGann executed his grub kick with delicate precision, Tom Grace outpaced the covering Peter Dixon to score in the corner and afford Kiernan the opportunity of supplementing his first half penalty with the conversion.

That raised a huge Irish cheer but then almost immediately, McLoughlin was penalised for not releasing the ball in a ruck and Hiller's radar was seen to be in working order again in extracting the maximum retribution. Twice Ireland spurned try-scoring chances, first when McGann held on too long after an overlap had been created and later when David Duckham's despairing interception deprived Tom Grace of a clear run to the line.

With just five minutes left, England were still leading 12–7 but then an inexplicable error by Beese in knocking the ball on behind his own line after Gibson's miscued penalty resulted in a scrum on the 25 and the chance for McGann to drop a trademark goal. At the time it seemed no more than a consolation score but this tumultuous struggle still held one more surprise.

Five minutes' injury time had already been allowed by the French referee, Roger Austry, when Ireland were awarded another scrum on the 25. Given what had just happened, the expectation was that the ball would be fed back to McGann for another drop at goal or, just possibly, moved along the line for Gibson to make the rapier thrust for glory. To counter that threat, Flynn's marker, Duckham, moved marginally to his right, to line up the tackle on the Ulster maestro.

It didn't go unnoticed by the Irish playmaker and when Moloney's arrowed pass bought him an extra couple of seconds, he sent Flynn racing through the narrow gap created by Duckham's injudicious decision and the veteran was past Hiller at speed before touching down behind the posts.

It was the perfect ending to the fairytale return by Flynn, famously enriched for history with the *Irish Times* headline which read, 'Try To Be Remembered For A Generation'. In one brilliant late flourish, the indignities visited on the Irish in London in the previous six years had been avenged and Hiller, so often the scourge of the men in green, was promptly dropped, never to play for England again.

Paul MacWeeney noted in his match report that on the last occasion Ireland won in Paris and London in the same season, the Grand Slam or equivalent title was secured in 1948. More than that, he noted that if Ireland were successful on home terrain in their remaining two games, it would be the first occasion the coveted Triple Crown was won at Lansdowne Road. Happy days.

Within eighteen hours of the gates being closed at Twickenham, the Irish selectors had again named an unchanged team for the next assignment, against Scotland in a fortnight's time. In the event, that announcement would be of mere academic significance after the Scottish Union, in a remarkable volte face, indicated that they would not now play in Ireland because of the civil unrest there.

Forty-eight hours before the game at Twickenham, officers of the four home unions had reviewed the deteriorating security situation in Ireland and agreed that all games there should go ahead. Now, two parties to that agreement were adopting a different stance on the matter of security and people here were perplexed. The immediate reaction saw Dom Dineen lead a six-man Irish delegation to Edinburgh in a last desperate attempt to persuade the Scots to travel but all to no avail. The Scots were not for turning and while they agreed to hold another meeting of their officers to review the position later in the week, the IRFU sensed that nothing would change.

Despite all the guarantees on offer and assurances of a major security plan being put in place for their visit, the Scottish Union considered that in light of the riotous scenes at the British embassy, it would be grossly unfair to their players and supporters if they permitted the fixture to go ahead as planned. Fears that the Welsh Union would follow suit were unhappily substantiated after Bill Clement, the Welsh secretary, announced that while they were willing to play Ireland in Cardiff or at a neutral venue, there was no question of them travelling to Dublin in the prevailing circumstances. The alternatives put forward by the Welsh were dismissed out of hand and Ireland's hopes of bridging a twenty-five-year gap in sport were, like so many other things, sacrificed in the violence that stained the image of the Irish in those dark, troubled days.

The actions of the Scottish and Welsh authorities were received in Dublin with quiet, if at times strained, dignity. Even in the most conservative centres, they were judged as disproportionate, but the effect was to deprive a golden generation of players of the opportunity of securing a prize which had attracted and tantalised for so long. And they were placed in perspective by the fact that the French authorities had no hesitation in accepting an invitation to undertake a replacement fixture in Dublin just a month later.

In time, normal relations were restored with Edinburgh and Cardiff, a process which was greatly facilitated by the decision of England's rugby hierarchy to honour their commitment to play at Lansdowne Road in February 1973. It yielded another prized win for the Irish but the abiding memory of a great occasion was the rapturous reception accorded to John Pullin's team as they took the field, an outpouring of gratitude and relief which lasted for almost five minutes.

In between, the seventh All Blacks touring squad had played its part in normalising matters by fulfilling their schedule of fixtures in Ireland. Thanks to Tom Grace's last-minute try, Ireland salvaged a 10–10 draw, their best result against New Zealand, and Kevin Flynn was able to take his leave of international rugby in a manner befitting one of the great players of his generation.

– Chapter 16 –

Soviet Coup

Football – Republic of Ireland v Soviet Union, October 1974

Don Givens, frequently an inspirational personality on the pitch and just occasionally an outrageous prankster off it, confessed that it was easily the most uncomfortable moment of his sporting career as he faced a battery of press photographers at London's Heathrow airport on the evening of 30 October 1974.

Some four hours earlier, he had been at the heart of one of the enduring dramas in Irish football history after the national team had opened their challenge for a place in the finals of the 1976 European championship with a superb performance against the Soviet Union at Dalymount Park.

Givens's performance was such that, long after they had locked the gates of the stadium on Dublin's north side, many of the London-based British national newspapers saw fit to record the return of the all-conquering hero to his adopted city where he was something of a cult figure in the blue and white strip of Queens Park Rangers.

The problem was that, because of a chain of bizarre circumstances, the celebrated Ireland striker was still in his mud-spattered Ireland tracksuit with the match ball tucked under his arm as he disembarked from the plane to face the cameras. And even for a man not unpractised in the art of pulling the odd stunt, his discomfort was plain for all to see.

'To be honest, I didn't know whether to laugh or cry,' he said. 'It's not every day a player travels in a plane in football strip, particularly if it is not particularly clean. I never expected to be confronted by photographers when I got ready to disembark and while I tried to explain that there were valid reasons for my odd appearance that evening, I'm not sure if they were believable. But in a strange way, it summed up for me what had been easily the most memorable day of my international career.'

The arrival of Givens on the stage of international football in 1969 coincided with the FAI's groundbreaking decision to appoint Mick Meagan as part-time manager of the national team and bring an end to the reviled system of five of the association's leading officials, taken from disparate roles in the game, selecting the side.

At that point, the FAI was among the last national federations in western Europe clinging to a selectorial policy that that had long been derided as outdated. And the clamour for change in the mindset of the powerbrokers on Merrion Square grew in intensity after the appointment of Alf Ramsey as manager of England's team had been identified as a key element in their World Cup success in 1966.

It would be some time before Meagan's contribution and that of his successor, Liam Tuohy two years later, began to come to fruition but by the time John Giles ascended to power late in 1973, the pieces were being put in place for the structure which some fifteen years later would see the Republic take their place at the top table of international football.

At that point, Giles was already fourteen years into a remarkably elongated international career which began with a spectacular strike against Sweden at the school end of Dalymount Park in 1959. Despite his success at club level, first with Manchester United and, later, Leeds United, his Ireland career didn't always run smoothly, culminating in his shock replacement by Billy Newman of Shelbourne for a World Cup game in Denmark in 1969.

That decision testified to the eccentricities of the old selection system and was almost certainly responsible for the dramatic change inherent in

Meagan's appointment. Significantly, Giles was among those at the fore-front of the lobbying campaign which eventually led to that shift in policy and as such, it was no more than appropriate that he himself should take control of the team in a player-manager role after Ireland's failure to make the cut for the finals of the World Cup in West Germany in 1974.

The men in green had won only one of their last seven fixtures when the new manager ventured into his first game in charge, a friendly at home to Poland in October 1973. At that point, meetings with Poland formed the centrepiece of the FAI's international programme and more than most, Giles was familiar with the abrasive nature of the teams sent out from Warsaw. On this occasion, however, all the indications were that the competitive qualities of the visitors would be even sharper than usual after they had upset England at Wembley en route to Dublin.

Their performance in London owed much to the theatrics of an unorthodox goalkeeper, Jan Tomaszewski who, for all his clowning, managed to defy the English with a string of improbable saves and in the end, they had to settle for a 1–1 draw. It was a vastly disappointing result for the home team which not alone ruined their chance of playing in the World Cup Finals the following year but effectively cost Alf Ramsey his job.

Fortunately for Ireland, that achievement appeared to sate the Poles' appetite for further heroics when they turned up at Dalymount four days later, and while the Polish goalkeeper produced a few more spectacular saves, he was powerless to stop Miah Dennehy's header which ensured that Giles's reign was off to a highly encouraging start.

In the event, it would prove Ireland's last home fixture before opening their European championship programme against the Soviet Union exactly a year later. Sandwiched between the two matches, however, was an alluring three-match South American tour in the spring of 1974 and the opportunity of confronting the mighty Brazilian team which was constantly pushing out the parameters of sporting excellence in the 1970s.

By common consent, the Brazilians were in a different league to all others at the time and the fact that the fixture was being staged in the giant Maracanã Stadium in Rio de Janeiro, merely served to emphasise the dimensions of the task awaiting Giles. The novelty of the fixture was sufficient to attract a crowd of 75,000 and one could only guess at the thoughts of those spectators as they watched the majority of the footballs being used by the visitors in the pre-match kick about end up in the moat surrounding the pitch.

Yet, when the real action got under way, the Irishmen played with sufficient composure to hold Jairzinho, Rivelino, Paulo Cesar, Luis Pereira and their colleagues scoreless in the first half. Eventually, Leivinha and Rivelino broke the deadlock with two goals in the space of six minutes early in the second half but when Terry Mancini scored twenty minutes from the end, the Irishmen got no more than they deserved for a highly creditable performance. Given the enormous work rate involved, it was perhaps inevitable that they would suffer a 2–0 defeat at the hands of Uruguay in Montevideo three days later. But when Eoin Hand and Jimmy Conway hit the target to ensure a 2–1 win over Chile in Santiago, Giles was entitled to look back with satisfaction on the ambitious tour.

It was the perfect riposte to those who had for so long opposed the notion of entrusting the selection of the team to the manager, and the effect was to heighten the sense of expectation for the first appearance in Dublin of the powerful Soviet Union team at the start of the qualifying programme for the 1976 European championship. The Soviets, one of the heavyweights of international football at the time, had won the inaugural European competition in 1960, lost in the final to Spain four years later and again reached the final against West Germany in 1972.

That presaged a hazardous test for the new management team, the more so since they wouldn't have the benefit of a warm-up game to prepare for the assignment after a five-month break from international competition. Unmoved, however, Giles was at pains to stress that the changes he had put in place on taking charge of the team were already beginning to have the desired effect.

For many years, Alan Kelly's agile goalkeeping had been a source of inspiration for Ireland teams but after making his forty-seventh appearance against Norway the previous year, he decided to call time on his international career. Initially, the manager sought to fill the vacancy by promoting Peter Thomas, a prime personality in Waterford's remarkable run of League of Ireland championship successes and later by calling up Mick Kearns of Walsall.

For the Soviet encounter, however, he decided to go with Paddy Roche, whose only previous Ireland appearance had ended in heartbreak and the concession of six goals as Austria overran what was essentially a League of Ireland selection in a European championship game at Linz three years earlier. In the intervening period, Roche had moved from Shelbourne to Manchester United and the graph of his progress was sufficiently encouraging to persuade Giles to give him the opportunity of joining his Old Trafford clubmate, Mick Martin, in the side.

The choice of Terry Mancini at centre back was equally interesting. Mancini, whose Cockney accent provided the aural evidence that he qualified for Ireland only through the ancestry rule, enjoyed a fine career with Queens Park Rangers and now, as a newly signed Arsenal player, he was given the chance of building on some impressive displays in the course of the South American tour.

Yet, the biggest talking point by far in the team announced by Giles was the inclusion of the much talked about Arsenal youngster, Liam Brady. At that point, Brady was only newly graduated from the Highbury Academy but asked to nominate the best prospect he had seen at the club, Alan Ball Jr, a former World Cup-winner with England, had no hesitation in putting forward the name of the lad from Whitehall. It was an opinion shared by many of the shrewdest judges of English club football.

At eighteen, Brady was a mere stripling but no less than his two older brothers, Ray and Paddy, who both played for Queens Park Rangers and later Millwall, he had a sharp competitive edge to his game that put him a cut above the rest. Allied to his sublime skills on the ball, it represented a package that was too good to ignore.

Oleg Blokhin, the Ukranian striker who would later be named as European Player of the Year, was one of several Dinamo Kiev players in the Soviet team and like Viktor Onischenko, he represented a major threat to the restructured home defence. Yet, if Giles harboured an inferiority complex about the gap which separated the teams in the international ratings, it certainly didn't show as they set about the challenge of upsetting the visitors with the pace and weight of their early attack.

With just minutes on the clock, Mancini was only narrowly wide with his header when a free kick from Giles found him in space, and then it was Givens's turn to hold his head in his hands after Ray Treacy's knock down had given him a clear sighting of goal. That miss didn't auger well for the QPR player and minutes later his hands were in the air again, this time after the Swedish referee had responded in the negative to his claims for a penalty when Olshansky's tackle tumbled him inside the area.

A crowd of 35,000 for the Wednesday afternoon kick-off groaned collectively when Steve Heighway just failed to make contact with Brady's pass but they were in full voice in the twenty-third minute after the Soviets stumbled into one error too many in the waves of pressure breaking across them. Giles, at the heart of everything that mattered, started the move by putting Joe Kinnear clear down the right flank and as the ensuing cross came in, Givens managed to get between the two centre backs to head his seventh international goal in twenty-five starts to that point.

Rarely had an Ireland goal received such acclaim, even by Dalymount standards, and suddenly an added element of self-belief imbued every green-shirted player on the pitch. With Brady's emerging skills complementing the experience of the player-manager in midfield, they began to string passes together in a manner which might have been unthinkable a year earlier.

The Soviets, by contrast, had scarcely launched an attack of any significance in the first quarter of the game. Unable to get a foothold in the battle for midfield control, they toiled to create anything of substance until Blokhin finally got away from Kinnear and made tracks for goal. His shot, on the run, was still rising as it cleared the crossbar by a couple of inches, but that cameo was enough to warn the Irish defence that they would ignore the Kiev player at their peril.

Blokhin's sudden burst also had the effect of damping down the enthusiasm of the crowd temporarily, but before the visitors could build on their new momentum, they leaked a second goal on the half hour. This time it was the persistence of Treacy which established the chance for Givens and in the manner of a man who sensed that things were beginning to go for him, the Irish striker again beat goalkeeper Viktor Pilgui from close range.

It was almost too good to be true for spectators who had long since stopped believing in little sporting miracles, but even as they waited for the expected Soviet rally to materialise, another incident which would have a profound bearing on the game erupted in the Soviet penalty area. When Mancini found himself being jostled by Vladimir Kaplichny as Giles prepared to take a free kick close to the penalty area in the thirty-second minute, he lashed out in frustration. The impact was almost certainly exaggerated as the Soviet player ended up in a crumpled heap on the ground, and having shown Mancini the red card, the referee waited for Kaplichny to 'recover' before dismissing him too.

Mick Martin, an outstanding utility man in many times of need, was taken out of the midfield formation to join Paddy Mulligan in the middle of the defence and the success of the move was such that Giles never saw fit to cap Mancini subsequently. After an initial scare which led to Onischenko going dangerously close to pulling a goal back for the visitors, the new defensive formation dovetailed so smoothly that Roche was rarely summoned to action in the second half.

The exception came in the sixty-first minute when the goalkeeper could only parry Valerey Fedetov's shot from the edge of the penalty but fortunately for the home team, Kolotov, lurking at the edge of the six-yards area, was unable to convert the rebound. In that moment, the outlines of a coveted win came more sharply into focus and the crowd knew for certain that the Soviets were doomed when Givens, on a flood tide of confidence, came across his marker to meet Giles's free kick with the glancing header that directed the ball well out of Pilgui's reach and completed his hat trick in the sixty-third minute.

It was the most exhilarating goals splurge by any Irish player since the peerless Paddy Moore rushed four past Belgium in a World Cup tie at Dalymount in 1934. And just 364 days later, Givens would emulate Moore's landmark achievement by putting his name on all the goals in the 4–0 demolition of Turkey at the close of their European championship programme.

After eulogising Givens in his post-match analysis of the Soviet game, Giles presented him with the match ball and unwittingly provided one of the props for the theatrics that followed. Restricted by the tight schedule of an early evening return flight to London, he didn't have time for a shower before dashing off in a taxi from Dalymount to the airport with the ball clutched under his arm.

Caught up in a traffic jam in Phibsborough, he abandoned the cab and ran past a long line of vehicles before flagging down an unsuspecting motorist half a mile further along the road. Bemused by the sight of an agitated man in a mud-spattered Ireland tracksuit and a football which had seen better times, the good Samaritan stopped and, totally unaware of the identity of the other person, agreed to convey him to the airport on being informed of the circumstances.

Givens got there just in time for the last check-in call and once through the departure lounge sprinted to the waiting aircraft as the door was being pulled closed. He was not to know then that, in London, a troupe of photographers was already on the way to meet him on his arrival and record in black and white images the faintly startled look of a dishevelled sporting hero.

'It was all a little embarrassing at the time for beneath the tracksuit, my legs and arms were covered in dried mud and the fact that I was carrying a football when I disembarked from the plane made it even worse,' recalled Givens. 'But in time, I came to regard it as a fitting end to a day which in so many ways had been a bit unreal for us all.'

As it transpired, Ireland's attempt to qualify for the finals of the 1976 European championship would founder on a shock 1–0 defeat by Switzerland in Berne some seven months later, but for Givens, the tournament was something of a personal triumph. Helped by the unforgettable hat trick which would resonate across the broad world of international football and the four-timer which followed against Turkey, he would go on to accumulate a then Irish record of nineteen goals.

Measured by today's extravagant standards and the opportunities which continue to expand for international players, it is not an imposing total. And yet, in the vastly different world of football in the leisurely seventies, it was still an acceptable calling card to any gathering of gifted strikers, not least in the sporting fortress of Moscow.

– Chapter 17 –

Dubs Get Dumped

Gaelic Football – Kerry v Dublin, September 1975

Growing up in Waterville, Mick O'Dwyer would have been well aware of the special qualities attaching to any meeting of Kerry and Dublin in Gaelic football. In good times and bad, the men in green and gold were feared opposition for any team, matching a natural talent for the game with a level of commitment that frequently put them in a different class to those who sought to invade their empire.

By 1955, they had amassed a grand total of seventeen All-Ireland senior titles, a figure which testified to the remarkable consistency of a county which, with rare exceptions, insisted on depending on home-grown play-ers in their relentless pursuit of titles. Dublin's tally at that point stood at fifteen championship wins but in this instance, they often had the pick of the country as young men arriving in the capital in search of work pledged their sporting allegiance to their adopted county.

That was before the Dublin County Board embarked on their 'natives only' policy and after the spectacular rise of the St Vincent's club, they chose to confront Kerry with a side which, in essence, was representative of the best of the local talent, carefully nurtured in the late 1940s and early '50s, in the showpiece of the Gaelic football season in September 1955.

It was the All-Ireland final which, the critics assured people, would change the whole concept of Gaelic football, a team of young pretenders projecting all the merits of clever, tightly patterned football against the side which had always identified the strengths of the catch and kick style of play. And it ended in a resounding win for the traditionalists.

True, Ollie Freeney achieved the distinction late in the game of shaking the net with a fourteen-yards free kick, unequalled in an All-Ireland football final before or since, but it merely had the effect of restoring an element of respectability to the eclipse of the Dubliners. Kerry won more comprehensively than the scoreline of 0-12 to 1-6 would indicate and a lot of people ended up eating humble pie.

Of all the Kingdom's title successes, that was the most gratifying, providing the script of a story which would be told and retold throughout the length and breadth of the county for years unending. Fast-forward twenty years and the climax of the 1975 season put the unassuming young man from Waterville at the heart of the drama in another gripping Kerry–Dublin final. It was the first meeting of the counties in the final since 1955 and the tales of undying sporting heroism were still vivid enough to fire his imagination.

In the intervening period, Mick O'Dwyer had been cast centre-stage on All-Ireland football final day, more often than anybody in history. Including the replayed 1972 final against Offaly, he played in no fewer than ten deciders, four of them successfully. Starting as a wing half-back, he filled the centre half-forward role for a couple of years before drifting, perhaps inevitably, into the full-forward line. By any standard, it was the textbook preparation for an aspiring coach/manager and once he had brought the curtain down on an eventful playing career, he let it be known that yes, he would be interested in the top job in the county.

At that stage, the Kingdom was ready to embark on one of the most extensive regrouping exercises in years and O'Dwyer was assigned the task of overseeing it. Since the 1972 defeat by Offaly at Croke Park, Kerry had failed to make it out of Munster, losing to Cork 5-12 to 1-15 in 1973 and again falling to their nemesis, this time by a seven-point margin the following year. Failure on that scale was suffered only with deep reluctance in all points south of Listowel and inevitably, it made for wholesale changes in personnel by the time the 1975 campaign commenced.

Donie O'Sullivan, a name which compared favourably with the best in Kerry football through the years, found himself redundant after a long association with the county team stretching back to 1964 and his fate was shared by four other defenders, Paud O'Donoghue, Seamus Fittgerald, Michael O'Shea and the team captain against Offaly, Tom Prendergast.

But the most notable loss was unquestionably that of Mick O'Connell, who at a remove of more than forty years is still widely regarded as the best Gaelic footballer of all. The man who redefined standards for friend and foe alike had judged it time to go at a stage when he was still playing well by general standards and with John O'Keeffe, his midfield partner in 1972, rerouted to full-back, it meant a new central combination of Paud Lynch and Pat McCarthy.

Brendan Lynch was the only forward to make the transition from the old regime in a formation which featured the arrival on the big stage of three players who would go on to fashion exciting careers, John Egan, Mike Sheehy and Pat Spillane, who found himself entrusted with the number fifteen shirt, a role which O'Dwyer himself had filled with distinction in the closing phase of his long stay in the team.

Seldom had a more inexperienced Kerry team been pressed into action at the start of a championship campaign. And yet, for all that lack of maturity, those close to the team contended that the newcomers were sufficiently talented to cancel out the disadvantage. For some, that smacked of bravado but it wasn't long before the GAA world at large came to acknowledge the accuracy of the assessment.

The opening assignment in Munster yielded an emphatic 3-13 to 0-9 win over Tipperary but the more pragmatic element in Kerry's support chose to await the evidence of their provincial final date with Cork in Killarney before passing judgement. For much of the preceding two years, the old aristocrats had been forced to operate in the slipstream of the Leesiders and many wondered aloud if the home team could escape the consequences of haemorrhaging so much experience right through the team.

It wasn't long into the game before those doubts began to recede and after Cork had asked all the pertinent questions, the Kingdom pulled away to win 1-14 to 0-7. That was more than even the most optimistic Kerry supporters dared hope for and the following morning the national newspapers were as one in their praise of O'Dwyer's new-look team. A 3-15 to 0-5 win over Sligo in the All-Ireland Semi-Final meant that they had accumulated 7-42 in just three games, of which John Egan claimed no less than four goals and seven points. If Dublin ever fretted about complacency, they now knew for certain the dimensions of the task ahead.

Dubliners old enough to remember the 1955 debacle believed that this was the game which would avenge the hurt of twenty years. Now, as then, they would take on Kerry as favourites to win but on this occasion they would go in as reigning champions after outplaying Cork en route to a five-points win over Galway in 1974. And they reckoned that this would give them a psychological advantage to complement their greater experience of big match pressures.

No less than O'Dwyer in the southwest, Kevin Heffernan enjoyed cult status in the capital after topping off an outstanding playing career by captaining the Dubs to victory over Derry in the 1958 final. And it was no great surprise that they should turn to the man from Marino to lead the way back to more fertile lands after being relegated from the top tier of the National League in the early 1970s.

Just as he had led from the front at the pinnacle of his playing career, Heffernan accepted the challenge of managing the team with a brand of enthusiasm which quickly infused tired players. And having identified higher fitness levels as a prerequisite of success, he contrived a situation in which the graph of the team's fortunes became a major focal point in Irish sport.

In 1963, he had been largely responsible for enticing Des Ferguson out of retirement to fill a perceived problem at full-forward and it was advanced as a major factor in their title success that year. Now he was well on the way to repeating the success of that audacious gamble by reintroducing another St Vincent's clubmate, Jimmy Keaveney, to lead the attack.

Keaveney's remarkable accuracy had been key to nearly everything that mattered in 1974. Leaner and sharper than he had been in years, he used all his skill and cunning to bring those around him into the game more often and it showed in the remarkable rate of improvement attained by players like Anton O'Toole, David Hickey and, not least, the highly influential Tony Hanahoe.

Midfield was manned by Brian Mullins and Bernard Brogan whose sons, Alan and Bernard Jr, would emerge many years later, to inspire a new generation of Gaelic heroes in the capital. Mullins, just out of his teens, was already on the way to becoming an outstanding player and on the basis of his contribution in the 1974 campaign, was tipped to sway the all-important midfield battle in Dublin's favour.

That registered well with supporters of the champions. Less acceptable were the growing doubts now being expressed about the quality of the home defence in which Gay O'Driscoll was the sole representative of St Vincent's. Ominously, they had conceded ten goals in the four games required to take them to the final and it was a statistic which Mick O'Dwyer was prone to use time and again in his motivational talks at Kerry's training base in Killarney.

The incessant rain hammering down in the capital from early morning wasn't the only talking point in the hours preceding the match. Dublin's unconvincing win over the Ulster champions Derry in the semi-final had been flawed by crowd violence both inside and outside the stadium. Disturbances on that scale were relatively rare in Gaelic Games and much was made of the fact that it appeared to have caught the security authorities off guard.

The negative publicity did nothing to soothe the anxieties of people who feared for the safety of women and children intending to watch the game – the first seventy-minute final – and the effect was to provide something of an unreal atmosphere for what should have been one of the GAA's biggest paydays in years. In the end, the attendance was returned as 66,346, which was almost 25,000 down on the figures for the 1955 game when some 5,000 gate crashers boosted the size of the crowd to an estimated 91,000.

The fact that the weather conditions on match day were the worst in years merely added to the champions' worries. Their margin of error at the back when facing the in-form Kerry forwards was always reckoned to be slim and now with a wet ball and treacherous underfoot conditions accentuating the problems of defenders on both sides, there was undeniably an element of alarm from the throw in. And within three minutes of the start of the action, it resulted in a Kerry score which would weigh heavily on them for the rest of the afternoon.

Gay O'Driscoll, normally an assured fielder under pressure, now failed to hold on to the ball after Sheehy had arced a free kick to the edge of the square. And when the error was compounded by the slow reaction of at least two other blue-shirted players, Egan grabbed the bouncing ball and, despite the close attentions of Sean Doherty, promptly dispatched it to the back of the net. The goal machine had worked again for Kerry and down on the touch line O'Dwyer's demeanour bespoke the delight on the challengers' bench.

Out on the pitch, accusing eyes were focused on a cluster of Dublin players gathered in close proximity to Egan when he struck for that lightning goal. In the space of just three minutes, Dublin had gone from confident champions to dishevelled challengers and O'Dwyer, scurrying up and down the sideline, merely had to glance around to note the body language of the protagonists which told him all he wanted to know.

The swell of confidence inspired by a second-minute point from

George Hardwick gets the better of a heading duel with Kevin O'Flanagan to clear for England in their 1–0 win over Ireland at Dalymount Park in September 1946. Other players pictured from left are Neil Franklin (E),Michael O'Flanagan (I) and Billy Wright (E). It was the first meeting of the countries in thirty-four years and a huge crowd turned up to mark the resumption of international football in Dublin after World War II.

Action in the Irish goalmouth as Tommy Goodwin saves in the memorable World Cup tie with England at Dalymount Park in May 1957.Irish players (left to right) are Noel Cantwell, Pat Saward, Charlie Hurley and Seamus Dunne. Tom Finney's last-minute equaliser for England ruined Irish hopes of qualifying for the finals in Sweden the following year.

Noel Cantwell (third from left) slides the ball just wide as Andy McEvoy (No. 10) looks on in the first instalment of the three-match World Cup tie with Spain at Dalymount Park in May 1965.Ireland were eliminated from the competition after a controversial 1−0 defeat at the hands of Spain in a play-off in Paris later that year.

Left: Jack Carey, one of the iconic personalities of Irish football, became the first player to receive the handsome statuette for twenty-five Ireland appearances, following his retirement as a player in 1953.Carey, seen here being presented with his trophy, was later appointed manager of the team.

Right: Don Givens's hat trick against the Soviet Union in a European championship game against the Soviet Union at Dalymount Park in October 1974 was the first by an Irish player since Paddy Moore scored all four goals in Ireland's 4−4 World Cup draw with Belgium in 1934.Givens went on to equal Moore's achievement the following year.

Packie Bonner, a study in concentration, was a key figure in the celebrated teams sent out by Jack Charlton during his time in charge of the national team. Bonner, who made his international debut on his twenty-first birthday in Poland, went on to win eighty caps before his retirement in 1996.

Kevin Flynn celebrates his return to international rugby by completing Ireland's brave fight back with the late try which consigned England to defeat at Twickenham in February 1972. Flynn had been recalled to the team after an absence of almost six years from the game.

Tony Hanahoe, the Dublin captain, lines up a shot at the Kerry goal in the 1975 All-Ireland Football Final, in a renewal of one of the great rivalries of Gaelic football. Kerry went on to win 2-12 to 0-11, but Dublin would have their revenge just a year later. (Sportsfile)

A youthful Liam Brady (extreme right) lines up alongside John Giles and Steve Heighway before Ireland's European championship game against the Soviet Union in 1975. It would mark the start of a splendid international career which established Brady among the best midfield players in Europe. (Connolly Collection/Sportsfile)

John Egan of Kerry finds the going tough as he attempts to get away from Offaly's Pat Fitzgerald in the 1982 All-Ireland Football Final at Croke Park. Seamus Darby's dramatic late goal ended Kerry's hopes of an unprecedented fifth consecutive title win. (Connolly Collection/Sportsfile)

All smiles from Jack Charlton, the Ireland manager, and his assistant Maurice Setters as they leave the pitch after Ireland's storied European championship win over England at Stuttgart in 1988. Some years earlier, Charlton had applied for the vacant England manager's job and didn't get a response from the English FA. (Ray McManus/Sportsfile)

Stephen Roche is on the wheel of his great friend and rival, Sean Kelly, during the Nissan Classic race in Dublin in 1986. Just two years later, Roche would go on to take his place among the finest riders in history by winning the Giro d'Italia and the Tour de France before completing his superb season by winning the road racing championship in Austria in September. (Ray McManus/Sportsfile)

Barry McGuigan prepares to unload his trademark short arm punches during his WBA World Featherweight Championship fight with Danilo Cabrera in Dublin in February 1986. He would lose his title in Las Vegas just four months later when dropping a points decision to the unconsidered Steve Cruz. (Ray McManus/Sportsfile)

Sonia O'Sullivan trails Sally Barsosia of Kenya and Ethiopia's Berhane Adere in the early stages of the Olympic 10,000 metres in Sydney in September 2000. O'Sullivan would later be central to some of the Games' enduring memories, taking on Gabriella Szabo of Romania in an enthralling finish to the Olympic 5000 metres championship. (Brendan Moran/Sportsfile)

Peter Stringer personifies the joy of it all after making a major contribution to Munster's first Heineken Cup win over Biarritz in Cardiff in 2006. Stringer's opportunist try had been key to Munster's success, a victory which would be repeated two years later, this time at the expense of Toulouse. (Brian Lawless/Sportsfile)

A cricket miracle in the making. Andre Botha celebrates with his Ireland teammates after taking a catch to dismiss Inzman Ul Haq and hasten the defeat of Pakistan in the biggest upset of the 2007 World Cup. It triggered unrestrained St Patrick's Day celebrations in Kingston, Jamaica. (Pat Murphy/Sportsfile)

Henry Shefflin eyes history in the making as he leads the Kilkenny hurling team in the pre-match parade for the replay of the 2012 All-Ireland Hurling Final against Galway at Croke Park. Together with Noel Hickey, a substitute on that occasion, Shefflin wrote a page of hurling history by becoming the first to win nine All-Ireland senior championship medals. (Sportsfile)

Mullins had been turned in one inspired moment by the talented Sneem club man and as the home defence sought to close ranks, so Kerry upped the pace to uncover different avenues to Paddy Cullen's goal line. First, Denis 'Ogie' Moran, one of two teenagers in the team, careered through twenty yards of empty space to shoot an excellent point, Sheehy tapped over a close-in free and when Bendan Lynch supplemented it with another, this time from forty yards, Kerry were five points clear after only ten minutes.

A frightening tackle on Michael O'Sullivan at the end of a fifty-yards run, resulted in the Kerry captain being removed to the Richmond hospital for an overnight stay with a suspected concussion after just twenty minutes but, undeterred, they were still pinning the opposition in the wrong end of the pitch. Then, when it looked as if the champions might collapse on all fronts, Keaveney and Pat Gogarty kicked points to lift the mood of the crowd on Hill 16. This was answered by three more Kerry points from Brendan Lynch, Sheehy and Moran but a second point from Gogarty meant that Dublin, for all their limitations on the day, still went in at the break only five points down, 1-6 to 0-4.

That flattered the men in blue for with Mullins and Brogan toiling against Paud Lynch and Pat McCarthy, the unsung Kildare club player who was rapidly emerging as the man of the match, Kerry had always looked the better team. If the Sam Maguire Cup was to stay on Liffeyside, they needed to minimise McCarthy's influence to lift the pressure off a disappointing half-back line. Most of all, perhaps, they were looking to Anton O'Toole and David Hickey to rediscover the form which on other, palmier days had sown the seeds of brilliance.

Hickey's flamboyant runs had never been in evidence in the first half but within ninety seconds of the restart he had sped through the Kerry defence, forcing Paudie O'Shea to concede the free which was duly pointed by Keaveney. That smacked of a recovery in the making but, alas, for the Dubliners, the signs were false.

Before long, the traffic was all one way again with McCarthy growing even more influential in midfield. Now, even the youngsters in Kerry's attack were playing with the self-belief of men in the prime of their years with Spillane, the other nineteen-year-old in the team, rampaging down the left flank after switching from the corner to play in the half-forward line. Egan, involved in a great man-to-man duel with Robbie Kelleher, was blatantly unlucky not to have a second goal after his effort had rebounded off the crossbar with Paddy Cullen in obvious difficulty, but nine minutes from time, Kerry's long threatened second goal finally materialised.

Moran, catching the mood of a carnival occasion for the Kingdom, released Egan down the right and when he crossed the ball, Ger O'Driscoll, on as a replacement for the unfortunate O'Sullivan, had the relatively straightforward task of directing the ball into the net. Suddenly, perhaps inevitably, all the escape routes had been cut off for Dublin and while they registered three of the last four points on the board, it merely had the effect of making the 2-12 to 0-11 scoreline a little more tolerable for the home supporters. In the end, the final whistle may have come as a merciful relief to a team which had underperformed on the day, and the headline in the next edition of the *Irish Times* merely rubbed salt into an open would for Dubliners – 'Oh, The Day Of The Kerry Dancers'.

Mick O'Dwyer's first All-Ireland success as a coach/manager had been achieved with a degree of ease which made a mockery of their pre-match billing as outsiders. 'The early goal settled us and once I saw the ball in the net, I knew that we would out-pace and out-last them,' he told the waiting press corps. 'It was a really great team victory and the age and quality of this team should see them win at least two more titles.' Prophetic words for sure!

Jimmy Deenihan, experiencing the exhilaration of All-Ireland success for the first time, was no less enthusiastic. 'That was the match of the decade to win and we played great stuff to win it,' he said.

Dublin's manager, Kevin Heffernan, shell-shocked but unbowed, was not about to disagree. 'We have absolutely no complaints – we were well beaten on the day,' he said. 'The team as a unit didn't do itself justice but there will be another day and another result.' And there was!

Twelve months later, the fallen champions were back with a vengeance, out-scoring Kerry 3-8 to 0-10 in the final and when they repeated that success at the expense of Armagh in 1977, redemption was indeed complete. En route to that success they had out-gunned Kerry on a 3-12 to 1-13 scoreline in the semi-final in a game viewed by some respected commentators as the best exhibition of Gaelic football ever witnessed. And one could only guess at Heffernan's inner thoughts as he reflected on the mood of that bleak post-match press analysis in an equally bleak room under the Cusack stand in 1975.

Yet, when the big questions were asked on that occasion, it was O'Dwyer who had the bragging rights. And as they shut the Croke Park gates that evening, Kerry didn't just have a clutch of winners' medals in their possession – they left in the reassuring knowledge that the astute man from Waterville had lain the foundation stones for another golden era in the history of Gaelic football in the county.

'Many of the young lads we took into the final against Dublin in 1975 walked away from Croke Park that day as men who could deliver in any company, in any setting,' he would later reflect. 'And when you think of it, wasn't that the biggest prize of all, not just for Kerry but for Gaelic football in general.'

Chapter 18

Darby's Dream Day

Gaelic Football – Offaly v Kerry, September 1982

Seamus Darby would have been readily pardoned if he felt he was merely making up the numbers as the coach conveying the Offaly Gaelic football team to the scene of battle inched its way along Clonliffe Road before wheeling left into the Croke Park enclosure some ninety minutes before the appointed throw in time for the 1982 All-Ireland Final against Kerry.

Darby, a member of one of the county's best-known GAA families, was only recently recalled to the squad and some days earlier had learned that he would not be in the starting line up to take on a Kerry team which, by most estimates, deserved to rank among the best of modern years. But even a place on the bench represented something of a coup as he headed towards the last big assignment in a long and colourful career.

A year earlier, he didn't warrant inclusion in the squad that lost out to Kerry by a margin of seven points in a final which saw the Sam Maguire Cup return to the Kingdom for a fourth successive year. Now, as Mick O'Dwyer's team regrouped and readied themselves for a record five-in-a-row success, Offaly's manager Eugene McGee was searching desperately for somebody who could help bridge that wide gap.

On the face of it, Darby was an unlikely choice for a recall. True, he was playing well for his club but with several emerging players beginning to push for promotion, nobody banked on the veteran being brought back on board. And yet, when supporters of the Leister champions attempted to unravel the reasons for his surprise inclusion, they were apt to hark back to the replayed All-Ireland Final of 1972.

He wasn't in the team which faced Kerry on the last Sunday in September that year when Offaly, in the manner of their calling, competed so abrasively with more experienced opposition that they were full value for a draw. A scoreline of 1-13 apiece testified to the Leinster champions' ability to go head-to-head with the most daunting team in the sport, but for all their courage and admirable skills, team officials decided they still needed more in the replay.

It was that rationale which saw Seamus Darby promoted to the attack in place of Murt Connor and the move would pay paid handsome dividends as Offaly triumphed 1-19 to 0-13 to retain the title they had won at Galway's expenses in the 1971 final. Now, ten years on, Eugene McGee was hoping that if push came to shove, Darby would be able to make a similar impact. It was, at best, an outside bet but even the astute manager must have been surprised by the dividends it yielded.

Nobody typified more accurately the rise of erstwhile fringe counties in the changing balance of power in Gaelic Games in the 1970s than Offaly. From a situation in which they were forced to operate in the slipstream of other, better-resourced counties like Dublin and Meath in Leinster, they were invariably numbered in the list of those teams who were expected to battle bravely without ever making it to Croke Park on All-Ireland Final day, until their 1961 meeting with Down.

That thrilling challenge ended in a heartbreaking one-point defeat but the effect was to change the mindset of Offaly sportsmen forever. And eight years later, they were making headlines once more when a formidable full-back line of Paddy McCormack, Greg Hughes and John Egan fronted a young, inexperienced goalkeeper, Martin Furlong, so effectively that they progressed to the final against Kerry, only to lose out on a scoreline of 0-10 to 0-7. McCormack, alone of that formidable trio, survived to savour the sweet smell of success in their groundbreaking wins in 1971 and '72 but ultimately, it was Furlong, illustrating the virtues of longevity in goalkeepers, who would enjoy the distinction of playing in all three of Offaly's All-Ireland football wins.

Nor was the county's ascent to sporting affluence restricted to football. Starting in 1980, they had the privilege of playing in the Leinster senior hurling final on no fewer than eleven consecutive occasions, going on to claim four All-Ireland titles in 1981, '85, 1994 and '98. Equally remarkable was the fact that in a county not accustomed to producing big performers in both codes, Liam Currams joined the band of elite players who secured All-Ireland hurling and football medals by partnering Joachin Kelly in midfield in the 1981 hurling win over Galway before going on to fill an equally important role in the football final meeting with Kerry a year later.

Coupled with John Dowling's presidency of the GAA, it represented a high-tide mark in the history of the county's fortunes but now, as they prepared themselves for the most talked about football final in years, they needed little reminding that if they were to preserve Offaly's reputation as a team which nobody could afford to ignore, they would have to reach exceptional levels to defy the Kerrymen in their march on history.

For all the justifiable praise Offaly teams had attracted in the 1970s, it still required a broad sweep of the imagination to give them anything other than a slim chance of doing so. After all, this was the Kerry team which the cognoscenti rated as one of the greatest of all Gaelic football teams, perhaps even *the* greatest. Had they not won four titles in a row and done so with a panache which brooked no argument? Courageous as Offaly were, it was difficult to see them succeeding where other, supposedly better teams had failed.

In the hot flush of excitement which pervaded the Kerry dressing room after their victory over Dublin in the 1975 final, Mick O'Dwyer predicted that his charges would win at least two more titles. Given the quality of the players he was managing, that assessment didn't seem overly presumptuous and still the most successful manager in the sport can only have been delighted with the manner in which his squad of players had evolved.

It wasn't as if the intervening years had been a story of one automatic success after another. Within a year of seeing off Dublin in '75, O'Dwyer was required to explain why they were forced to hand back the Maguire Cup to the most enduring of their rivals and again the following August when they lost out to Kevin Heffernan's team in what was almost certainly the best celebration of Gaelic football any of us had witnessed.

But the badge of Kerry teams in that era was their facility to regroup and return. In 1978, they luxuriated in the knowledge that they had shaken the netting behind Dublin goalkeeper Paddy Cullen on no fewer than five occasions en route to a resounding 5-11 to 0-9 win and it was still largely one-way traffic when the teams met again in the 1979 decider with the men in green and gold winning 3-13 to 1-8.

By now, the callow youths whom O'Dwyer had taken to Croke Park for the 1975 final had grown into superb, mature athletes and the curtain had come down for a talented generation of Dublin players. Even as one accomplished team left the arena, another, perhaps even more gifted side moved centre stage. Suddenly, we discovered that Kerry, spoiled for success for so long, had found a new target for fulfilment – five titles in a row – and names which had to be checked twice only a few short years before, were now household around the country.

Charlie Nelligan had made the goalkeeping job his own and immediately in front of him, Paud Lynch and the two O'Keeffes, Ger and John, were every bit as intimidating for opposing forwards as the full-back line which brought Offaly to prominence some twenty years earlier. Tim Kennelly, flanked on either side by Paudie O'Shea and Tommy Doyle, barred the central way to goal in the half-back line and in midfield, Sean Walsh partnered Jack O'Shea who, no less than Brian Mullins, was responsible for rewriting the template for the sport with the concept of the square to square runner.

Of the six players who formed the attack in the starting line up, it can be said with some certainty that as a unit they reached a level which had rarely if ever been surpassed. So rich was their talent that Pat Spillane had to settle for a place on the bench before being introduced as a replacement for Denis 'Ogie' Moran during the half-time break – compelling testimony to the quality of the full-forward line of Mike Sheehy, Eoin Liston and John Egan.

For all that talent and experience, however, those close to the Kerry camp were preaching the need for vigilance as they eyed the glittering prospect of a fifth consecutive title at the start of the championship season. And they knew for certain that the road ahead was stony when Cork forced them to a replay of a tensely fought Munster final. Victory came readily enough in the second meeting, however, and when they powered to a 3-15 to 1-11 victory over Armagh in the All-Ireland Semi-Final, everything was back on track.

That was markedly different to Offaly's experience when, after retaining their Leinster title with a 1-16 to 1-7 win against Dublin, they tottered on the brink of defeat in their meeting with Mattie McDonagh's Galway team. In the end, they scraped home by a point but afterwards Eugene McGee was quick to acknowledge that when the pressure came on in the closing stages, it could have gone either way. Yet, victory was sweet for it meant that after being swept aside by Kerry in the final a year earlier, they now had another opportunity of going toe to toe with the best in the land.

Richie Connor, the Offaly captain, felt that the 1-12 to 0-8 result on that occasion was not a true representation of the game, pointing out that it was Kerry's ability to poach scores at critical stages of the game which distorted the scoreline. In making the case for his team's chances of turning the tables, he stressed the need to avoid conceding what he called 'the killer scores' that had won so many big games for the Kingdom. He was not to know it then that when the 'killer goal' materialised the following Sunday, it would be the Offaly fans who celebrated.

Even as Offaly were making their way towards the dressing rooms beneath the old Cusack Stand, some of the Kerry players were huddled in a group catching snatches of the county's minor team in action in the Croke Park curtain raiser. And what they saw was not encouraging. The Kingdom was struggling against Dublin and that was a sight rare enough to disturb the composure of any son of the sod.

So, too, was the sight of Liam Currams, rampaging far from his allotted role at left half-back, taking out at least three Kerry players in the process, before firing the opening point from long range after just five minutes. Kerry led briefly through points from Tom Spillane and John Egan but every time the champions threatened to put clear day light between themselves and the Midlanders, they were reined in by men who, in terms of pedigree, scarcely deserved to share the same pitch with them.

More than that, Offaly were matching them in style, frequently deploying the angled kicked pass to open gaps in the opposing defence. That was an art more associated with Kerry teams of the past and with the champions only too willing to take them on in the skill stakes, the opening half probably deserved to rate as the best in years. It ended with the Leinster team leading by a point, 0-10 to 0-9, after Eoin Liston had spurned a great chance in front of goal. And Pat Spillane's arrival in the game by the time the teams reappeared for the second half bespoke O'Dwyer's growing sense of agitation.

It also coincided with a cloud burst and while players on both sides required time to adjust to a greasy ball on the damp surface, the tempo soon picked up again as the teams went in search of the scores to act as insurance against the dangers inherent in a long, tense finale. Ominously, Jack O'Shea and Sean Walsh were now beginning to turn the screw in midfield for the holders and early points from Sheehy and Pat Spillane were interpreted by the team's supporters as the start of a decisive charge.

And it was at the height of more intense pressure that the first of the game's pivotal moments arrived in the forty-seventh minute. John Egan, in the act of pulling the trigger after a flowing Kerry move, was hauled down in the square and when the match referee, P. J. McGrath, awarded the penalty, Sheehy addressed the ball in the manner of a man who had never previously been found wanting in similar situations.

Crucially, this was different and after sacrificing accuracy for power, he succeeded in driving the ball only marginally to the right of goalkeeper Martin Furlong. Furlong, playing in his sixth All-Ireland final, duly parried the shot and given Sheehy's justified reputation as one of the most skilled finishers in the game, Offaly had just been handed a massive reprieve.

Yet the miss didn't appear to worry Kerry unduly and when they landed four points between the fifty-fourth and sixty-first minutes to open up an advantage of three, they had one hand on the cup with the other ready to write the names of this squad into history. It was at that point that Eugene McGee went for broke and decided to dismantle his established midfield pairing of Padraic Dunne and Tomas Connor and recall Gerry Carroll and Richie Connor from the half-forward line in a desperate damage limitation exercise.

By this stage, Jack O'Shea's influence had expanded to the point where he was claiming almost every ball dropping in midfield, and alongside him, Walsh's contribution was enriched with two excellent points from distance. To have any chance of forcing their way back into contention, the challengers needed their revised central partnership to start firing immediately. And the measure of the input from Carroll and Richie Connor was that, within minutes of the switch, Kerry were sliding into trouble.

Matt Connor, precise to the point of perfection in his role as free taker, had halved the deficit to two points by the time McGee made his second master move by withdrawing John Guinan and sending Seamus Darby into action in the front line seven minutes from the end. To many in the crowd of 62,309, there was scarcely enough time left for the substitute to make an impact but in the event, they were proved wrong, gloriously wrong from an Offaly perspective.

There was just two minutes of normal time left when full-back Liam Connor, reflecting the desperation of Offaly's race against time, abandoned his allotted position to lend extra experience in the search for the goal needed to retrieve their sinking hopes. Taking a pass from Richie Connor in full stride, he progressed down the right flank before lofting the ball to the opposite wing where Tommy Doyle, under pressure from Seamus Darby, raced to catch it.

What happened next would provide one of the sport's enduring talking points. Either by miscalculation, or perhaps a push in the back, Doyle, seldom less than dependable in such situations, misread the trajectory of the cross, leaving Darby in splendid isolation to grab the ball and sprint towards the posts at the Railway end of the ground. In a situation demanding nerves of steel, the substitute was not found wanting and retained his composure to shoot past Charlie Nelligan for the decisive goal.

Could a player of Tommy Doyle's experience have committed such a fundamental error without being fouled? Or was it a case of Darby using all his vast experience to entice his marker into the error which would effectively destroy Kerry's chances of pushing out the boundaries of Gaelic football?

That incident survives to bear testimony to the dimensions of the challenge awaiting any county aspiring to put five All-Ireland football successes back to back. It also serves to remind of the folly of minimising the value of experience when young bloods seek to pit ambition and exuberance against the lessons of history.

Reflecting on the score which earned him a place among the game's immortals, Seamus Darby would say simply, 'I found myself in open country when the ball dropped into my arms and knew instantly that I had to stay cool. It helped that out of the corner of my eye I saw Charlie Nelligan beginning to leave his line and that swayed me to shoot when I did. I could never even have dreamed of a moment like that.'

That was the voice of maturity and so too were the utterances of

Martin Furlong, the only man to have played in all six of Offaly's All-Ireland final appearances to that point. Drawing on a cigarette in the jubilation of the winners' dressing room, he said simply, 'I just gambled on the line of Mikey Sheehy's penalty and my luck was in. At thirty-six, I reckon I was too old to start throwing myself about.'

For Kerry, the dignity of their demeanour in their failed attempt on history matched the admiration which they had demanded on so many other, happier days. 'Of course, it was tough to lose the game in those circumstances,' said Jack O'Shea. 'The goal, coming when it did, gave us no chance of recovering and for that, all credit to Offaly. Now, it's up to other Kerry teams to succeed where we failed today and I've no doubt that they will.' More than thirty years on, it's an aspiration that still awaits fulfilment.

– Chapter 19 –

Heaven in Helsinki

Athletics – World Championships, September 1983

Of all the distinguished names Eamonn Coghlan encountered in an international athletics career which was his life for the greater part of twenty years, none is recalled with greater anguish than Miruts Yifter, a small, balding Ethiopian with a personal life to match his extraordinary talent on the track.

Nobody knew Yifter's age, which was given variously as thirty-three, thirty-six and forty-two. Questioned on the point on one occasion, he responded through an interpreter, 'I don't count the years. Men may steal my chickens, men may steal my sheep. But no man can steal my age.' On one point, however, all were agreed. Standing just 5 foot 4 inches tall and weighing little more than 8 stone, Yifter the Shifter was one of the finest distance runners in history, with Olympic gold medals at 5,000 and 10,000 metres to prove it.

In the first week of August 1980, he would cross Coghlan's bow in a fashion which has stayed with the Irishman ever since. The immediate consequence was to wreck his hopes of achieving the goal which had motivated him since childhood, an Olympic title in the 5,000 metres final at Moscow. Although two other runners, Sulieman Nyambui and Kaarlo Maaninka, also finished ahead of him, it was Yifter's explosive surge on the last lap which effectively destroyed Coghlan's best chance of Olympian conquest.

Out of the depths of his disappointment on that occasion however, would come the motivation for the biggest achievement of his career in Helsinki three years later when all the pieces finally slotted into place and he became the first Irishman to succeed in the newly established world championships with a spectacular success in the 5,000 metres final.

If Yifter was inadvertently the catalyst who would influence Eamonn Coghlan's search for global vindication, the moments of destiny he experienced in Finland were a long time in the making at that point. Ever since his days in collegiate completion in Ireland in the early 1970s, he had been identified as one of the outstanding prospects in Irish sport, first at Drimnagh CBS and later during a short stay at St Vincent's, Glasnevin.

In due course, he was offered an athletics scholarship at several universities in the United States and with a similar degree of inevitability, he chose to enrich a fine Irish tradition at Villanova. We have seen how Jumbo Elliott, the legendary Villanova coach, first worked with Irish athletes in 1947 when Jimmy Reardan, and later John Joe Barry and Cummin Clancy pioneered the journey to Philadelphia and the opportunity of receiving a third level education to complement their athletic skills.

Ronnie Delany would attribute much of the credit for his Olympic 1,500 metres triumph at Melbourne to the Villanova influence and later came Frank Murphy, a European championship silver medallist at Athens in 1969 and the talented if unfulfilled Corkman, John Hartnett. With the exception of Reardan and Clancy, all started their Villanova careers in the mile or 1,500 metres events and in those circumstances, it was always probable that Coghlan would choose to hone his talent for middle-distance running with the assistance of Elliott's experience.

The measure of that progress is that less than three years after establishing base in America, he was on the start line in Montreal for the Olympic 1,500 metres final, the first Irishman to do so since Delany twenty-one years earlier. This was progress on a spectacular scale and Coghlan, largely unproven at the highest level, was even rated as a possible threat to New Zealand's John Walker and the man most likely to follow him home, Ivo Van Damme of Belgium.

On the eve of the final, Coghlan, with the approval of his Dublin-based coach, Gerry Farnan, decided that he would curb his natural exuberance on this occasion and attempt to win the race from behind. And he would later confess that it was only a telephone call from Elliott just hours before the 'off', pointing out that there were at least two other athletes in the race with the ability to out-kick him if it came to a sprint finish, which caused him to revisit that decision.

The effect was to sow seeds of doubt in his mind which would later prove ruinous. After running in the slipstream of Walker for the first 400 metres, Elliott's message flooded his mind and, changing tack in mid-race, he unwisely decided to quicken the pace by bolting into the lead. If his rationale was that Walker and Van Damme would respond by sharing the pace-making, it was grievously wrong and when he was left alone in the lead for the next 800 metres, he knew for sure that he was in the wrong place at the wrong time.

Thus it proved and when Walker and Van Damme glided past him going down the back straight for the last time, the game was up. Having set himself up for the big 'kickers', he simply didn't have the acceleration to get back into contention and when the German Paul Heinz Wellman reined him in just a metre from the finish line to secure the bronze medal, Coghlan's indignation was complete.

The measure of the man's character, however, was that within days he was back competing successfully on the Grand Prix circuit, and his rehabilitation was well advanced by the time he started his preparations for the next big event on the international track and field programme, the European championships at Prague in 1978. Across the Irish Sea, two rising stars of the track were embarked on careers which would bring them universal acclaim and while Sebastian Coe wasn't yet ready for top-class 1,500 metres competition at that point, Steve Ovett was prepared to take on all comers.

Ovett, a controversial personality who never quite got the credit for an outstanding career after falling out with the British sporting press, was noted for his ability to accelerate decisively in a matter of strides. And fatally, Coghlan was not in position to cover the vital break in the final when the tall Englishman pressed the accelerator 180 metres out and was gone, irretrievably gone, from the pursuit.

The Dubliner, back in sixth place between the last two bends, quickened sufficiently to run a personal best time of 3 minutes 35.6 seconds in capturing the silver medal, but that didn't quite make up for the lost opportunity of taking on the flying Brighton runner down the finishing stretch. Observers were quick to remember that Frank Murphy had lost in similar fashion to another English runner, John Whetton, in the 1969 European final over 1,500 metres, as had Ronnie Delany after being caught out by Brian Hewson's finishing speed in the European 1,500 metres championship eleven years earlier.

History was one thing, but absorbing the harsh lessons of two tactical blunders in his first big championship races was a lot more relevant if Coghlan was to deal with the pressures of successful competition at the highest level. Compared to his earlier assignments, the European indoor 1,500 metres final at Vienna the following year was less demanding and three years after the disappointment of Montreal, he was at last able to savour success.

That race was memorable for the fact that it was another Irishman, Ray Flynn, who was posing the biggest threat to the new champion until a dramatic last lap fall in an incident involving the Finn, Antti Loikanen. Whether Flynn would have beaten Coghlan is a moot point but it gave birth to a colourful post-race quote when he said, 'One second, my head was clear and I was racing for a medal. The next second, the floor was coming up to meet me.'

If Coghlan's outdoor career had promised more than it delivered in the early years, the same could never be said of his indoors record. Following in the tradition established by Delany, Murphy and Noel Carroll at Villanova, he proved himself so adept in this facet of the sport in the US that he would earn the title of Chairman of the Boards after a couple of world records and a string of outstanding wins in the famed Wannamaker mile at New York's Madison Square Garden. And it was on the back of another flamboyant indoor campaign, supplemented by a couple of fast outdoor races, that he headed for the Moscow Olympics and the chance of exorcising the ghosts of Montreal.

By now, he considered that his best days in the metric mile were behind him and with the encouragement of Gerry Farnan, he was concentrating on the 5,000 metres during the outdoor season. That put him on course for a new challenge and the even bigger task of coping with the gifted African athletes who were beginning to dominate middle- and long-distance running. Of these, Miruts Yifter was the man identified as the one posing the biggest threat for every European or American with designs on winning the Olympic 5,000 and 10,000 metres titles.

Yifter, never less than fascinating for the newsmen in search of the unusual story, first came to prominence in 1971 when he competed in a match between the US and Africa in North Carolina. His biggest opposition in the 5,000 metres was Steve Prefontaine, a gifted if ill-fated American who had recently graduated from 1,500 metres competition. With 600 metres to go, Yifter had established what looked like an unassailable lead, only to pull up abruptly just 200 metres later. Prefontaine went on to win and the Ethiopian later explained that he had miscounted the laps and stopped running because he thought the race was finished. Unperturbed, he turned up the next day and this time got the lap count right in the 10,000 metres event to emphatically beat the formidable Frank Shorter.

When the Munich Olympics rolled around the following summer,

Yifter was still unfortunately accident prone. After finishing third in the 10,000 metres behind Lasse Viren of Finland and the Belgian, Emiel Puttemans in one of the most dramatic Olympic finals on record, Yifter was thought to have a great chance of turning the tables on the Finn in the 5,000 metres just a couple of days later. That was until he failed to show up on the start line for the heats.

He was confirmed as being on the coach conveying the athletes to the stadium but then the trail went cold. One report suggested that he had been refused entrance to the arena after presenting himself at the wrong check-in gate. Another story was that he got lost on his way from the toilet to the track. Typically, Yifter failed to furnish an explanation for an omission which in all probability cost him a medal, and little had changed at the Montreal Olympics four years later when the African boycott of the games deprived him of another golden opportunity.

It was against that background that he travelled to Moscow in 1980 in search of Olympic fulfilment and it duly materialised in another memorable 10,000 metres final in which the three Ethiopian athletes contrived to wreck Lasse Viren's hopes of a third consecutive win in the event by chopping and changing the pace, a tactic which ultimately set up a thrilling 200 metres sprint by Yifter for his first gold medal.

That success was never likely to satisfy him however, and despite the fact that the organisers saw fit to include an extra qualifying round for the 5,000 metres final, the little Ethiopian had no hesitation in confirming that he would attempt the double. John Treacy, who had come to grief in the 10,000 metres, also confirmed his entry for the shorter event but for all their durability, the consensus was that those earlier exertions would tell against them.

Coghlan had his own problems after being affected by the onset of diarrhoea less than twenty-four hours before the final but as the plot of the final unfolded, he appeared to be untroubled, covering every attempted break to be only inches adrift of Yifter's teammate, Mohammed Kedir, at the bell. Then, midway down the back straight, he made his big move with Nyambui at his shoulder, Kedir immediately behind him and Yifter trapped on the kerb in fourth place.

In a move which would have grave implications for the other athletes, Kedir then stepped aside to allow Yifter though the gap, losing a shoe in the process, and suddenly, with space opening up in front of him, the old man was off on his journey into history. Coghlan can only have been startled as he glanced across to discover the favourite overtaking him and in a matter of strides the dream of a golden Irish success was gone. The Ethiopian in full spate was never going to be caught and to add insult to injury, the erstwhile leader was run out of the minor placings by Nyambui and Maalinka with Treacy back in seventh place.

Treacy would later recall that for a split second he thought Coghlan had won. 'He was placed so well and running so strongly when I last saw him, that I felt sure he had won when I got to the finish line. Then I saw the photographers crowding around Yifter and I realised that it had all gone wrong for Eamonn over the last 150 metres. To lose out in those circumstances after his experience in Montreal four years earlier was cruel and I could have cried for him.'

Those were the feelings of Irish people everywhere and even for a man of iron determination, the exasperation of finishing just out of the medals for the second consecutive occasion in the biggest sporting carnival of them all, can only have been difficult. And yet those closest to him knew that at the age of twenty-eight, he still had many better days ahead of him. When the good times eventually returned, most of them were on the boards in the United States and yet he never lost sight of the fact that he still required a major title win outdoors to secure a place among the elite of the track.

That opportunity presented itself at Helsinki in 1983 after the International Amateur Athletics Federation, in its wisdom, had decided to inaugurate world championships, a move motivated more by the opportunity of generating extra funding for the sport than fulfilling the wishes of those athletes who believed that the continental championships were insufficient to sustain a high level of public interest between the four-yearly Olympic Games.

Life post-Moscow was complicated for Coghlan by an injury which caused him to miss most of the 1982 season until it finally yielded to treatment in Germany. At the time, it was interpreted as a serious setback but he would later recall it as the misfortune which changed his career. 'It gave me the rest I urgently needed but would never have taken in normal circumstances,' he said. 'And when I eventually got the all clear to return to training, I worked so hard that I was probably in the best condition of my career in the build up to the world championships.'

It helped, too, that by now Yifter had finally drifted into retirement and with Nyambui and Maalinka also marked absent, the line up in the Finnish capital was markedly different from that which had toed the line in Moscow's Lenin Stadium. And yet, there was no shortage of experience in the field which, in addition to the European title holder, Tomas Wessinghage, included Wojado Butoi (Ethiopia), Doug Padilla (US), Marrti Vainio (Finland) and not least Dmitry Dmitriev of the Soviet Union. No less than Coghlan, all sensed that that in the wake of Yifter's abdication, this final offered the chance of an exciting reign for the new monarch of 5,000 metres running.

And the importance of the spoils awaiting the new champion was reflected in the manner the race was run, with nobody prepared to take on the responsibility of setting a decent pace in what was developing into a cagey, tactical struggle. That was until Dmitriev decided to bolt 800 metres out and in an instant, caution was abandoned.

Coghlan, at one point closer to the back of the field than the front, moved immediately to extricate himself from the pack, as did Butoi, Wessinghage and the unfancied East German, Werner Schildhauer. At the bell Dmitriev was still eight metres clear of the weakening Wessinghage and it was at that point the Irishman realised that if the bespectacled Soviet was to be reeled in, the hard work was now down to him. Metre by metre the gap closed until he finally loomed alongside the leader at the crown of the bend.

A quick glance at Dmitriev's pained face told him all he needed to know. The Soviet runner had come to the end of his challenge and Coghlan was able to indulge himself in the thrill of victory, taking time off to wave to the crowd as he crossed the line in a time of 13 minutes 28.53 seconds. The erstwhile leader was to experience the anguish of Coghlan's Montreal and Moscow defeats, being caught by both Schildhauer and Vainio in the last 50 metres of a remarkable race to finish fourth.

After years of heartbreak, the Dubliner had finally vindicated himself on the big stage and was promptly installed as the long-range favourite to win the Olympic 5,000 metres title at the 1984 games in Los Angeles. Alas, he never made it to California after another injury threw his career off course and by the time he arrived in Seoul for his third and final Olympic appearance in 1988, he just didn't have the legs to achieve the success that had attracted him since his boyhood dreams in Drimnagh.

It meant that for all his long train of achievement, he never got to join the other distinguished Irish athletes who stood on an Olympic presentation podium. And yet, his claims to a special place in Irish athletics are undeniable. In 1995, he became the first forty-year-old to run a mile in less than four minutes and that statistic, one imagines, will stand the test of time long after the bitter experiences of those early Olympian escapades have been forgotten.

– Chapter 20 –

Waterford's Iron Man

Athletics – Olympic Games, July 1984

John Treacy didn't look much like an endurance runner when he presented himself to the Irish sporting public for the first time in the late 1970s. It's true that well-fleshed mortals seldom had a future in this facet of athletics, but even by the most generous standards, Treacy's sparse figure scarcely looked capable of concealing an engine capable of propelling him through the extremes of this, possibly the toughest of all disciplines.

First impressions were of a young man who, perhaps, had strayed into the wrong sport, better fitted for a more leisurely pastime than the hard grind of battling through ploughed fields or the piercing solitude of a long, lonely road with only nature for company. The measure of that miscalculation is that by the time he'd run his last competitive race, he had redefined the standards in cross country and road running for generations of Irish athletes still unborn.

Long before Ronnie Delany succeeded in switching the focus to track running with his stunning success in the Olympic 1,500 metres championship final in Melbourne in 1956, Irishmen had a fascination for cross country running at a time when the notion of a modern parkland course as the setting for a major championship was so far off the radar that it didn't merit a second thought.

As a child, I had watched Steve McCooke, the renowned East Antrim athlete, pick his way through thick, clinging mud and deep, cavernous ditches to win the Irish cross country championship out at the headquarters of Clonliffe Harriers in Finglas and wondered why he never appeared to run on the track, at least not according to the newspapers I was reading. Before that of course, Bob Tisdall, a citizen of the world, had worn an Irish vest when he won the inaugural Olympic 400 metres hurdles championship in Los Angeles. But look back through the pages of history and you'll discover that it was Dr Pat O'Callaghan's successful defence of the hammer championship which demanded most of the attention in Ireland that momentous week.

The manner in which born weight throwers won Olympic titles for the United States and in some instances Britain in the early Olympic celebrations are well documented, but following O'Callaghan's premature retirement after missing out on the chance of a third consecutive hammer throwing title at Berlin in 1936, that art form and the near certainty of an Irishman ascending the presentation podium on major athletics occasions was irretrievably lost.

But just as one golden era faded, Tim Smythe's success in the international cross country championship at Baldoyle in 1931 opened up the vista of another. Smythe, from County Clare, seldom achieved significant success on the track but he remained the trailblazer for cross country running until an unlikely young man from Villierstown, County Waterford emerged on the scene some forty-five years later.

As so often happened in Irish sport in that era, it was a local priest, Fr Michael Enright, who introduced John Treacy to athletics at the age of twelve. At the time, he can scarcely have been robust enough for the more popular sporting disciplines of hurling and football in the region, but years later Fr Enright would recall that it was the sense of natural movement and balance which put him apart from the others.

That judgement was well made. Before long the youngster, together with his brother Ray, was making steady progress in his newly chosen sport, first at local level and then on an international stage. It helped that he was offered an American athletics scholarship at Providence College but his first statement of intent was when he finished third in the Junior International Cross Country Championship in 1976 and repeated the achievement the following year.

The effect was to short-cut his apprenticeship in international competition. Ever since its inception, this championship has been acknowledged as the barometer of the best of the emerging talent across the broad world of athletics, a race which invariably identified the contenders for the biggest titles in cross country competition in the years that followed. And yet, for all the merit of those two runs, the Waterford teenager did not, perhaps, receive sufficient credit for his spectacular progress since setting down in America.

That may have been down to the fact that collegiate competition, no less than indoor athletics on the other side of the Atlantic, received scant media coverage in these parts. Equally, Treacy's inclination to shrink from the public spotlight was such that it discouraged all but the most invasive news people in search of stories. Either way, the Irishman arrived in Scotland from Rhode Island beneath the radar as the great and the good began to assemble in Glasgow for the 1978 staging of the international championships.

A dozen possible champions were mentioned in the British press previews of the race but ne'er a word of Waterford's pride and glory. Instead, the spotlight was on people like Alexander Antipov of the Soviet Union, Bernie Forde, the British champion, and Carlos Lopes of Portugal who had won the title two years earlier. Karel Lismont, an iron man from Belgium, was at this stage of his career concentrating on marathon running but, no less than Antipov, he fancied his chances over a hilly, demanding course which put a heavy premium on strength.

To accentuate the difficulties faced by athletes, heavy rain greeted them on their arrival at Bellahouston Park, ensuring that the climbs became even more treacherous. Only the most nimble footed could hope to cope in these kind of conditions and in this instance, Treacy's sparse frame and his reputation as a balanced runner in any conditions, amounted to a big plus.

Right from the start, the twenty-year-old Irishman made his intentions clear, joining Antipov and Lismont in a three-man group which would go on to dominate the race. Twice Lismont tried to get away on steep climbs and twice he was reeled in without too much difficulty. It suggested that if Treacy was to break his rivals, it would have to be achieved in one short, sharp burst and to the delight of the Irish supporters in the crowd, it materialised early on the last lap.

Pressing the accelerator, he opened up a gap in a matter of strides and while Antipov, in the manner of a great competitor, gathered himself for one last counter attack as they began the surge for home, Treacy was in no mood to concede. Gradually, the piston-like drive left Antipov's legs and as his strength emptied, so the confidence of the man in front increased. The race, over 12,300 metres, still held one more scare for him when, for the first time, he lost his foothold momentarily on the run in. Fortunately, he recovered his poise almost immediately and at the finish he had eight seconds to spare over Antipov in recording a time of 39 minutes 25 seconds.

Stretched out in the distant pursuit were many of the finest long-distance runners in the world. Craig Virgin (US) and Tony Simmons (Wales) were almost out on their feet in finishing in the top ten and even more remarkably, neither Willie Polleunis, the Belgian champion, nor Carlos Lopes of Portugal, winner of the race in 1976, managed to make it to the finish line. It was the first occasion that Treacy encountered Lopes on a big occasion but it certainly wouldn't be the last.

It had been a journey of distinction for the Waterford man who arrived in Scotland as a largely unknown international runner and departed as one of the most talked about long-distance runners in the world. But it didn't turn his head in a manner which might have been expected of one so young. The next morning he was out training on the roads of a Glasgow suburb and before nightfall he was on his way back to Rhode Island to resume his accountancy studies at Providence College.

From the perspective of the International Amateur Athletics Federation, there could scarcely have been a more appropriate winner. The championship was scheduled to be held at Limerick the following year and with an Irishman defending the title, it now had all the makings of a financial bonanza. So it proved with two strong performances in the European track championships at Prague in the autumn, followed by a string of impressive indoor runs in the United States in the spring, ensuring that when Treacy eventually got to Limerick in March 1980 he was an even more formidable international runner.

Not since Raphael Pujazon, the renowned French runner, achieved the distinction of back-to-back successes in the premier cross country race in 1948 had a champion retained his title and Treacy merely had to look at the quality of the field lining up alongside him to realise that, on such occasions, champions can be vulnerable. Erik De Beck and his Belgian compatriot Leon Schots could both testify to the pressures weighing on the shoulders of reigning title-holders but now, freed of these impositions, they relished the chance of taking on Treacy, even on his home terrain.

In there, too, were the familiar names of Leon Schots, Carlos Lopes, Christophe Herle (West Germany) and not least, Bronislav Malinowski of Poland, who, at Prague six months earlier, had upstaged some of the biggest names around by winning the European steeplechase championship. But it was the familiar figure of Alexander Antipov that almost certainly worried the champion most. It was only after a tense struggle that Treacy saw off the challenge of the Soviet athlete in Glasgow and in the intervening period, Antipov had finished a long way ahead of the Irishman in securing a bronze medal in the European 10,000 metres title race in the Czech capital.

In that era, 10,000 metres specialists dipping beneath the twenty-eight minutes barrier were a rare breed and now, on the grassy plains of Greenpark racecourse, four of them were seeking Treacy's crown. It was enough to persuade thousands of Irish people to venture outdoors on a foul day of wind and rain in support of their man and by the time the big race started, it was estimated that some 25,000 spectators were on hand to watch the drama unfold. Among them were his parents, availing of a rare opportunity of watching two of their sons – Ray was again in the support team – compete at the highest level of the sport and no less than the rest of the crowd, they must have wondered how the champion would react to the pressures now building on his slim shoulders.

In Glasgow, he had gambled successfully on going out strongly from the gun but now things were somewhat different. Aware of his intentions, the opposition resolved to close down the spaces around him as they set off in the driving rain and when the field passed the stands for the first time, he was back in the pack chasing Schots, Herle and the English runner Nick Rose. But once in open country, Treacy powered on to join Schots in the lead and those in the know quickly realised that the decisive duel was about to ensue.

Schots, a member of the Belgian army, had looked unbeatable when winning the international military championship in Mallow the previous week and now, as a former winner of the world title, he sensed that the long arm of opportunity was again about to reach out to him. But the vociferous home crowd told him a different story and before long, the self-belief he took into the race had dwindled to the point where he was struggling to match the man running alongside him.

In contrast, Alexander Antipov had improved from an uncommonly slow start to work his way through the field and, together with Malinowski, was now the principal threat to the champion. But Treacy, coated in mud, was in no mood to surrender his kingdom and having spurted clear at half way, he was running on his own for much of the last

3,000 metres. This was proving a lot easier than the hard graft which had brought him safely through the ordeal of Glasgow but now, as then, the plot held one last surprise.

Even as he eyed the vast throng willing him to victory in the distant stands, he stumbled and fell on his shoulder and for the second time in twelve months, his supporters held their breath. On this occasion, he wasn't able to prevent himself hitting the ground with all the risks involved and for a few nerve-wracking moments, it looked as if his dream might be over. Then, happily, he picked himself up, got back into stride quickly and from that point coasted home alone in a time of 37 minutes 20 seconds, significantly faster than a year earlier and nine seconds clear of Antipov.

'The only time I was worried was when I saw the crowd converging on me just beyond the finish line, all intent on clapping me on the back,' he recalled. 'I know they meant well but at the end of a long cross country race, you could be doing without that extra punishment. Yet, I shouldn't complain. I think Leon Schots was frightened by the crowd early on and once in the clear, I felt I was going to win. In that sense it was a lot easier than Glasgow.'

Some five months later, Treacy was reporting for an even bigger assignment. This time, there were no exuberant supporters in close proximity to threaten his safety as he lined up for the start of the Olympic 10,000 metres championship in Moscow's Lenin Stadium. But danger of another hue threatened when he collapsed inexplicably midway through the race and had to be stretchered from the track.

That appeared to be the end of his Olympian dreams but incredibly he was back in the stadium within days and showing no effects from his earlier ordeal when achieving a top-seven finish in the 5,000 metres final. It was just another example of the phenomenal strength crammed into his sparse frame and it proved that, physically, he was up for the challenge of making it three-in-a-row in the world cross country championship in Paris the following March.

He arrived there on the back of some big performances in indoor competition and so confident were his compatriots of yet another big result, that long before it became fashionable for politicians to align themselves with successful sportspeople, Jim Tunney, Minister of State with responsibility for sport, travelled to Longchamps racecourse in anticipation of another captivating performance by Treacy. In the manner of the man, the defending champion left nothing behind him on the course but on this occasion, his best just wasn't good enough to repel the challenge of his old adversary, Carlos Lopes.

No less than Treacy, Lopes was a man who believed implicitly in the maxim that titles are won and lost on the training ground. And the word coming back from Portugal was that Lopes, like the Irishman, was preparing like never before in the hope of signing off on his career in the grand manner with an Olympic title in the 1984 Games in Los Angeles. By now, Lopes was channelling his energies into road running and in that context, those eyeing the marathon championship knew that another big player had arrived on the scene with the pedigree and ambition to warrant the closest scrutiny.

From his base in America, Treacy let it be known that in spite of his brave run in the 5,000 metres final in Moscow, he was targeting the 10,000 championship as his priority in California. While he had never run a competitive marathon previously, he was also allowing his name to be included in the list of entries for the road race. That was interpreted by the local press as nothing more than a statement on his ambitious long-term plans at a stage of his career when the edge would have left his track speed.

After his ordeal in the 10,000 metres in Moscow, it was logical that the Waterford man should want to focus on this event in the hope of proving that he was still capable of transferring his imposing cross country form to track competition. Alas, that conundrum would endure long after Moscow, for in spite of leading at the halfway mark, he never figured with a chance when it mattered most and eventually finished a long way behind the Italian Alberto Cova, who added the Olympic title to his European championship success in Helsinki the previous year.

Still, there was no disguising the sense of disappointment among the press contingent in Los Angeles as they pondered the likely consequences of his eclipse in the last 2,000 metres. Imagine the surprise then when we learned on the eve of the marathon, the last major event of the twenty-third Olympic Games, that Treacy would in fact face the starter for the first major road race of his career. It was only then that we discovered that he had been preoccupied with his marathon training in the build up to Los Angeles, a revelation which went some way towards explaining his decision, some nine months earlier, to resign his post in Dublin and return to the United States.

Making one's marathon debut in an Olympic championship was rare enough even in those days – to do so on a day when the temperature topped 90 degrees on the steamy highways in and around Los Angeles made it still more unbelievable. Yet, at twenty-six, Treacy believed that he was young enough, and thanks to his cross country exploits, experienced enough to handle the intense pressure of it all.

In there with him were two of the durable men of the road, America's Alberto Salazar and Robert de Castella of Australia. There also was Carlos Lopes and in a strange, bizarre way, that merely added a badge of authenticity to the occasion. On occasions such as this, it appeared as if Tracey was almost fated to confront the great Portuguese runner in his search for a gold medal. Back in 1976, at a stage when his career was only beginning to take off, Lopes surprised almost everybody by securing a silver medal in the Olympic 10,000 metres championship at Montreal.

He never quite delivered on the promise of that outstanding run in subsequent track appearances but now, at the venerable age of thirty-seven, he was seeking to become the oldest ever to win an Olympic marathon title. That mammoth tilt at history, even more than Treacy's debut run, demanded the enthusiastic attention of the colour writers in

Los Angeles on the morning of the race.

As it turned out, the two were at the cutting edge of the race throughout. To the astonishment of many, Salazar began to feel the heat, literally and metaphorically, when the leading pack of eleven runners began to break up after eighteen miles. He was followed soon afterwards by the reigning European champion, Wim Najboer of Holland, as well as the talented Japanese runner Toshihiko Seko, and when de Castella stopped at a water station at the twenty miles mark, the race developed another twist.

The Australian, who appeared to be running reasonably comfortably, was suddenly ten metres adrift by the time he threw away the water cup and even more surprisingly, he began to drop farther and farther behind over the next mile. Now we knew for certain that the Los Angeles marathon would produce a shock winner and with Treacy and fellow Irishman Gerry Kiernan in the leading group of seven at that point, we dared to dream that Ireland might even emerge with two medals.

Kiernan, who had done so well to extricate himself from the pack and make contact with the leaders, expended too much energy in the process to progress to the medal placings, but even as the Kerryman's challenge came to an end, his fellow Munsterman was continuing to battle up front. For all his resilience, however, he still couldn't respond when Lopez threw in a 4.30 mile after passing the twenty-four-mile mark and from that point, Treacy and England's Charlie Spedding were searching for silver. And despite Spedding's two marathon wins en route to California, it was Treacy who surprisingly prevailed.

'At one point late in the race, I thought I had the gold medal in my grasp,' he recalled, 'but in the end, Lopes had just too much strength and too much speed for me. Still, it was a nice way to mark my first marathon.' As ever, the self-effacing man who would subsequently go on to head the Irish Sports Council was right on the button!

– Chapter 21 –

Great Fight Nights

Boxing – Championship Bouts, February 1980 to June 1986

The date 10 May 1981 is one neither Barry McGuigan nor Charlie Nash is likely to forget. For one, it was the start of a long and distinguished journey to fulfilment on a global stage in professional boxing; for Nash, it was the evening he discovered that his search for riches in a trade as hard as the blacksmith's anvil, was over.

Earlier in the day, a big crowd had watched Galway beat Roscommon in an all-Connacht final to claim the National League football title. Unfortunately, a pitifully small crowd, measured in hundreds rather than thousand, turned up to witness the return of professional boxing to Dalymount Park. And given the significance of the occasion, that was a pity.

Chastened by Philip McLoughlin's experience, fellow promoters shunned Dalymount like the plague after that financial hit, and having regard to the high profile of the two Ulstermen, it would prove a lost opportunity of re-establishing outdoor boxing at a venue which had in the past been central to the sport's existence in the capital.

While McGuigan's second-round win over Selwyn Bell, a journeyman pro with little pretence to boxing's bigger prizes, marked a successful start to a fine career as a prize fighter, the evening, alas, would shatter Nash's reputation as a master craftsman after he had ducked through the ropes to put his European lightweight title on the line against the Spaniard, Joey Gibilesco.

In a fashion, there was a symmetry in the lifestyles of the two men. Although separated by some ten years in age, they both graduated through juvenile competitions in Ulster to box in the Olympic and British Commonwealth championships. And inevitably, they chose to try their luck in the professional game after they had travelled all the avenues in the amateur sport.

Having competed well without attaining medal status in the 1972 Olympics at Munich, Nash made his professional debut against fellow Derry boxer Ray Ross, the man who had interrupted his sequence of five national senior lightweight championship successes in the amateur code to win the vacant Northern Ireland professional title in their home town on 2 October 1975. There followed the customary introductory programme with Nash having his arm raised in victory on twelve occasions, most of them inside the distance.

That was a dangerously deceptive statistic, for the Derry man, whose day job was in the printing trade, was never known in his amateur career as a damaging puncher. And perhaps it led him unwittingly into his first professional defeat in October 1977 when he allowed himself to be lured into a slugging match with Adolpho Osses, and in front of a startled home town crowd he was stopped in five rounds.

This came as a shock to the senses but eight months later he would take his revenge by knocking out Osses in just three rounds. In between, he had beaten Johnny Claydon for the vacant British lightweight title and five successful fights later, it would lead inevitably to a shot at the vacant European title. That represented progress on the grand scale and Nash, by now strutting his stuff in a manner which was beginning to capture the imagination of a much wider public, went back to his old, classical, upright style to beat Andre Holyk on points.

For a man who had earned just a modest income from boxing in his first four years as a professional, the world was beginning to open up and within six months of claiming the European championship, he was on his way to Copenhagen for a first title defence against the former world champion, Ken Buchanan of Scotland. In his prime, Buchanan was a proven showstopper, a man who could box or fight as the occasion demanded.

Although now on a downward curve, Buchanan was still a dangerous opponent and the fact that he was being mentioned as a likely opponent for Jim Watt, a fellow Scot who was by now rejoicing in the title of champion of the world, testified to the fact that he was still highly regarded by his peers. British promoters thought so too, for the speculation was that the two Scots were being lined up for a winner-take-all prize of World and European champion in an open air bout that would be expected to attract a summer crowd of 50,000 to Hampden Park in Glasgow.

As it transpired, Nash, a modest, gentle person in private whose public persona frequently seemed a cruel caricature, was equal to the task of out-pointing Buchanan over twelve rounds and that put him directly on course for a tilt at Watt's world title in the Kelvin Hall, Glasgow on 14 March 1980. For those of us in attendance, it would prove an unforgettable occasion for all the wrong reasons.

Many football people will tell you that the most intimidating atmosphere in the game is to be found in the same city in the derby fixtures between Celtic and Rangers. Now, the same raw ingredients of hatred and fear, spawned by historic religious and political differences, was being transported indoors. And the end product on that rowdy night in the Kelvin Hall was chilling.

It was the first Irish-British title fight since Rinty Monaghan drew with Terry Allen thirty-one years earlier, and the cramped odds of 1/2 on Watt keeping his title in front of a capacity crowd of 5,000 derived in part from the fact that three British officials, Syd Nathan, James Brimell and John Clarke, would 'score' the contest. 'They say that if I'm to win the contest, I'll have to take ten of the fifteen rounds,' opined Nash before climbing into the ring. 'But I'm ready to take that chance.'

Mathematics, as it turned out, would not be required to determine the outcome after an explosive fight that lasted less than five rounds. The din was such that it is doubtful either boxer heard the opening bell – the people at the ringside certainly didn't – and the decibels rose still higher when Watt walked straight into a battery of punches and dropped to the canvas. But this was his home town and pride demanded that he rise immediately before a count was started. The unfortunate consequence was that Nash somehow was enticed into believing that he could take on the champion in a slugging match and it proved disastrous. And when he emerged from a tangle on the ropes with blood flowing from a cut above his left eye, it was already obvious that the contest would not go the distance.

From a situation in which he had originally planned to out-jab and out-run the thirty-one-year-old champion, the Irishman now found himself committed to a mini war of attrition and as the raucous home crowd demanded more punishment for the man in the green trunks, so Watt grew more and more authoritative in fourth round. Twice he dropped Nash to the canvas before bringing across the left hook to the jaw that ended the fight after 2 minutes 12 seconds of the round.

Nash, lurching onto the punch, accentuated the impact and even as he hauled himself up with the aid of the bottom rope, his cause was irretrievably lost. Syd Nathan, the referee, counted to eight and then, with an outstretched gesture of his arms, indicated that Nash's attempt to become Ireland's first undisputed world champion in thirty years was, indeed, finished. Significantly, the brave Irishman accepted the decision without demur and Watt had successfully negotiated his second defence of the title.

For a man who had frequently looked so elegant in jabbing his way to victory in both amateur and professional contests, this was a spectacle which ill fitted him. So also was the sight of a broken man at Dalymount

Park some fourteen months later when Joey Gibilesco, a fighter who would scarcely have lived with Nash when the sap was still rising, took away his European title with a sixth-round knockout.

Charlie Nash, who lost a younger brother in the Bloody Sunday massacre in Derry in 1981, would have four more fights before announcing his retirement from the ring in May 1983. But before taking his leave, he had achieved enough to fire the ambition of a young man living some forty miles south of him in Clones, County Monaghan.

As an exponent of the art of boxing, Barry McGuigan was cast in a different mould to Nash. His apprenticeship in the amateur sport was not nearly as long as that of the Derry man and while his skills at long range were adequate, it was his capacity to take a punch and, more crucially, to throw an even bigger one which stamped him out at a relatively early stage of his career as an excellent professional fighter in the making.

Also important was the fact that his father, Pat, was one of the leading vocalists in Irish entertainment in his prime and this background in show business would in time transfer to the next generation. 'If you stand out in the rain, you're going to get wet,' was one of Pat McGuigan's favourite expressions in his assessment of the fight game, and it was this unshakable belief in the abnormal strength and character of his son to prevail in any crisis that sustained the family on big fight nights.

Barry would say that it was chores like lugging sacks of potatoes and similar weights around the family shop in Clones which accounted for his inordinate strength in the first instance, but whatever the source of his greatest asset, it stood him in good stead when it came to sorting the men from the boys in the featherweight division. One such occasion was in the Commonwealth Games in Edmonton, Canada in 1978 when, after beating Michael Anthony (Guyana) and Bill Ranelli (Canada) on his way to the final, he came up against Tumat Sogolik of Papua New Guinea.

For two rounds it all looked to be going well for him, so well that he may have allowed his concentration levels to drop in the last three-minute session. It almost deprived him of the biggest accolade of his career in amateur boxing but after taking two standing counts and incurring a public warning for holding, he survived to gain a disputed points decision. He wasn't so fortunate in the Olympic Games in Moscow two years later, when he was involved in another tense bout against Wimfred Kabunda of Zambia. On this occasion, the decision went against him and it may well have been this disappointment which hastened his decision to quit amateur boxing and go punching for pay.

Barney Eastwood, the Northern Ireland bookmaker, was announced as the man who would manage McGuigan's new career and inevitably it meant that, with few exceptions, Belfast would be the professional base for the man who later enjoyed a huge following throughout Ireland. Eastwood had a background in professional boxing locally but some may have questioned his managerial decision-making after an apparent misjudgement had landed his man in trouble at a stage of his development when it ought to have been problem-free.

After beating Selwyn Bell and Gary Lucan on stoppages, one in two rounds, the other in four, it was decided to confront Peter Eubanks in his home town of Brighton. A member of a noted boxing family, Eubanks proved that he wasn't in the ring just to capitulate and over eight hard-fought rounds, he emerged with a points decision. That was a shock to the system for everybody in the McGuigan camp, but four months and two fights later came redemption in the form of an eight-round knockout of Eubanks, this time in Belfast.

The lesson of the Eubanks saga was that, in professional boxing, it is folly to take anything for granted. But nothing could have prepared McGuigan for the trauma which followed his contest against a West African boxer who went under the name of Young Ali on 14 June 1982. It topped the bill at a black tie show at London's Grosvenor House and was remarkable only for the immense courage shown by the African fighter in this most artificial of all settings.

Nobody intervened to halt the one-sided affair until a knockout punch by McGuigan finally brought it to an end in round six. Young Ali eventually recovered consciousness after being lifted to his corner, was able to leave the ring unaided but then, almost immediately, collapsed again. After being removed by ambulance to hospital, he was to spend the next six months in a coma before eventually succumbing. Young Ali, a man who earned a paltry living from one of the most dangerous of all sports, left behind a young wife and a child who was born, even as his father clung to life on a ventilator.

That was a tragedy to shake even the most resolute and Barry, a sensitive family man, was said to be so deeply upset that at one stage he agonised about his future in the sport. But persevere he did and after beating Vernon Penprase to win the British featherweight title, he was crowned champion of Europe by knocking out Valerio Nati in six rounds in Belfast on 16 November 1983.

Three successful defences of his European title inevitably led to speculation about a shot at Eusabio Pedroza's WBA featherweight title and eventually it was confirmed that he would meet the legendary Panamanian at the grounds of Queens Park Rangers FC in London on 8 June 1985. With just one defeat in twenty-seven contests, he felt he was now sufficiently mature to go in against one of the most celebrated of all world champions at the time.

Only one of McGuigan's twenty to that point had gone the full distance and oddly, it was the exception, against Juan Laporte from Puerto Rico in Belfast at the start of 1985, which probably convinced him that the time was ripe to take on Pedroza. Laporte, who had gone the full championship distance with Pedroza, was by some way the best fighter McGuigan had met since turning professional and in the course of the ten rounder, he twice rocked the Irishman with big punches. In each instance, however, McGuigan recovered in a matter of split seconds and at that point, his corner men knew for certain that he was ready to venture out in the rain.

At the behest of the champion's handlers, it was agreed that eight-ounce gloves would be worn by the boxers instead of the six-ounce ones which were customary up to the middleweight class. This was interpreted as recognition by Pedroza of the Irishman's punching power and the threat it posed to his hold on the world title, a thought which surely sustained the challenger as he came down to the ring with the *Rocky* theme ringing in his ears.

Rumour had it that Pedroza, at 5 feet 10 inches, unusually tall for a featherweight, was having trouble in making the 9 stone weight limit but if this was true, it certainly didn't show in the early rounds. After Pat McGuigan had discharged his pre-fight responsibility of stoking the atmosphere by climbing into the ring to sing 'Danny Boy', the ageing champion in his twentieth defence of the title repeatedly picked off the challenger with accurate jabs to presage a difficult evening ahead for the green hordes in the ground.

At times, it was as futile as attempting to trap mercury but all that would change over the next few rounds as Pedroza slowed marginally and McGuigan's feared short arm punching began to hit the target more often. And then in the seventh round came the decisive twist when the champion went down under a fusillade of punches in a neutral corner and suddenly, we sensed that the old order was about to change.

Deprived of his aura of invincibility, Pedroza had to call on all his experience to escape the indignity of being beaten inside the distance as the challenger stalked him relentlessly over the last three rounds. Befitting a man who had reigned with such authority for so long, the Panamanian managed to keep the floor beneath his feet throughout that tempest but at the final bell, the title and the glory belonged to the man they now called the Clones Cyclone.

Just four years after turning professional, Barry McGuigan had arrived at the summit of his trade and the financial rewards that would flow from his victory at Loftus Road suddenly became topical. Not so long ago, his wife Sandra was working as a part-time hairdresser in Clones to supplement the family income, but now his reputation as one of the most marketable persons in sport meant that he could look forward with confidence to some big pay nights.

Successful title defences against Bernard Taylor in Belfast and Danilo Cabrera in Dublin yielded satisfactory profits, but to achieve the financial security he coveted, he needed to impose himself on the American scene. In that situation it was no surprise when Barney Eastwood confirmed that his next championship fight would be in Caesar's Palace, Las Vegas in June 1986 against Fernando Sosa, an Argentinean fighter who had previously been mentioned as a possible opponent for McGuigan in Dublin.

Injury prevented him from accepting that challenge and he discovered that nothing had changed when, just ten days before the Las Vegas bout, a medical test revealed two detached retina in his eyes. Bob Arum, the promoter of the show, then offered McGuigan the choice of four possible replacements and eventually the Irish camp settled on the lowest ranked of the quartet, Steve Cruz.

On the face of it Cruz, a man of Mexican extraction but now based in Fort Worth, Texas, was not a dangerous opponent. True, he had won twenty-five of his twenty-six bouts, thirteen of them inside the distance, but despite his Golden Gloves pedigree in amateur boxing, he appeared to have little of McGuigan's punching power. On this false assumption, the fight many regarded as an obvious mismatch, would turn into a nightmare for the man from Clones.

It didn't help that the champion's preparations were clouded by a reported ankle injury and allied to the steamy heat in the arena where the temperature was recorded at 110 degrees for the 6 PM (local time) start, it showed as the Irishman retreated from a position of calm authority in the opening rounds, to suffer palpably in the second half of the contest. Most ringside observers had him in a clear lead going into the tenth round in which he was dropped for the first time by a left hook to the jaw and, thus encouraged, Cruz was a man inspired in the closing stages.

After being penalised for a low punch in the twelfth round McGuigan, to his credit, appeared to regain his composure in the thirteenth round only to be shaken again by another barrage of punches in the closing minute of the fourteenth. At that point, it was still all there for both men but crucially, it was the Texan who finished the stronger. McGuigan, his feet blistered by the scorched canvas and restricted still further by damage to both eyes, simply couldn't avoid the punches raining in on top of him. And after taking two counts, he must have realised in his heart of hearts that he had lost the round and by extension, the title he prized so much.

The man who had endeared himself to boxing enthusiasts around the world with his courteous demeanour in victory, was no less gracious in accepting a defeat which must have come like the clap of doom. He would answer the bell on just four more occasions before closing his career in Manchester in 1989, leaving behind the memories of some marvellous nights for the multitudes he attracted to his cause.

– Chapter 22 –

Roche's Golden Year

Cycling –Tour de France and World Championship,
June to September 1987

Look back through the pages of sporting history and almost certainly you'll be refreshed by the riches of relatively small countries which, at different times, produced gifted contemporary athletes who went on to make their mark in major international competition.

Only in terms of landmass could England ever be described as a small country. And yet, even with a population of 50 million plus, it was remarkable that Sebastian Coe and Steve Ovett should emerge at much the same time to establish a friendly domestic rivalry which would expand to embellish middle-distance running in the late 1970s into the '80s. Ireland has just a tenth of that population, but per capita it is right up there with the best in the context of local rivalry which spilled on to the broad stage of international sport.

Take, for example, Sonia O'Sullivan and Catherina McKiernan. They were born within days of each other in 1969 at opposite ends of the country and, after a diligent apprenticeship served in the underage coaching structures put in place by Bord Luthchleas na hEireann, graduated to senior competition while still in their teens. In time, O'Sullivan would be acclaimed as one of the most successful female track athletes in the world with McKiernan complementing her outstanding achievement of finishing in the top two on four consecutive occasions in the world cross country championship, with some class performances as a marathon runner in the 1990s.

Ollie Campbell and Tony Ward were both born in Dublin in the 1950s and, in line with expectations, went on to dominate schools rugby in Leinster. Unfortunately, out-half was their specialist position and eventually their rivalry would develop into an enduring source of debate for rugby commentators world-wide. At a time when Irish rugby wasn't exactly blessed with a surfeit of talent in other positions, the national team selectors attempted on occasions to accommodate both players, with Ward allocated the number thirteen shirt. But far from providing a definitive solution, that was viewed by many as no more than an uneasy compromise.

And then there was the riveting story of Sean Kelly and Stephen Roche in cycling. There was a stage early on in their careers when either man could walk down Dublin's main thoroughfares without turning a head. And that was all the more remarkable when viewed in the context of the public recognition they received in France and Belgium where the sporting press was quick to acknowledge the latent talent of both riders. The measure of the transformation in the mindset of the Irish sporting public is that by the time they retired, Kelly and Roche were numbered among the nation's sporting icons.

Kelly, a tall, raw-boned athlete from Carrick on Suir, was at one point reputed to be among Europe's biggest earners in sport, outside football, despite the fact that he never won the Tour de France. That was ample testimony to the longevity of his career and the manner in which he managed to surf the well-documented problems of professional cycling.

Roche was the city kid who grew up in Dublin with dreams of becoming a footballer. That ambition was quickly superseded after he received his first bike and from this relatively low-key background, he went on to fashion a career which, at the summit of his reign, brought him to the attention of millions. If the glory days of 1987 were lost all too quickly, his legacy was such that it inspired a whole new generation of cyclists in the capital, headed by a talented son, Nicholas.

Remarkably, for a country in which the bicycle was far and away the most common mode of transport for much of the twentieth century, there was no great tradition of competitive cycling in Ireland. That was down in part to the fact that the sport was riven by divisions in much the same manner as athletics suffered because of the political influences at the time.

A case in point was the controversy which resulted in the exclusion of an Irish cycling team in the 1948 Olympic Games in London. Cumann Rothaíoct na hEireann (CRE), the internationally recognised organisation for the sport, nominated riders to participate in the games, but after objections by the rival National Cycling Association(NCA), the International Olympic Committee ruled against the inclusion of a team which the NCA claimed was unrepresentative of a thirty-two-county Ireland.

One of those affected by the ban was Jim McQuaid, a native of Dungannon, who began to dominate the sport south of the border soon after moving to Dublin. McQuaid brought a new flair to cycling and with other promising young riders beginning to emerge, Billy Morton saw fit to include a modern cycling track, the first such facility in Ireland, when the specialist athletics stadium he built for Clonliffe Harriers at Santry opened its gates to the public for the first time in 1958.

Sadly, Jim McQuaid never got to realise his ambition of competing in the Olympic Games but two of his sons, Oliver and Kieron, would go on to achieve that distinction in the 1980s. Pat, the eldest sibling, lost his chance of riding in the 1976 Games at Montreal because of an international suspension, but his rehabilitation was such that he later ascended to the top administrative post in international cycling.

Peter Doyle, an accomplished amateur, promised much when he began his career with a local club in Bray, but it was another rider from the County Wicklow seaside town, Shay Elliott, who pioneered the way for a new generation of Irish cyclists when he became the first to turn professional in 1957. After more than fifty years, Elliott is still remembered as one of the more influential personalities of his era, a man who was never fazed by the task of fashioning firsts.

At the time, cycling was very much a minority sport and what little publicity it received in the national media was devoted almost exclusively to the amateur code. In the 1950s the biggest domestic cycling event was the Rás Tailteann, promoted by the NCA, and it was this marquee race which first brought the talented Dublin rider Shay O'Hanlon to the notice of a wider audience. But by pledging his loyalty to an association outside the mainstream of the sport, O'Hanlon unselfishly turned his back on the possibility of bigger, more prestigious honours which might have been his in other circumstances.

At the other end of the spectrum, Elliott saw the opportunities offered by international competition and reached out for them with a brand of enthusiasm which made no provision for failure. His first important international success came in the Isle of Man when, against all expectations, he upstaged other, more experienced riders at that level of competition. That confirmed his enormous promise but on a return visit there a year later, he knew the other, harsher side of the sport when he came down at the last corner and eventually had to settle for fourth place.

Twelve months later, however, his fortunes were on the rise again when in the 1954 Tour of Ireland, he defied atrocious weather conditions of snow and ice to win the King of the Mountains award. His prize was a place in a training camp in France the following year, an opening which would launch his career on the Continent in the grand manner in 1955. In the course of that year, he finished fifth in the world amateur road racing championship in Italy and on the back of that achievement he was invited to participate in an international amateur race in the Parc des Princes in Paris to coincide with the finish there of the Tour de France.

In the manner of the man, he grabbed his chance with open arms to

achieve the biggest win of his career to that point in front of a huge attendance, and after making the decision to base himself in France, he
announced that in future he would ride as a professional. Ireland now had
a direct interest in professional cycling and it was reflected in the fact that,
for the first time, it began to intrude onto the sports pages of the national
daily newspapers.

Many of his better performances in French domestic competitions still
went unreported, however, and it was not until 1962 that he at last
received the recognition he deserved when finishing second in the world
championship. At the time, the annual Caltex awards were among the
most coveted of their type in Irish sport and Elliott's achievement was duly
rewarded by the sports editors of the national papers who selected the winners. Ironically, his nomination would be at the expense of another Bray
rider, Peter Crinnion, a close friend who had earlier put himself in line for
the Caltex prize by winning the Route de France amateur race.

Within a short span of time, he announced himself on an even bigger
stage by winning a stage in the 1963 Tour de France and then retaining the
yellow jersey for a couple of days. That was an achievement so great as to
be off the radar for earlier generations of Irishmen and while he never got
to realise his ultimate ambition of winning the Tour, his would be the
torch that lit the way for other, equally ambitious fellow countrymen after
his untimely death at the age of just thirty-five.

On Elliott's demise, Peter Crinnion and later Ian Moore from north of
the border would represent Ireland creditably in professional cycling until
the arrival of an even greater luminary in the person of Sean Kelly. It was
Dan Grant, later to become his father-in-law, who nurtured Kelly's fledg-
ling talent with Carrick Wheelers, and it was from this base in Carrick on
Suir that he planned his challenge for Olympic glory at Montreal in 1976.

Unwisely or not, he undertook to compete in South Africa at a time of
growing militancy in the anti-apartheid movement and even before the
precipitous move which resulted in an African boycott of the games, he

was blacklisted by the Olympic Council of Ireland. That was a severe set-back for Kelly, who like most talented amateur cyclists had viewed the Olympics as a passport to a lucrative professional career. But in a positive sense, it made up his mind for him on the time scale of his departure from Carrick on Suir.

Soon afterwards, he took off for mainland Europe to sign professional forms for Jean de Gribaldy's team in southern France before moving eventually to take up residence in Belgium, close to the French border. And de Gribaldy's faith in the Irishman's ability was quickly vindicated when he formed part of the Skil-Sem team which won a couple of stages in the 1978 Tour de France.

Set down in foreign climes with none of his compatriots around to lend moral support, the Tipperary man might have been forgiven if, at times, he questioned the wisdom of his move abroad. But those close to him contended that it was never an issue, merely part of the development programme which, over a period of eighteen years, would bring him legendary status in a sport where acclaim has to be earned the hard way.

His first big impact on the international stage materialised in Italy in 1982 when he finished third in the world road championship, the highest placing by an Irishman since Shay Elliott's achievement some twenty years earlier. Then, in 1983, came his first classic success in the Tour of Lombardy. Later his successes would include the prestigious Tour of Spain in 1988 and the Tour of Switzerland (twice) as well as four spectacular victories in the showpiece of the Irish season, the Nissan Classic.

The great omission, of course, was his failure to win the Tour de France at times when he was riding at the top of his form and it remains the only blot on a career which is frequently advanced by connoisseurs of the sport as a model of its type. In fairness, it ought to be stressed that at different times he finished fourth, fifth, seventh and ninth in the overall standings, compelling testimony to his consistency in the most punishing race of all. Even more remarkable, however, was his feat in topping the points table and with it securing the green jersey on no fewer than four occasions.

That was down in the first instance to his qualities as a sprinter, acknowledged by friend and foe as the best in the business. 'If it comes to a sprint finish, you sure as hell don't want Sean Kelly on your wheel,' was Greg LeMond's assessment of the Irishman's proven record in tight finishes and it reflected the opinion of the great majority of those involved on the circuit.

Various reasons have been advanced for his failure to win the top prize, among them the fact that within the sport he was regarded as less than expert as a climber. Towards the end of his career, that assessment was shown to be questionable, lending credence in the process to the frequently expressed opinion that in his early years under de Gribaldy's tutelage he was advised to ride conservatively on the climbs to ensure that he was that much fresher than the opposition for the time trials.

More valid perhaps is the argument that, unlike many others, Kelly never laid out his season to win the Tour de France. Lance Armstrong was typical of those who structured their season in a way that ensured they peaked in late July. The Irishman, on the other hand, frequently started his season in late January and continued right through to October, to take account of one-day classics and promotional appearances which contributed to his reputation as a big earner. And his misfortune on the days it really mattered was graphically illustrated when he lost out in a race which, professionally, was set up for him to win – the world road racing championship in Austria in 1987.

Significantly, that accolade went to Stephen Roche and in a fashion, it illustrated probably the biggest differences in the records of the two Irishmen who frequently dominated professional cycling in the 1980s. Roche's introduction to the sport was a result of the morning newspaper round he undertook as a twelve-year-old before heading off to school in Dundrum, County Dublin. A neighbour, Pat Flynn, noted his dexterity on the bike he used for this work and advised him to attend a meeting of some Orwell Wheelers members in the car park of H. Williams supermarket in Dundrum the following Wednesday. It was the start of a journey that would take him to the pinnacle of his trade in a modern sporting fairytale.

Unlike Sean Kelly, Roche got to achieve one of his great ambitions after being named in Ireland's team for the 1980 Olympic Games at Moscow, where the disappointment of finishing down the field in fortieth place in the road racing championship was offset by an introduction to Lucien Bailly, technical director of the French national team, during a pre-Olympic seminar in Dublin. Bailly liked what he saw of Roche who, at nineteen, had became the youngest-ever winner of the Rás Tailteann the previous year. Bailly invited him to go on a six-month trial in France and having secured leave of absence from his employers, the apprentice fitter was on his way to join the Athletic Club de Boulogne-Billancourt.

Following an impressive win in the Paris-Roubaix amateur race, he was offered a professional contract with the Peugeot club and for a wage of 5,000 francs a month, he was soon on his way to pit his wits, strength and courage against the best in the business. It helped that he won his first big race, the Tour of Corsica, early on in Peugeot's colours and that led to even greater opportunities as a member of Carrera's high-profile team in 1985. And the Dubliner, thriving on the challenge of repaying his new employers, delivered almost immediately, finishing third in the Tour de France to the thinly veiled astonishment of older, more experienced rivals.

Within months, however, his career was in crisis after he had damaged his knee so severely during an indoor meeting at the Bercy Stadium in Paris that surgery was necessary to repair crushed cartilage. Later, a second operation was deemed advisable and the upshot was that from a position in which he rated as one of the best prospects in the world just months earlier, the level of his performances in 1986 dropped to a point where his future with Carrera was in real doubt. That was reflected in a mutual decision to postpone talks on a new contract until April 1987, when Roche hoped to be back to something approaching his form of two years earlier. In the event, the dimensions of his rehabilitation would prove truly spectacular.

Twelve months earlier Roche had set aside his personal problems to help his teammate, Roberto Visentini, fulfil the hopes of a nation in securing victory on home terrain, in the first of the season's major classics, the Giro d'Italia. Now the roles were starkly reversed as the Irishman risked the ire of many of his teammates and the naked hostility of the Italian crowds by upstaging Visentini for the biggest success of his career. That was a triumph of character as much as anything else and it raised the stakes for the start of the Tour de France in West Berlin just sixteen days later.

In defying the odds in Italy, Roche had occasionally pushed himself to the brink of physical collapse and while the absence of the reigning champion, Greg LeMond, and the recently retired Bernard Hinault, made the 1987 renewal of cycling's most famous race one of the most open in years, the critics wondered if the Dubliner could recover in time for the marathon twenty-six-day event over some 2,400 miles.

Roche was more advanced than most in the mind games which permeate modern sport and he planned to demoralise the opposition as much as reassure his supporters by making some pertinent points early on in the race. As it transpired, he finished third in the prologue and from that point, the man who appeared to be in turmoil at the start of the year was now the one everyone else had to beat in the Tour de France.

Pedro Delgado, the accomplished Spanish rider whose powers on the steep climbs were legendary, threatened to rain on his party when he took a slim lead into the twenty-third stage of the race and the mountaintop finish at La Plagne. This was Delgado territory and when he opened up a two-minute advantage on the last, tortuous 5 kilometres climb to the summit, some were already proclaiming him as the new champion.

But Roche, dredging inspiration from the depths, was not about to concede without a fight and closing the gap metre by metre in the gathering gloom on the winding roads to the top, he emerged from the final corner just four seconds down. That astounding recovery still left him twenty-nine seconds behind going into the time trial at Dijon the following day, but with the roles now starkly reversed, Roche quickly put daylight between himself and the Spaniard to seal one of the outstanding Irish victories of recent years.

Only one man, the celebrated Belgian Eddy Merckx, had won cycling's three major titles in the same year but now that goal was opening up for Roche as he prepared for the world road racing championship in Austria six weeks later. The complication was that his great friend and rival, Sean Kelly, was leading the Irish team and after his misfortune in breaking a collar bone in the Tour de France, everything would be geared to getting him across the line first.

Unfortunately, Kelly missed the break after Roche had led out for him approaching the finish and with his teammate lost in the group, Roche, who had chased down breakaways assiduously throughout the race, surged on to take his place in history, just a second ahead of Moreno Argentin of Italy.

Speaking at the post-race press conference, Roche astounded his audience by saying his victory had been a mistake. 'The understanding was that I would work for Sean and that my turn to be champion would come in time. With so many sprinters in the bunch on the last lap, I felt I couldn't win but when I looked back for Sean, he wasn't there. So I just took the bull by the horns and kept going.'

For Kelly, who eventually finished fifth, it was the crowning misfortune in a year which had gone horribly wrong for him. But incredibly, when he crossed the line his arms were in the air celebrating an Irish win that should have been his. It was the supreme example of the remarkable camaraderie which supersedes all else when Irish athletes pit themselves against the world's best.

– Chapter 23 –

Wine and Roses

Football – The Jack Charlton Era, February 1986 to December 1995

Jack Charlton recalls his first visit to southern Ireland as a member of the Leeds United squad which played an exhibition game in Waterford in the late 1960s with a curious combination of hilarity and disbelief.

The party travelled by air from Leeds to Cork and then on to Waterford by road in a fleet of privately owned cars. Unlike the modern setup in which the bigger clubs frequently commute by air to away games in domestic competitions, road travel was standard at the time for even the bigger, more affluent clubs in the old English First Division championship.

What made this one different for Charlton was the number of unscheduled stops at licensed premises on the journey to Waterford. 'We must have stopped four of five times, all at the behest of the driver and I can tell you that some members of our party were in a pretty happy mood by the time we finally arrived at our destination,' recalls the man who would help revolutionise Irish sport.

It was an experience which would colour his judgement of Irish people in a largely benevolent manner in the ensuing years. It hinted at a comfortable, vaguely unstructured lifestyle which contrasted so starkly with his experience of southern England and it resonated immediately with this son of Northumberland.

In a fashion, it may help to explain the inordinate love affair the Irish had with Charlton and he with them. And the fact that he was driven in part in his crusade to put Ireland at the centre of the world of international football by the disillusionment he experienced after being snubbed by the English FA for the challenge of managing their national team, was an added bonding influence.

All of which served to heighten the build up when the team that Jack built arrived in the finals of the 1988 European championship in Germany by a circuitous route and, prize of all prizes, found themselves on course for a mouth-watering meeting with England at the start of an adventure which, on good days and bad, would hold the nation in thrall for the next seven years.

One of the great myths of the Charlton era was that Ireland teams were never competitive in international football before his arrival and that the public had no empathy with them as a consequence. The fact is that the FAI's teams had come close to qualifying for the finals of the World Cup on at least two occasions and history shows that those who could afford it were following them abroad on different occasions in the previous sixty years.

Charlton's enduring achievement was to introduce the national football team to a much wider public and by extension popularise the game in areas where it hadn't previously flourished. The proof, if needed, was everywhere in evidence on the approach roads to the Neckarstadion stadium in Stuttgart on that memorable afternoon in 1988, where people from all thirty-two counties helped swell the number of those supporting the team in green to something approaching 20,000.

The fact that Charlton had been on FA coaching courses with Bobby Robson, by now managing England and that the Ireland No 2, Maurice Setters had once been a regulator babysitter for the Robson family when they were both playing for West Bromwich Albion, added to the piquancy of the occasion. But in truth, the historical rivalry between the countries didn't require any embellishment.

What was required to set the match aflame was the spectacle of the ball nestling in England's net and right on cue Ray Houghton delivered. It was no thing of beauty but was still acclaimed like a World Cup winner with Houghton, the smallest player in the park, scoring with a looping header which caught Peter Shilton, the England goalkeeper, in no-man's land. Only five minutes had elapsed at that point and with the Irishmen determined to protect that lead above all else, it made for the longest countdown any of us could recall.

Twice Gary Lineker got through in one-on-ones with Packie Bonner and twice Bonner denied him. Then, in injury time, Lineker was menacing the peace of mind of 20,000 Irish spectators once more, timing his run precisely to make contact with Glen Hoddle's free kick. But Bonner, twisting in the air, knocked the ball to safety via a post and the wages of John Atyeo's last-minute equaliser for England some thirty years earlier were at last paid back in full. Ireland had achieved an historic win and the era of the Celtic Tiger in sport was born.

It was a remarkable introduction to big-time competition for the FAI, who had known only heartache in the past and it opened up a whole new vista for the players Charlton had attracted to his cause. Europe, it seemed, was unprepared for his mantra of direct, no-frills football, a tactic so outdated that few knew how to counter it. To capitalise on their achievement in Stuttgart, they needed to beat the Soviet Union at Hanover, but in spite of Ireland's best away performance in years, they had to settle for a 1–1 draw.

Taken in conjunction with the 1–0 defeat at the hands of the Netherlands at Gelsenkirchen four days later, it meant the end of the line for the Irish but for nine eventful days, the team and its supporters had announced their arrival in international football in a manner demanding the respect of football people across Europe.

That England should unwittingly help Charlton to secure his place in local sporting folklore was hugely ironic and given the importance attached to meetings with the most respected but stubbornly unyielding of our sporting rivalries, it was inevitable that Big Jack's tenure in charge of Ireland's team would be largely defined by results against the English.

In that context, he was helped substantially by his share of good fortune as the two countries were drawn in the same group in the finals of the World Cup in Italy in 1990 and even more so by the fact that they would play each other twice in the preliminaries of the major competition which followed it, the 1992 European championship. In terms of drama, the 1990 game in Cagliari did not quite compare with that unforgettable afternoon in Germany two years earlier and yet, it was equally significant insofar as the 1–1 scoreline confirmed that the Stuttgart result was no mere sporting eccentricity.

On this occasion, it was England who got the early break with Lineker capitalising on a couple of defensive errors to open the scoring before sweat had been broken. However, with the self-belief which characterised Irish teams of the period, Charlton was able to oversee a fine recovery, culminating in Kevin Sheedy, one of the understated members of the squad, beating Peter Shilton from the edge of the penalty area for a second-half equaliser. That 1–1 draw would provide the springboard for an eventful contribution to the competition, leading to a successful penalty shootout with Romania in the round of sixteen and ultimately, a heartbreaking 1–0 defeat against Italy at the quarter-final stage of the competition.

The measure of the success of that Italian adventure was that in the space of just four years, the national team had climbed from the ranks of the also-rans at the start of the preliminaries for the 1988 championship to a place in the last eight in the global competition. Equally significant was the fact that without winning any of their five games in Italy – if one excludes the penalty shootout finale in Genoa – the squad was greeted on their arrival back in Dublin by a multitude of not less than 400,000.

Nobody could argue with that kind of progress and with their growing maturity now reflected in a marginally more rounded game, it set the scene perfectly for the two European championship qualifiers with England. It had been a long time in the making but now any Ireland team could look their time-honoured rivals in the eye and ask, 'Why not?' Graham Taylor, who had succeeded Bobby Robson as England's manager, knew that too, and pointedly warned against false presumptions for those travelling to Dublin for the first-leg game in November 1990.

It was England's first visit to Lansdowne Road in twelve years and Taylor's decision to dispense with seven of the players who had started in Cagliari five months earlier, looked likely to be rewarded when David Platt arrived late at the far post to convert Lee Dixon's cross for the lead goal in the sixty-seventh minute. Ronnie Whelan's return to central midfield after missing out on almost all of Italia '90 hadn't gone as well as anticipated and it was only after Alan McLoughlin replaced him that Ireland developed the momentum which led to Tony Cascarino's belated equaliser.

For the third time in as many competitive games, England had failed to assert their historical supremacy but almost certainly, Charlton felt the more frustrated of the two managers leaving the stadium. It didn't help that injuries prevented Mick McCarthy and Whelan playing in the return match before a sell-out crowd of 83,000 at Wembley and Irish fears were heightened when Lee Dixon's shot took a wicked deflection off Steve Staunton to leave Packie Bonner stranded after just nine minutes.

That was ominous and yet, from this troubled start, the Irish team contrived a recovery which deserved to rate high on the list of the best they had achieved to that point. After Niall Quinn had detached himself from his old Arsenal colleague, Tony Adams, to level the scores some fifteen minutes later, Ireland were quite the better team as they sensed the opportunity of securing the win which would enable them to top the table. At least two scoring chances were squandered, however, before Ray Houghton spurned the best opportunity of all by shooting wide late in the game. It was an untypical miss which would come back to haunt Big Jack in his attempt to lead his team to the finals in Sweden the following summer.

Charlton never quite understood why Ireland prized victories over England above all else in sport, to the point where they occasionally lacked motivation against supposedly lesser opposition. Having played so well at Wembley without winning the game, he secretly feared that the two group matches with Poland could yet erode all the merit of the performances against Graham Taylor's team. And in this, he would unfortunately be proved right.

A controversial refereeing decision which cancelled John Aldridge's apparently legitimate goal, could not disguise the lack of quality in a scoreless draw at home to the Poles and when they allowed a 3–1 lead to slip from their grasp in the return fixture at Poznan in October 1991, the Ireland manager may have sensed that the game was up. To pip England as the qualifiers from the group, they needed to beat Turkey in Istanbul and then hope that Poland could somehow rediscover the skill to defeat Taylor's squad.

Thanks to John Byrne's finest game in a green shirt, they delivered on the first part of the equation and with word filtering through from Poznan that Poland, against all the odds, were leading England late in the game, hope was high that the Irish might yet escape unpunished from their failure to deliver wins in earlier games. Then, with Irish players already back in the dressing room, came word that Gary Lineker had plundered a late equaliser against the Poles and the realisation dawned that Ireland had been eliminated from the championship without losing a game. The sense of shock would stay with Charlton for years to come.

'In my time in football, I had been through the whole range of emotion, from joy to despair, cynicism to schoolboy enthusiasm but nothing I'd seen prepared me for the desolation of our dressing room in Istanbul that night,' he recalled. 'Tough professionals who, like myself, had seen it all, just sat there staring into space, not uttering a word. I left the room, came back twenty minutes later and nobody, it seemed, had moved a muscle while I was away.

'One minute, they were on their way to the European finals, the next they were out – and they just couldn't take it all in. I think the sense of hurt was deepened by the realisation that, for some of them, the chance of playing in the finals of another big championship was now lost forever. And my heart genuinely went out to them.'

That was an extraordinary evening for all the wrong reasons. In the opinion of many, the 1992 European championship represented Ireland's best chance of making it into the final of a major tournament – and the possibility of getting lucky on the big day. After participating in the finals of two championships in 1988 and 1990, some of the key members of the team were probably in their prime that year and the widely held feeling that the European finals in Sweden were the most open in years would be illustrated in varying degrees of admiration and astonishment when Denmark, who only got into the finals after Yugoslavia pulled out, went on to lift the Henri Delauney trophy.

In the ledger of Charlton's emotions during his Ireland years, that rated as one of his worst experiences. The highlights of the closing phase of his career were undeniably qualification for the 1994 World Cup Finals, finally confirmed on a volatile, disturbing night in Belfast, and the ecstasy of bringing Italy to heel on their first outing in the finals in New Jersey the following summer. In seven previous meetings with the Italians, Ireland had come up short every time, but for ninety exhilarating minutes in Giants Stadium, the roles were reversed in a manner which brooked no criticism.

In some respects, Ray Houghton's match-winning goal was even more important than that in Stuttgart six years earlier. This was a bigger, more elaborate stage on which to confirm the dramatic progress the national team had made in his term of stewardship, but deep down his pragmatism told him that the sun was setting on the most remarkable era any of us could remember in the colourful history of Irish football.

Yet few could have foreseen the depth of the disillusionment which followed the friendly international game with England at Lansdowne Road on 15 February 1995. It was the fifth time in seven years that Charlton prepared a team to face his native country and in each of the four previous fixtures, the Irishmen had demonstrated beyond question that the chasm which once separated the countries in international football had now dwindled to almost nothing. And they were apparently on the way to reinforcing that point when bedlam descended on the old stadium.

Shortly after David Kelly had established the home team in the lead with a finely executed goal in the twenty-third minute, a section of the England supporters rioted in the west stand and for the first time, the local public experienced the crowd violence which had brought the sport in Britain into disrepute in the preceding years. By the time riot police and baying dogs cleared the arena, the image of football had been tarnished still further and Lansdowne Road had, in the short term, lost its prized reputation as a theatre of family based sport.

That hurt Charlton deeply, the more so since it was the hooligan element in England's support which precipitated the trouble. For all the resentment he was entitled to hold for the dismissive attitude adopted by the English FA after he had been advised to apply for the job of managing England some ten years earlier, he deplored the bad publicity which English football was attracting because of the actions of a small minority of thugs.

The effect was to turn the first half of 1995 into a huge anticlimax for him and it got even worse as he noted the decline of the squad he had nurtured so diligently in some ninety-four games, only seventeen of which were lost. After a 1–0 home win over Portugal had established Ireland as favourites to top Group Six in the qualifying section of the 1996 European championship programme, the wheels came off at the end of the 1994/95 season when they were held to a scoreless draw by lowly Liechtenstein in

Eschen before losing at home to Austria a week later. And when Austria repeated that 3–1 win in Vienna in September, the Irish found themselves on course for a play-off with Holland at Anfield on 13 December.

Nobody was more aware of the impending crisis than the Irish manager. At one point early on in the qualifying campaign, he reckoned he could postpone the breakup of the team he had built, for at least another year. But those two disastrous performances against Austria told a different story and even before the withdrawal of Roy Keane and Niall Quinn, he sensed that the task of containing a young, emerging Dutch team in Liverpool would be difficult to the point of being impossible for a squad running on empty.

Much as he had feared, it was all of that as a youthful Patrick Kluivert, embodying the grace and power of a Dutch team that promised more than it ultimately delivered, scored twice to consign the men in green to a defeat which may have fallen like a death knell for players and manager alike. Before the game, the manager who had won the hearts of a nation confided in his assistant Maurice Setters that he would resign if Ireland failed to make the finals, a decision which was in turn relayed to the FAI president, Louis Kilcoyne.

The Irish supporters, unaware of what was happening, were chanting for Charlton and Setters to walk back out on to the pitch some twenty minutes after the final whistle and as strains of 'The Fields of Athenry' rang out across the ground, the manager, acknowledging the significance of the moment, admitted to shedding a tear tor two. His understanding at that point was that he would announce his retirement publicly some seven weeks later when he would have been a full ten years in the job.

In view of the fact that the next international match was not until March, it seemed a reasonable request. He was not to know then, of course, that some in the FAI hierarchy had other plans and after being pressured into announcing his retirement, he left the association on 21 December. It was, at best, an insensitive decision and it set in train a sequence of events which would culminate in the infamous Night of the Long Knives and, ultimately, the resignation of Kilcoyne and the Hon Treasurer, Joe Delaney.

It was an unfortunate ending to the most astute appointment in the history of the FAI – a credit attributed to the foresight of long-serving official Des Casey – and watching from afar, at least some in the English FA appeared to be not unfamiliar with the happenings in Dublin. A couple of weeks later a letter arrived at the Charlton household, enquiring if Jack Charlton, by that stage among the best-known managers in international football, would be interested in participating in an upcoming FA coaching course at Lilleshall. The two-word response was in the negative.

– Chapter 24 –

Pride of Dublin

Boxing – Olympic and World Championship Successes,
July 1992 to November 1996

Sport was one of the more obvious beneficiaries in the days when the Celtic Tiger motif identified Ireland's economic buoyancy for the world and money flowed in a manner which contrasted starkly with the relative penury of earlier generations.

Starting from a low base in the 1970s, government funding for sport increased tortuously at first, until the profile provided by some outstanding achievements in international competition resulted in Taoiseach Bertie Ahern awarding sport a seat at the cabinet table and, as a consequence, a much improved budget, some twenty years later.

For the first time, disciplines which had previously been largely ignored now found themselves with a regular source of funding to supplement other streams of revenue and the effect was to raise the boats of all national federations. Boxing, historically among the most successful disciplines, headed the list of those who profited most from that infusion of finance and few made the point more powerfully than Dubliners Michael Carruth and Steve Collins.

In their different ways, Carruth and Collins were men who epitomised the spirit of the Fighting Irish, a proud title which derived from the exploits of many of our diaspora after professional boxing began to take root in the United States in the late nineteenth century. Men of Irish descent were hugely influential in that development and apart from full-blown Americans, no country provided more world champions until the emergence of African boxers began to change the ground rules many years later.

For all that proud heritage, however, the task of tracking down Olympic gold proved beyond the capabilities of Irish amateur boxers for more years than we cared to remember. Back in 1939, Jimmy Ingle and Paddy Dowdall became national celebrities after winning European titles in Dublin, but the outbreak of World War II just months later meant that they never got to build on those successes in the aborted Olympic Games of 1940.

John McNally, a skilful bantamweight from Belfast, was the first to reach an Olympic final in Helsinki in 1952, but undoubtedly the best Irish performance in that period came from a man who had failed to win a national title in Dublin before setting off in search of the Olympic welter-weight championship in Melbourne in 1956. Fred Teidt would later be named as the most stylish boxer in the championships but that was a poor consolation prize after a clutch of eastern European judges had somehow contrived to make Nicolae Linca of Romania the points winner of a final which Teidt dominated for much of the three rounds.

Over the next thirty years, amateur boxing would become a pulpit for the dissemination of political ideologies, first by the Soviet-led Eastern European bloc and later by Cuba, where the dual Olympic champion Teofilo Stevenson became the first in a series of exciting ringmasters who would bring the sport to a whole new level of proficiency. As such, it was no great surprise when the IABA, in its collective wisdom, turned to Fidel Castro's regime to augment the intuitive talents of generations of Irish box-ing trainers after the state funding came on stream.

If the name of Nicholas Hernandez Cruz did not immediately resonate with regular patrons at Ireland's international matches in the National

Stadium on Dublin's South Circular Road, it provided a guarantee of excellence among the policymakers of the sport. In his time, Cruz had been responsible for honing the natural talents of many of his compatriots and it was on the back of that outstanding record that he was invited to Ireland to work with the indigenous coaches. It was Michael Carruth's good fortune to be one of the first to benefit, on this side of the Atlantic, from that treasure trove of experience.

Carruth, the middle member of a set of triplets, had a solid family background in boxing. Martin Humpston, a maternal uncle, was the first winner of the national light-middle title after it was decided to introduce two new weight divisions in 1957. More than that, his father, Austin Carruth, was a founding member of the Greenhills Club in the expanding south Dublin suburb. Now, Cruz joined Austin in his corner as the serving soldier prepared for his second attempt to track down the alluring prize which had attracted him ever since he was old enough to appreciate the unrivalled fulfilment of Olympian success.

At that point, Michael Carruth had boxed in more than 250 contests after being introduced to the sport as a schoolboy in short trousers. Some shrewd judges rated Billy Walsh from Wexford as the better medal prospect in the welterweight division, immediately above Carruth, and when they were both included in the team to participate in the Olympic Games in Seoul in 1998, it offered an unprecedented opportunity to assess the merits of both men at the highest level of competition.

As it transpired, Walsh, later to develop into an outstanding coach in his own right, failed to make it through the preliminary stages and Carruth fared no better when, after defeating a Japanese boxer in the first series of bouts, he encountered George Gramme of Sweden in the next round. Months earlier he had beaten Gramme with some ease in Copenhagen and now he appeared to be on his way to a repeat success – until the Swede brought the roof in around him with a sucker punch that could have been detected by a juvenile.

Moving forward, the Irishman dropped his right hand and never had a chance of escaping the consequences of that error after the oncoming left hook from the Swede detonated on his chin. For the first time in his career, Carruth was on his back on the canvas and while he got to his feet at the count of six, the referee decreed that he was in no condition to defend himself and promptly stopped the contest. Before setting off for South Korea, the Dubliner had bought a bottle of champagne in expectation of celebrating a medal success on his return and to that extent, his first-round exit represented the deepest disappointment of his career.

Nor did he attempt to cloak his feelings when he eventually made it back to base. 'I find it difficult to describe the sense of desolation,' he said. 'I realise that I let down my family and my friends and that hurts an awful lot more than the punch which cost me the chance of progressing to the quarter-finals.'

That shabby performance was followed by another defeat in the European championships in 1989 before a journey to Moscow, and the chance of rehabilitation in the world championships there, eventually began to roll away the dark clouds of self-doubt. Victories over Pierre Rahilou (France) and the American Skipper Kelp ensured that Carruth was assured of at least a bronze medal, his biggest achievement to that point in major international competition.

Sadly, his semi-final meeting with the feared East German boxer, Andreas Otto, was less satisfactory. Otto, strong and immensely skilful, was in a different class to anybody he had previously encountered and while the eventual scoreline of 18–1 was an affront to fair-minded people at the ringside, it served to remind the Dubliner that he still had a vast amount of work ahead of him if he was to make a decent showing in the upcoming Olympic extravaganza in Barcelona.

For one thing, he would have to devise a whole new fight plan if he came up against Otto for a second time in Catalonia. All the indications were that the East German was targeting an Olympic gold medal to decorate a superb career before hanging up his gloves. Nobody with any knowledge of the sport could have concurred with the margin of Otto's win in Moscow. And yet his supremacy was sufficiently clear to suggest that Carruth needed something of a sporting miracle to reverse that result on the biggest stage of all.

His build up to the games was anything but inspiring. For one thing, he lost to Billy Walsh in the national senior championships and then, even more disturbing, he suffered a double misfortune in breaking a bone in each arm in the space of just six months. The effect was to plunge him into the biggest crisis of his career. But in spite of the fact that he had now dropped out of the top fifteen ranked welterweights in the world, he still retained the confidence of the selectors when they named the Ireland squad to travel to Barcelona after avenging his 1991 defeat by Billy Walsh in full.

If the wider boxing fraternity had already written off his chances of finding gold in Spain, the Dubliner still hadn't given up on his dreams and with bookmakers now quoting odds of 100/1 on his chances of succeeding, his last words to his brother Austin before boarding the plane for Barcelona were to take the plunge and gamble.

'We were just about to walk through the departure gates at the airport when I turned and advised him to go for it,' he recalled. 'And like any sensible, newly married man, he asked what would happen if I lost. In that case, I reassured him, I'll pay you back your stake.' In the event, he was never required to make good on that pledge.

Two wins over a boxer of Walsh's class – they were required to meet again in a trial bout shortly after their championship showdown – proved that Carruth had made a good recovery from the hand problems which had earlier threatened his preparations for the Games. He was not to know then, but before he would set foot in Dublin again he would find himself plunged into another injury crisis which almost drained him of self-belief.

He also enjoyed moments of good fortune in Barcelona, not least when he was awarded a bye into the second series of bouts in the welterweight division. Instead of meeting the renowned Cuban Juan Hernandez first time up, he now enjoyed the bonus of having one bout less than the majority of the other title contender, and it would prove invaluable!

Mindful of the salutary lessons of his defeat at the hands of George Gramme in Seoul, he resolved that he would not allow his concentration to wander and it showed as he punched out an emphatic 11–2 points win over Maselino Tuifo of Western Samoa in his first appearance in the championship. That was as convincing as he could have wished and it put him on course for a return meeting with Andreas Otto, the elegant German who had had ended his world championship hopes in Moscow.

Two years on from the hurt of the judges making Otto an 18–1 winner on that occasion, Carruth still harboured deep resentment about the vagaries of the scorekeeping system. And his mood was not improved when it transpired that in the course of his meeting with Tuifo, he had damaged a hand, an injury later diagnosed as a fracture of a small bone. It was only after a long discussion that his handlers decided to permit him to go on and take his chance against the tall, athletic German

In Moscow, the Dubliner had allowed his opponent to take charge from the opening bell, but not here. Determined to meet fire with fire, he refused to cede the centre of the ring to his opponent and after leading 3–0 at the end of the first round, he survived a potentially disastrous public warning to take the decision on a count back. The indignities of his misadventure in Russia had been exorcised in nine eventful minutes and suddenly, new, exciting vistas were opening up for him.

The man who had been dismissed as a no-hoper by so many boxing critics was now just two bouts away from Olympian fulfilment and two became one after he outpointed Arkom Chengli of Thailand in a semi-final which curiously held little of the tension of his win over Otto. With Wayne McCullough scoring a thrilling 21–16 points victory over a tough North Korean, Gwang Li, it meant that Ireland, without an Olympic boxing finalist for almost fifty years, now had two representatives in the ring on the last day of the Barcelona championships.

McCullough's bout against Joel Casamajor of Cuba would be his last as an amateur before embarking on a professional career which led to a world title success, and the little man from Belfast gave of his all in a contest which ranked high on the list of the best of the Barcelona Games. Casamajor, a master craftsman who could switch from boxer to fighter and back again in less time that it took to relate, took the first two rounds in a manner which was hugely impressive.

But the Irishman, nothing if not brave, was not about to capitulate without emptying the tank and for much of the last three minutes, he was driving the Cuban before him in a marvellous two-handed attack. Even the most grudging Cuban could only watch and admire the ferocity of that late charge but sadly, he had left himself with too much to do and instead of gold, he departed the ring with a silver medal.

Back in the dressing room, Carruth had followed every punch of McCullough's courageous stand on a television monitor. And he secretly vowed that he would learn from his friend's early tactical blunders and take the fight to Juan Hernandez, the man he might have met in the first round but was now, like himself, on the cusp of the biggest triumph of his career.

The Dubliner, who knew Juan Hernandez only by reputation, would later confess that he was surprised by the abnormality of his reach when the bell went and he came face to face with a man who was rated on a par with some of the title contenders in the professional welterweight rankings. Allied to his technical skills and proven punching power, it established Hernandez as one of the stand-out performers in the twenty-fifth Olympic festival. And it convinced Carruth's handlers that if their man was to have any chance of upsetting the tall odds against him, he would need to get beneath the Cuban's jabs and depend on his short-range punches to sway the decision in his favour.

It was a fight plan fraught with risk and yet, it worked sufficiently well in the opening round to establish Carruth in a 4–3 lead. That was better than any of us watching the action in the Pavollo Joventat arena could have expected and it fostered the hope that there might yet be a golden lining to the day. But before that could materialise, he would have to deal with the revised strategy now being hatched in the startled Cuban's corner.

Hernandez was too good a fighter to go down without a big stand and sure enough, the bell had barely sounded when it started. From a situation in which he never really got going in the first round, he was now hunting his quarry with menace. Most of the short arm punches thrown in clusters were blocked by Carruth's gloves but on those occasions when they got through, they certainly left their mark.

Yet the Irishman was still composed under the pressure until, in a moment of crass carelessness, he appeared to forget the dimensions of the prize at stake and wrestled his opponent to the canvas. The point's deduction for the public warning which followed from the Indian referee Kishen Narsi had the effect of establishing the favourite in the lead for the first time. That was a high price to pay for a silly error but to his credit, Carruth soon reassembled his wits to catch his man with a couple of good hooks to tie the scores 8–8 at the end of the second round.

By the start of the last round, Carruth was ready to stake his title challenge on his ability to score on the counter and with the Cuban becoming increasingly frustrated in his failure to land with a decisive punch, the man earlier dismissed as a no-hoper found the openings to go back in front as the contest reached towards its conclusion.

'I remember looking up at the clock and noting there were only twenty-three seconds to go – twenty-three seconds between me and the win that the experts said was impossible,' Carruth wrote subsequently. 'Then the bell went to signal the end and truly no sweeter music has ever reached my ears. It was all over and now Hernandez, for all his huge reputation, couldn't get to me. I was safely back in port and the gold medal, I felt sure was mine.'

'Son,' Dad told me. 'Son you've nicked it. And as our eyes met, we saw the sweat and the pain, the joy and the tribulation of eighteen long years pass in front of us. Minutes later, my win was official and next morning I read in the papers that the age of sporting miracles was not yet past.' Unfortunately, my brother didn't have the nerve to lay the bet I had suggested but as Dad said later, an Olympic gold medal is worth more than £10,000 of any bookmaker's money.

Like Carruth, Steve Collins grew up in a family with a proud boxing tradition. His father, Pascal, was on the card for the first tournament televised by RTÉ after the station launched in 1962 while brother Roddy was also a skilful boxer before embarking on a much-travelled football career which included a stint in England. But unlike Carruth, who didn't turn professional until he had scaled his Everest in the amateur code, Steve Collins made it clear that his time in the ring was motivated primarily by money.

There are, unquestionably, easier ways of making a living than by boxing professionally and in choosing to take up the trade, he was following in the footsteps of many of the sport's most illustrious practitioners in sourcing his inspiration from the size of his paycheques. And once he had identified his career path, he followed it with the dedication of a Spartan. By the time he climbed out of a ring for the last time in Glasgow in 1997, he had amassed a small fortune but nobody could question either his integrity or his industry in making that possible. Like Barry McGuigan, he had lost just three times in thirty-nine fights and in the process did his part in embellishing the image of Irish boxing by the manner in which he deported himself inside the roped square.

It was on the undercard of American promotions that he learned to look after himself in the rough and tumble world of the fight business. Starting with a third-round win over Julio Mercado at Lowell in 1986, he put together an imposing sequence of sixteen victories before crossing the path of Mike McCallum some four years later. At stake in his adopted city of Boston was the WBA middleweight championship of the world and while Collins left nothing behind him in the ring, he came up just short at the end of a bruising twelve-round contest that thrilled his growing band of admirers.

Over the years, the middleweight division had produced some of professional boxing's greatest moments and if McCallum was no Sugar Ray Robinson, he still fitted the description of a strong, durable fighter who had arrived at the top only after a difficult journey. After Collins had pushed him to the limit of his capabilities, the consensus was that the Dubliner was now well on the way to winning a world championship belt.

Ever since Randolph Turpin won and then lost the world title to Robinson in the space of sixty-four eventful days in the summer of 1951, Britons had been fascinated by the perennial battle for power among the best middleweights in the business. And when Chris Eubank and Nigel Benn emerged to enrich that tradition some forty years later, it gave the prize fight game there a timely fill-up. It also enabled Collins to share in the rivalry which enriched the annals of Anglo-Irish competition.

Eubank, an unashamed showman who compensated for relatively modest ring skills with a towering sense of theatre, was embarked on an outrageous schedule of a defence of his world super middleweight title every month for a year, to justify the biggest television deal ever negotiated by a British fighter. Ultimately, it led him unwisely to the risky decision to take on Collins at Millstreet, County Cork on 18 March 1995. It was an unlikely venue for Ireland's biggest fight night since the heydays of Barry McGuigan and it gripped the imagination of the public like few other sporting attractions.

Eubank came to work that evening on a souped-up Harley Davidson but in terms of drama, the manner of his arrival far outweighed anything else he had to offer. Collins, unmoved by the hyperbole on show in the opposite corner, fought efficiently, if seldom brilliantly, to expose the defending champion for what he was and by the eighth round, he had already built up a commanding lead.

Then, inexplicably, his concentration lapsed and after being caught by a flurry of leather, he dropped to the canvas to take a count. Had Eubank pressed home his advantage at that moment, it is just possible that he could still have salvaged his title. Fortunately for the home supporters, he allowed the habits of a lifetime to prevail, preferring to prance around the ring after Collins got to his feet instead of going after his stricken opponent. It provided the Irishman with precious extra seconds to regain his wits – and in the end, that proved decisive.

That unlikely knockdown took some of the gloss from the biggest win of his career, and in a perverse way it helped to sell tickets when the rematch was confirmed for Cork city some six months later. On this occasion, Eubank was notably less strident in his pre-fight assessments and with the psychological advantage now transferred to the Collins camp, the new champion proceeded to hold his dominion intact without undue stress.

There remained at that point the latent threat presented by Nigel Benn, another overhyped British fighter who had languished in Eubank's slipstream in the closing stages of his career. Unlike his nemesis, Benn enjoyed the advantage of fighting on home territory when he ventured in against Collins in Manchester on 6 July 1996, but the bottom line remained unchanged when the Dubliner forced the referee to stop the bout in the fourth round.

Benn, bellowing belligerence that weary arms were unable to substantiate, suffered a similar fate in their second meeting at the same venue later in the year and at that point, Collins could claim with some authority that he was, indeed, the best of the bunch in the WBO's super middleweight ranking list.

Even at that stage, however, there were indications that the champion was growing increasingly disillusioned with the sport and after two more successful title defences against Frederic Seillier and Craig Cummings, both achieved inside the distance, he announced his retirement. Steve Collins's star had finally burned out and a significant epoch in Irish sport was over.

– Chapter 25 –

Sonia Trailblazer

Athletics – Olympic Women's 5,000 Metres Final, September 2000

Sonia O'Sullivan, a shy, unpretentious person for much of her adolescence in sporting stadia across the world, would never subscribe to the notion, but at different times in the last twenty years she has been described as the athlete who more than anybody changed the perception of women in sport in Ireland. It is an opinion with which many would readily concur.

Over the years, athletes of the quality of Catherina McKiernan, Mary Purcell and, in the first instance, Maeve Kyle represented the country with distinction on the track. And in women's golf, names such as Philomena Garvey and Mary McKenna were evocative in any discussion on how the gender imbalance began to change in sport in the second half of the twentieth century.

O'Sullivan's achievement was to bring the country to a standstill on those occasions when she raced in Olympic, World and European championship finals and millions clustered around television sets to monitor the progress of the runner in the green singlet at venues from Atlanta to Sydney. And if they weren't always rewarded with the reflected glory of success, the constant in every performance was the manner in which she deported herself in victory or defeat.

By the time the book was closed on an international championship career which stretched from 1990 to 2004, she had accumulated an impressive number of trophies and, more importantly, the respect of people with diverse interests in this, the most global of all sporting disciplines. In that, her contribution to the new Ireland has been considerable.

Aside from the occasional media endorsement of an exceptional teenaged talent in Cobh, I knew little about Sonia O'Sullivan until I saw her run in the European championships at Split in August 1990. For all the enthusiasm of the local organising committee, Croatia in late summer held little of the colour and excitement of Italia '90 just a couple of months earlier. And yet, for the small corps of supporters who, hail or shine, continued to show up in distant climes in support of Irish athletes, it was a journey wisely undertaken.

The golden area which produced runners of the quality of Eamonn Coghlan, Frank O'Mara, Marcus O'Sullivan and Ray Flynn among others, had drawn to a close and we wondered aloud when the next trailblazer for middle-distance running would emerge. In a tall, slim girl with an impressive stride pattern, we stumbled on the answer in Split. At that point, the grandeur which once attached to these championships hadn't yet diminished and only the elite could aspire to making it onto the presentation platform.

O'Sullivan, just turned twenty, was always going to be numbered in the supporting cast in her first major international championship; and yet in reaching the final in the 1,500 metres in Split, she had surpassed the expectations of those who ventured there in search of a new star on the horizon. From the town which nurtured the emerging talent of Roy Keane and, before him, the colourful Jack Doyle in boxing, another name was ready to demand the attention of the headline writers.

Back home, the reaction to that promising performance was to heighten expectations for the Olympic Games in Barcelona two years hence. The old guard had disappeared into the shadows and in spite of her limited background, O'Sullivan was identified as the athlete most likely to step into the breach. Even for one of such abundant natural talent, it was a big ask.

From the perspective of those with designs on winning the 1,500 metres title in the Barcelona Games, the lessons of the European championships were that a new face was ready to burst forth in Olympic middle-distance running, one with the potential to be a significant influence in the distribution of the major accolades in the sport for the following ten years. And the effect was to expand the dimensions of the challenge she faced in Catalonia.

At that point, the 3,000 metres event, soon to be replaced by the 5,000 metres in championship competition, was perceived as the second part of the double which defined all the great middle-distance runners and O'Sullivan, who had acquired some experience at the distance during her college career at Villanova, elected to emulate the example of the Olympic and world champion, Tatiana Dorovskikh, among others, in undertaking a dual programme.

The preliminaries went very much to plan as she eased to victory in the last of the heats and on the back of that performance, she was regarded as a credible contender for a medal. That optimism seemed to be well founded as she made all the right moves in the final, tucking in just behind Yvonne Murray as the Scot surged into the lead at the bell. Inexplicably, however, Murray failed to go through with her run and O'Sullivan, to her obvious disquiet, suddenly found herself where she didn't want to be, in the lead with 200 metres to go.

She was still showing the way coming off the last bend but when she pressed the accelerator to deal with the threat of the two Russian athletes, Dorovskikh and Elena Romanova immediately behind her, she discovered, to her shock, that she was running on empty. And after the Canadian, Frances Angela Chalmers passed her in the last few strides, the Irishwoman experienced the singular frustration of finishing in fourth place. It was a harsh introduction to the cutting edge of athletics at the highest level and when she failed to make the final of her specialist event, the 1,500 metres, just four days later, she knew for sure that she still had much to learn in the art of panning for gold.

A capacity to learn from bitter experience has ever been the hallmark of champions in the making and for O'Sullivan, that examination of character was not long delayed. The fourth world track and field championships at Stuttgart in August 1993 would at once offer the opportunity of rehabilitation and the need to prove that when months of preparation condense into seconds of critical decision-making at a time when mind and body are severely tested, she was conditioned to make the right calls on the track.

The fact that China's newly taken fascination with the profile offered by international sport was now being manifested in the presence of several athletes in the middle-distance events, heightened that element of challenge. Thanks in the main to the patronage of Lord Killanin immediately before and after his ascent to the presidency of the International Olympic Committee in the summer of 1972, China had been brought into the Olympic family. And their arrival was interpreted as the most significant development since the emergence of athletes from the African continent some twenty years earlier.

At a time when the Cold War was still dominating world headlines, China's inclusion in the Stuttgart programme was viewed with distrust by some, the more so after some previously unknown athletes had begun to post big performances in the preceding eighteen months. This was attributed in part to the fact that many of the discredited coaches who had conspired to make East Germany one of the dominant players in international athletics in the 1960s and '70s, were now plying their dark trade in China.

They, in turn, spawned an even more controversial home-grown coach in Ma Junren. In Junren's book, the secret of success in athletics was diet and among his recommendations were turtle blood soup and a concoction which had caterpillars as one of its principal sources of nourishment. Moreover, he was reputed to have advised against his women athletes involving themselves romantically until the age of twenty-two. Whatever about romance, subsequent revelations suggested that the intake of substances was a lot more devious than Chairman Ma suggested.

Qu Yunzia was one of those who appeared to follow his advice to the letter, and having marked her arrival on the international stage by taking the bronze medal behind Hassiba Boulmarka and Lyudmila Rogacheva in the 1992 Olympic 1,500 metres championship in Barcelona, she was identified among O'Sullivan's most dangerous rivals in the 3,000 metres in Stuttgart. More ominous still, Qu was joined on the start line for the final in the Gottlieb-Daimler stadium by two of her compatriots, Zhang Linli and Zhang Lirong, and their impact on the race would be profound.

The trio promptly destroyed the plans of the other finalists by running as a team, all three taking turns to make the pace at the dictates of a mysterious man positioned in the front row of the stand, halfway down the back straight. 'I first noticed him on the third lap,' remarked the Scottish athlete, Yvonne Murray, in her post-race interview. 'At his command, they changed places at the head of the field throughout the race, talking non-stop among themselves and generally ignoring the rest of us. The effect of that was to disrupt the tempo and in the end it cost us dearly.'

Murray would later complain that O'Sullivan had declined to join her in a similar stratagem but, as it transpired, neither was able to cover the break when the Chinese increased the pace 600 metres out and went on to achieve the first clean sweep of the championship medals, with Qu leading Linli and Lirong across the line in a disarming exercise in Asian intrigue.

O'Sullivan's sense of indignation was accentuated by the knowledge that each of the new champions in Stuttgart would be presented with a spanking new Mercedes car by the championship sponsors. And a subsequent disclosure that Qu didn't even possess a driving licence did nothing to appease her disappointment.

'I'll now go back to base and treat this like every other race I've lost to people whom I had never previously competed against,' she said. 'I always learn something from a defeat and this one will be no different. Hopefully, it will show when I come back to this stadium for the start of the 1,500 metres championship in three days' time.'

In that prediction the Irish champion was proved to be right. Running in the 1,500 metres final, she again found herself immersed in an engrossing tactical struggle. This time, however, her nous was not found wanting and in the end the timing of her late charge was sufficiently precise to beat all but the pre-race favourite, Dong Liu. For the second time in a week, the Chinese had deprived her of that coveted winners' bonus, but a silver medal still represented the biggest prize of her career to that point.

By now, the international career which had been launched in the relatively obscure setting of Split three years earlier was already beginning to flower and we knew for certain that she had the character to cope with the pressures of an expanding media presence after justifying favouritism in the last running of the 3,000 metres in the European outdoor championships in 1994.

That was hugely encouraging but for all the merit of her performance in Helsinki, nobody could have foreseen the train of triumph which, in the space of the next twelve months, would take her to the top of the rankings in international women's athletics and a place among the four highest-paid athletes of either gender on the Grand Prix circuit. Only Kelly Holmes, running on home territory in a low-key meeting in Gateshead, finished in front of the Irish champion in 1995 when she ran with imperious authority at venues across Europe.

By far the most important of her wins was in Gothenburg, where victory in the world 5,000 metres championship confirmed her rating as an athlete approaching the summer of her career. By now, the Chinese coup in Stuttgart two years earlier had been exposed for what it was and O'Sullivan, seemingly invincible, was confirmed as the one every woman had to beat in the middle-distance events in the Olympic Games in Atlanta the following summer.

In the space of just a couple of years, the athlete from Cobh had grown from ambitious contender to a place where she frequently looked to be in a different class from those lining up with her at the start of every Grand Prix race. At that point every analysis of the likely outcome of the Olympic 1,500 and 5,000 metres championship started and ended with Sonia O'Sullivan. By the time the Atlanta Games were consigned to history, every assessment of the two events started and ended with the same question – how had it all gone so terribly wrong for the athlete who had finished the 1995 season in a position of supreme authority?

A wide diversity of excuses, from illness to a breakdown in the relationship with her agent and long-time friend, Kim McDonald, were advanced by way of explanation for perhaps the biggest anticlimax in Irish sport in modern years. Track athletes in particular are regarded as a hypersensitive breed and there were occasions, rare occasions, when the pressures of having to perform at a consistently high level in every facet of the sport appeared to impact on O'Sullivan. The scars of a painful fortnight in Atlanta would endure for much of 1997 but it is to her credit that she recovered sufficiently to emerge from the world indoor championships in Paris with a silver medal in the 3,000 metres.

Through it all, however, she invariably managed to retain her love affair with the Irish public and in 1998 it was all systems go again after a return to something approaching the form which had wooed the masses three years earlier. It began in the steamy heat of Morocco in March when, on consecutive days, she won the world long and short course cross country titles in a style which belied her relative inexperience in this facet of athletics. That was reassuring and some six months later the good times were still rolling with a 5,000/10,000 metres double in the European championships in Budapest.

Even when she was struggling to get back to where she was pre-Atlanta, Sonia O'Sullivan was always big news and just months after her Budapest victories, she was in the headlines once more, this time for an announcement that she intended to take a break from athletics in 1999. It later emerged that she was pregnant with her first daughter, Ciara, and wholly in character, she was back in training within weeks of the happy event.

In a very real way, that was a statement of intent for the 2000 Olympic Games in Sydney and the need to address the deep hurt of her experience in Atlanta. For all the gratification of securing two world cross country titles in Marrakesh and the fluent nature of her track double in Hungary, she still craved the fulfilment of Olympic success and the opportunity of decorating her career on the biggest stage of all.

By now, she had abandoned her early dreams of conquering the world over 1,500 metres and was concentrating on the 5,000 metres event with ambitions of moving on to even longer distances. That was a plan shared by several athletes who had cut their teeth in international competition in the four-lap event, among them the highly talented Romanian, Gabriella Szabo.

Romania, whose sporting history had been adorned by the legendary gymnast, Nadia Comanaceci, a multiple gold medallist in the 1976 and 1980 Games, quickly realised that they had stumbled on another rare talent when Szabo, a tiny girl with a big smile, began to make waves in under-age running. That brought her to the notice of many athletics people in western Europe and at one point there was speculation that she was about to be fostered by an Irish family after those directing her sporting career concluded that she would develop her talent more quickly in the West.

With Sonia O'Sullivan and Catherina McKiernan already in situ, that represented a glittering prospect for Irish athletics for a few short weeks, but as it transpired, she didn't leave Romania until her devastating finishing pace established her as a top of the bill attraction for all athletics promoters around the world. Ultimately, allegations of taking performance-enhancing drugs would tarnish her reputation, but at her peak she was a truly outstanding runner.

Those who doubted O'Sullivan's ability to regain a racing edge after taking time out to start a family reckoned without the singular dedication of the woman who had sacrificed so much to make it big in her chosen sport. By the end of 1999, she was already well into her customary training schedule in Australia where all the hard work was done to sustain her during the track season the following summer. And the word on the grapevine was that, at thirty, she was again heading for another eventful campaign.

Ever since the trauma of her encounters with the Chinese in Barcelona eight years earlier, she had coveted the chance of getting into the type of condition required to launch a credible title challenge on the biggest stage of all in sport. And the fact that the Olympics were being held in her adopted country, albeit in a green singlet, heightened that ambition in the approach to the Games.

It showed in the manner in which she eased into the 5,000 metres final in the vast Sydney bowl which, for the better part of three weeks, held the world captive as one spectacular performance superseded another in perhaps the most memorable Games of recent times. By the time she arrived for her date with destiny on 25 September 2000, she was ready to undertake her role on what would come to be remembered as a magic Monday in Sydney.

In turn, Anier Garcia (men's 110 metres hurdles), Jonathan Edwards (triple jump), Michael Johnson (men's 400m), Maria Mutola (women's 800m) and Haile Gebrselassie (men's 10,000m) would reach out for the acclaim of the thronged stadium. But it was another, more familiar face which occupied the Irishwoman's attention when she arrived to join the assembled glitterati in the warm-up area adjoining the main arena.

Cathy Freeman, the darlin' of the crowds, was the Australian athlete primarily responsible for generating such a memorable atmosphere that evening. But as a former partner of Nic Bideau who, by that stage, was engaged to Sonia O'Sullivan, it meant for a difficult relationship between the two athletes. More than that, less than half an hour separated Freeman's appearance in the 400 metres final and O'Sullivan walking onto the track for the 5,000 metre race.

O'Sullivan, in fact, was just finishing her warm-up when a vast explosion of noise told her that Freeman's race was already in progress and the decibels rose still higher as the Australian, garbed so oddly that at times she resembled an invader from space, came with a superb late run to collar Lorraine Graham and the British runner Katherine Merry down the finishing straight and win in 49.11 seconds. The jubilant scenes which followed will long live in the memory and the stadium was still rocking as O'Sullivan took her place on the start line for the 5,000 metres final.

With no Australian athlete in the field, the enormous volume of home support now switched to their adopted daughter, but with less than 1,500 metres gone they, like the Irish, can only have been shocked as she receded from the leading group, to run at the back of the field for a couple of circuits. Not for the first time, however, the signs proved false and with just over a lap to go, the race for gold condensed into a duel with Szabo.

A sharp burst of speed and in a matter of strides the Romanian was in the lead. But O'Sullivan hadn't come this far to concede easily and, centimetre by centimetre, the gap closed until she was running at Szabo's shoulder out of the last bend. Then she surged and with more than eighty metres separating her from a life's ambition, we were on our feet, waiting for the great moment.

Many, many times we had watched that late surge retrieve causes that had appeared lost but sadly, not this time. Hard as she tried, there was simply no way she could get away from her arch rival and when Szabo, running on the inside lane, surged again close to the line, the divide of gold and silver had been settled.

O'Sullivan had come up short by a mere footfall in her quest for Olympian glory, but in every other aspect it had been an occasion to savour. And yet for some, a career which encompassed so much triumph would be defined by that searing heartbreak. And as we made out into the long night, that was the unkindest cut of all.

– Chapter 26 –

Roy Keane and Mick McCarthy

Football – World Cup Finals, June 2002

Brian Clough, at the summit of his managerial career at Nottingham Forest, was probably closer to the truth than many of his contemporaries in his assessment of Roy Keane, when he was asked how he dealt with the raw, emerging firebrand he had just bought from the League of Ireland First Division club, Cobh Ramblers.

'I don't understand a word he says but the lad's self-belief on the ball and his capacity to see things that are beyond the ken of others, makes him a very special young man,' said Clough. 'So I just bite my tongue and let him get on with it.' Their partnership at City Road lasted just three seasons, but long after he had departed the midlands, Keane would continue to admire the pragmatism of his old Guv'nor.

It was a template which wasn't always observed by others and the sequel was a series of well-publicised spats which occasionally earned him headlines he could have done without. In the end, Roy Keane and controversy were intimate bedfellows and that reputation would follow him into his initial managerial stints with Sunderland and Ipswich.

Keane was still under the wing of Clough when he made his first international appearance in the Republic of Ireland's team in the friendly game against Chile in May 1991. At that point he had still to play in Forest's first team but Jack Charlton was sufficiently impressed with his progress in

Ireland's underage sides to shortcut his apprenticeship against the South Americans.

In that assessment, he was proved right. Soon, the young Corkman was holding down a regular place in the team and making a big enough contribution to emerge as an automatic choice by the time Ireland made it into the World Cup Finals for the second consecutive occasion, in the United States in the summer of 1994. And it was there that he first found himself taking Keane aside to discuss issues which had evolved in the media.

Maurice Setters was supervising a training session in Big Jack's absence on a reconnaissance mission in New Haven, when he got involved in a shouting match with Keane, and later Charlton had occasion to take the player to task for not reporting an injury problem in the run up to the first game against Italy in New Jersey.

Charlton recalls, 'There was a bit of shouting after Roy had raised Maurice's dander in a training session but as usual, the media blew it out of all proportion. On the second occasion I was genuinely annoyed when I discovered that he was carrying a groin strain without telling me, just days before we played Italy. He informed me that he intended to run it off in training but that wasn't good enough and I told him so.

'Now Roy was never the easiest person to deal with. He was basically a shy lad who would never volunteer conversation and unless you approached him on a specific matter, he'd tell you nothing. But on this occasion, he was out of order – and I think he knew it. I have to say that these were isolated incidents. There will always be the odd hiccup in manager/player relationships but normally he was very responsible in the manner in which he prepared for matches.'

Alex Ferguson also had a way with Keane and in time, it would be a hugely important factor in consolidating Manchester United's place at the forefront of club football worldwide. The man whom Fergie was apt to describe as his 'Irish warrior' fitted his concept of a box-to-box player in the mould of Bryan Robson. He also liked what he termed Keane's intense commitment and the old-fashioned work ethic which put him apart from so many others.

He was aware too of the player's fiery temperament. 'His Irish fire was fundamental to his immense value as a footballer but his tendency to stray beyond the bounds of acceptability had to be curbed,' recalled Ferguson. 'To his credit, he was always conscious of his responsibility to his team-mates and it meant that we didn't have too many disputes over the years.'

It was different with Mick McCarthy. As a recent recruit to senior international competition, Keane was happy to beaver away under McCarthy's captaincy in their tantalising failure to qualify for the finals of the 1992 European championship. True, harsh words were exchanged by the pair in Boston in 1992 after Keane had shown up late for a coach journey in what was McCarthy's last overseas tour as a player, but generally they managed to co-exist. The rapport between the two dwindled over the years, however, and by the time McCarthy took over the management of the team from Jack Charlton at the start of 1996, they appeared to have little in common.

McCarthy, it ought to be said, was quick to acknowledge that, in the mood, the Manchester United midfielder was Ireland's biggest asset and he sought to underline the point by naming him to captain the national team for the first time during the close season tour of the United States later that year. Keane had been unavailable for four of McCarthy's first five games in charge but in a bold show of faith, the manager nominated him to wear the captain's armband in the games against the USA, Mexico and Bolivia.

One could only guess at his inner thoughts when he discovered, late in the day, that Keane had pulled out of the tour without prior notice. Yet, after meeting the player in clear-the-air talks in a London hotel later in the year, McCarthy was sufficiently reassured to recall him for the 1998 World Cup qualifying campaign. And the relationship blossomed when, on Andy Townsend's retirement, Keane was appointed to replace him as captain for the European championship programme that followed.

Yet the perception was that the interaction between manager and team captain wasn't always what it should have been and the issue was again in the public domain when, after leading out the team for the first leg of the 2002 World Cup play-off against Iran in Dublin, Keane missed the return game in Tehran just five days later. Later he explained that he was having treatment for an injury at the time and was freed by Alex Ferguson for the first leg of the tie on the condition that he would not risk aggravating the damage in the second Iranian game. Not everybody was enthused by Ferguson's rationale and inevitably, Keane's commitment to the national team was questioned once more by his critics.

The player's indignation at that criticism was only thinly veiled and it had the effect of damping down the celebrations which followed qualification for the World Cup Finals for the third time in the previous four attempts. What followed in the Far East some six months later was a public relations disaster which, in the context of notoriety, put everything which had preceded it, in the shade.

Even at that advanced stage of his playing career, Roy Keane was still the name which identified Ireland for the world of football at large and as such the news of his walk-out from McCarthy's squad at their training base in Saipan a little more a week before the start of the World Cup Finals was recorded in varying degrees of annoyance and astonishment by the international media corps.

For those monitoring developments from a local base, the final break between McCarthy and Keane was, perhaps, less surprising. The last phase of the preparations before the squad set off on their great adventure encompassed an exhibition game in Sunderland on 13 May followed three days later by the meeting with Nigeria at Lansdowne Road on the eve of their departure to Saipan. Keane sought and was given permission to absent himself from Niall Quinn's testimonial match in Sunderland, an odd decision in the opinion of some given the proximity of the action in the Far East.

McCarthy would later explain that he had facilitated Keane in order that he could travel to Paris for treatment of a persistent knee injury. Significantly, the request came from Manchester United rather than Keane and it testified to the lack of communication between manager and player in the approach to one of Ireland's biggest games in eight years in the Far East.

Harshly, perhaps, Keane was seen by sections of the media as the party most at fault for the Sunderland fiasco and his frustration showed in verbal spats with those involved on the long haul to Saipan. And when he discovered that the FAI had been wayward in the preparations for their stay there, it was the tipping point as far he was concerned. He indicated that he wanted to return home and after being talked out of an overnight trip to the local airport by McCarthy, he found the management team in a less accommodating mood when he strayed over the line once too often and the meeting broke up in disorder.

Recalling the scenario at his final meeting with Roy Keane at the team hotel in Saipan, McCarthy wrote, 'For about eight minutes, he hurled every expletive in the book at me. I was a crap player, a crap manager, a crap coach, I couldn't organise training, I couldn't make a decision, couldn't get inside players' heads. I had never seen any human being act like this before, let alone a footballer. And with that he upped and left.'

The effect of that bust-up, without parallel in Irish football, was to reduce all other team news to insignificance and it's probable that the vast majority of the people monitoring events back in Ireland, missed the story that Mark Kinsella was the man being earmarked to step into two of the biggest boots in football. Kinsella, a product of the famous Home Farm nursery, had started his professional career in the modest surroundings of Colchester United some twelve years earlier. But it wasn't until he joined Charlton Athletic in 1997 that his career took off and the skills which had earned him so much praise as a schoolboy player found a new outlet for expression. In terms of publicity, he didn't even begin to compare with

Roy Keane, but those who had followed his development from Whitehall to Japan sensed that he would not be found wanting in his central midfield partnership with Matt Holland.

Fortunately for McCarthy and his battered back-room staff, they were proved right. At thirty, Kinsella was ready for the job of bossing midfield alongside Holland and in the sense that it overturned the predictable game plan which ordained that everything be routed through Roy Keane in midfield, it could be said that in some aspects it improved the attacking build up.

The draw for Group E in the first phase of the finals in the Far East lumped Ireland with Cameroon, Germany and Saudi Arabia in that order. Barring a mishap of monumental proportions, victory over Saudi Arabia was always in prospect but nobody could be under any illusions about the task awaiting the reshaped Irish team in their opening two games.

After their exploits in the Olympic Games and the African championship, Cameroon were widely identified as the new face of African football, a strong, athletic team with the skills to match their physical attributes. And the fact that they were first up for the Irish, invested the match at the Big Swan stadium in Niigata on Saturday, 1 June with a significance befitting the first-ever meeting of the countries.

Apart from the inclusion of Kinsella, the big talking point in the team sent out by McCarthy in Niigata was the choice of Jason McAteer on the right side of midfield. McAteer's goal against Holland at Lansdowne Road had been key to Ireland's qualification for the finals but in the weeks preceding the action in Japan, there was persistent speculation about his rate of recovery from a recent injury.

In the manner of his management, McCarthy was loyal to his senior players and after some agonising, decided to go with the veteran Sunderland midfielder. In the event, it proved an unwise decision and for the second half, McAteer was replaced by Steve Finnan, effectively ending his World Cup adventure. By that stage, Cameroon were in the lead and apparently heading for victory after Patrick Mboma, epitomising the Africans' swashbuckling style, had angled a shot beyond the reach of Shay Given six minutes before half-time.

That was a notion soon dispelled in the second half, however, when Kinsella and Holland took over in the critical struggle for central control to turn the game undeniably in Ireland's favour. Fittingly, it was Holland who came up with the equaliser in the fifty-second minute and they went close to winning the match nine minutes from the end when Robbie Keane was denied only by the width of a post. Ireland had been good value for their 1–1 draw and suddenly, the loss of Robbie's namesake didn't look so serious after all.

For all his pre-match apprehension, it was a scoreline which didn't fully satisfy the Ireland manager, who contended that on the basis of their late supremacy they deserved more. Given the moments of crisis which erupted at regular intervals in the Cameroon penalty area in the closing quarter, McCarthy's frustration was not without foundation and yet the quality of the performance can only have reassured him in the approach to the fixture against Germany in Ibaraki four days later.

Over the years, Ireland had put together some good results against one of the enduring powerbrokers in European football and while Rudi Voeller's German team was occasionally hugely impressive in the preliminary phase of the competition, McCarthy was even more moved by what he saw in the second half of the Cameroon game in which Damien Duff's confidence on the ball was surpassed only by his decision to join the singsong on the coach taking the players back to base. That was uncharacteristic of the normally diffident winger and in the strange ways of football, the manager interpreted it as an encouraging augury for the meeting with Germany.

Just nineteen minutes into the game, the Irish manager can only have been alarmed by a German strike which embraced all that is best about the old aristocrats. After winning the ball in their own half, they moved it at speed to Michael Ballack and the midfielder's through pass was precise enough to take Ian Harte and Gary Breen out of the game and set up Miroslav Klose for the finely executed finish. The ease with which his defence had been undone was disturbing enough to conjure up all kinds of dark images for the Ireland manager but some forty minutes later the Irish players had regained sufficient poise to persuade him to go for broke in the search for an equaliser.

The decision to replace Harte and his uncle, Gary Kelly, with Niall Quinn and Steven Reid enabled McCarthy to deploy three specialist forwards. And from a situation in which they had earlier presided with authority at the centre of the German defence, Tomas Linke and Carsten Ramelow suddenly began to struggle in the face of the challenge posed by Quinn's height, and it showed as Oliver Kahn's goalkeeping skills were soon increasingly in demand.

Then, with the game in the fourth minute of injury time and the Danish referee, Kim Nielsen preparing to signal full time, Steve Finnan floated a hopeful cross into the goalmouth, Quinn chested it into the path of Robbie Keane and while Kahn got a hand on the ball, the shot had sufficient weight to finish in the net and earn the men in green the most dramatic of draws.

Barring a catastrophe, that result was always likely to earn them a place in the round of sixteen and much as people expected, Ireland made light of the challenge offered by Saudi Arabia in their final group game. Remarkably, almost 66,000 people crowded Yokohama's International Stadium to watch the one-sided affair in which Gary Kelly was again preferred to Jason McAteer on the right side of midfield. A heavy sense of inevitability settled on the game from the kick off with Robbie Keane's goal after only seven minutes, opening the way to a victory which was polished by second-half scores from Gary Breen and Damien Duff.

The fact that Ireland would be meeting Spain just five days later at the South Korean venue of Suwon, just outside the capital Seoul, for the right to enter the quarter-finals of the championship, merely heightened the element of authenticity in this, the biggest test of McCarthy's managerial career. Ever since that memorable afternoon when Paddy Moore's acclaimed goal earned Ireland a 1–1 draw in Barcelona, the rivalry between the countries had been sharp and pungent and if history favoured Jose Antonio Camacho's Spanish team, the graph of Ireland's performances suggested that they were not without a chance of advancing.

Before the game, McCarthy made a point of emphasising the need for early vigilance after conceding first-half goals to both Cameroon and Germany. Events would prove that he spoke in vain for within eight minutes of the kick-off, Shay Given was bending his back to retrieve the ball from the net after Fernando Morientes had stolen in ahead of Breen to head a cross from Puyol beyond the reach of the goalkeeper. Given the passion of McCarthy's pre-match talk, that was a wounding blow but as in the German encounter, the Irish found inspiration in adversity and thriving on the artistry of Damien Duff, they proceeded to torment the Spanish defence for the remainder of the game.

It wasn't reflected on the scoreboard, however, and when Ian Harte, catching the mood of an unhappy tournament for him, saw his penalty saved by goalkeeper Iker Casillas in the sixty-third minute, it threatened to bring the roof in on this team of battlers. That was until a brave call from the Swedish referee, Anders Frisk, gave Ireland a second penalty chance in the last minute of normal time and this time Robbie Keane extracted the maximum price for Hierro's silly foul on Niall Quinn.

With Spain down to ten players following the departure of Albeda, the Irish team spurned the opportunity of winning the game in extra time and thus, for the second time in twelve years, they found themselves involved in a penalty shootout at this stage of the competition. Sadly, there was to be no repeat of the joyous scenes we had been privileged to witness in the shootout in Genoa when David O'Leary's successful penalty triggered days of national celebration.

Now the tears were of sorrow rather than joy as Matt Holland, David Connolly and Kevin Kilbane in turn wilted in the pressure and Spain, who had missed two of their own, scrambled home 3–2 on penalties with the last successful spot kick from substitute Gaizka Mendieta. An honourable journey, undertaken with courage and commitment in equal measure, had come up short but the Irish public was sufficiently moved to turn out in multiples of thousands to welcome the manager and his players back to Dublin.

No less than Jack Charlton before him, Mick McCarthy had earned the gratitude of a nation and as he left the Phoenix Park with the applause of the masses ringing in his ears, he was entitled to believe that his love affair with Ireland would continue long into the future. Nobody could have anticipated that within another five months he would be dismissed by the FAI or that his old friend Roy Keane would return to the national team two years later in Brian Kerr's failed attempt to qualify his team for the 2006 World Cup Finals.

– Chapter 27 –

Munster Abu

Rugby – Heineken Cup Final, May 2006

Anthony Foley didn't have far to look for a role model when he embarked on a career which would decorate Irish rugby. Back in 1978 his father, Brendan, was in the celebrated Munster team which made history by defeating the All Blacks 12–0 at Thomond Park, an achievement which continues to rank among the more significant milestones in Irish sport.

Coming from that background, it was always in prospect that the only son of the colourful Shannon second-row forward would end up pursuing an oval ball for much of his early life. Less obvious was the fact that in time he would captain a Munster side which, almost thirty years later, eclipsed even the monumental achievement of his father's teammates.

Foley Snr was present in Cardiff's Millennium Stadium on that historic day in May 2006 to watch his pride and joy establish the warriors in red at the pinnacle of rugby in the northern hemisphere and enrich the tradition of a province which, over the years, frequently played to a standard that was greater than the sum of its component parts.

Ronan O'Gara travelled a different route to that captivating Heineken Cup Final against Biarritz. His family roots were in the west of Ireland and unlike Foley, who delights in recalling that as a toddler he was regularly taken into the Shannon dressing room by his father to savour the atmosphere created by a proud parish team, O'Gara didn't get involved until he went to secondary school.

Once established in the Presentation College, Cork team however, his talent shone like a beacon and as he made his way through the various underage categories, it was already apparent that, with luck, he could develop into that most precious of all rugby assets, an out-half of rich creative talent to complement his goal-kicking skills.

Like Foley, a highly competitive back-row forward with the innate ability to run all day, O'Gara thrived in the extra pressures of professional rugby and on these two pillars rested many of Munster's hopes as they sought to get a foothold in a competition which, in a relatively short span of time, caught the imagination of millions in the rugby strongholds of Europe. Thanks to the benefits of saturated television coverage, the European Cup competition sponsored by Heineken succeeded in bringing the sport to a wider public than anybody could have anticipated.

Ulster, seldom found wanting in innovation, was the first Irish team to adapt to the new priorities of the professional game and while decidedly light on players with international experience, they demanded the admiration of a capacity Lansdowne Road crowd by outplaying Colomiers in the 1999 Heineken Cup Final. That was down in large measure to Simon Mason's siege-gun placekicking and David Humphreys' leadership at number ten and the effect was to create a whole new support base for the competition on this island.

That success was flawed only by the fact that no English clubs took part in the competition, but all the outstanding issues with the Rugby Union authorities in London had been resolved by the time the 1999/2000 season kicked off. And this time, it was Munster rather than the men from the north who spearheaded the Irish challenge for the coveted silverware.

The previous year they had come up short against Perpignan in the Stade Aimé Giral, failing to match the sheer intensity of the French team at the breakdown as they receded to a 41–24 defeat and when they fell again in France, this time against Colomiers in the quarter-finals, they knew they had to address a recurring problem.

Playing in their own fortress at Thomond Park in front of some of the most passionate supporters in the world, they were capable of beating anybody. It was a different story on the road, however, where apart from a win over the lowly Italian club Padova, they had never been able to reproduce their best form. Results proved that they still had much to learn in the transition to professionalism and having identified the problems, they set about solving them.

Expeditions to France, in particular, showed that they needed to up the tempo of their play and having worked on this aspect, they then focused on adjusting their game plan to get more in tune with the interpretation of the laws and decisions of referees. Away from the pitch, they employed a local chef to take charge of their culinary requirements and equally important, they resolved to travel to assignments abroad by charter rather than scheduled flights.

On a bleak November day in November 1999, they knew for certain that they were on the right road when, after trailing 9–21 at the interval, they hit back to defeat a Saracens team led by the great South African, Francois Pianarr, at Vicarage Road. From there on, it was all systems go for the Munster men and landmark away wins over Stade Français and Toulouse, took them into the Heineken Cup Final against Northampton at Twickenham. Having eliminated the best teams in France en route to London, supporters travelled in their thousands in expectation of securing the ultimate prize but in spite of David Wallace's fine try, O'Gara's late penalty miss meant that they returned unrequited after an agonising 9–8 defeat.

They were not to know it then, but the disappointment of that result would be replicated more than once. Twelve months later Foley, at his predatory best, scored a hat trick of tries to eke out a home win over

Biarritz – and an inviting semi-final tie against Stade Français at Lille. History showed that Stade Français were seldom better than fragile when forced to leave their home base and while this match was being played in nearby Lille, the Irishmen fancied their chances.

They might well have done so had the referee allowed what looked like a perfectly legitimate try from John O'Neill. The English official, Chris White, ruled otherwise however, and for the second consecutive occasion the post-match mood of their supporters bordered on despair after Munster had again failed by just a solitary point.

If there was a silver lining to that cloud it was that Declan Kidney's team had proved that even without Keith Wood, by now back in England with Harlequins, and fiery flanker Eddie Halvey who had aligned himself with London Irish, they still possessed the raw power to blast a way through Europe. And with the distinguished Australian Jim Williams now on board at number six, they proved it by reaching the final once more, against Leicester at Cardiff in 2002.

A momentous day for the province was given added significance by the fact that it would mark the last big day in the colourful careers of Peter Clohessy and Mick Galwey. But Munster couldn't provide them with the send-off they craved after Neil Back had perpetrated an outrageous professional foul minutes from the end and Leicester, reprieved, held out to achieve a success they scarcely deserved.

By now, the nearly men of Europe were attracting even the most grudging to their cause. Declan Kidney left to join Eddie O'Sullivan in a new national management team but the arrival of Alan Gaffney, the Australian who was formerly number two to his compatriot, Matt Williams at Leinster, provided an excellent solution to a potentially tricky problem. Not unexpectedly perhaps, he settled on the maturity of Jim Williams, rather than the exuberance of the younger Foley, when he came to name a replacement captain for Mick Galwey.

It wasn't the easiest of starts for Gaffney and defeats on the road to

Gloucester and Perpignan raised the spectre of Munster failing to qualify for the knock-out stages of the competition for the first time in six years. For some, that was an unthinkable scenario after losing two Heineken Cup finals and a Celtic league decider to Leinster in the space of three years. But if the challenge of digging themselves out of trouble fazed the Australian, it certainly didn't show. Perpignan were duly put to the sword in the return game at Thomond Park and then, memorably, John Kelly's thrilling late try ensured that they met their target of beating Gloucester by no less than twenty-seven points at the second time of asking.

The manner of the response to that daunting task would serve to heighten the appeal of Munster for the masses. Here indeed was a team which refused to be derailed by refereeing decisions or other impediments on the road to fulfilment in Europe and the mission assumed an urgency that fringed on compelling for even those with only a tiny affinity for the southern team.

The reward for the demolition of a Gloucester team regarded as one of England's finest was another tilt at the reigning champions, Leicester. Neil Back's dark ploy in denying Munster the probability of the late try, which might well have produced a different result at Cardiff the previous year, was not forgotten and it meant that Gaffney did not have to work hard to motivate his players for the quarter-final tie that everybody wanted to watch in Leicester's compact Welford Road stadium.

Together with Toulouse, Leicester were rightly regarded as the heavy-weights of European rugby at that point. Even in the most intimidating stadia, Martin Johnson's team demanded the respect of all opposition when they ventured away from home. Playing in the fortress that was Welford Road, they were well nigh invincible and the ploy of dispersing visiting fans to different areas of the ground can only have accentuated the mood of apprehension as Foley bounded out at the head of his fired-up team mates.

The fact that the Munster players were not informed of a ten-minute delay in the starting time – to facilitate the thousands of fans still seeking to access the ground – did nothing to sooth jangling nerves. And by the time Johnson, who had embarrassed friend and foe alike in what was seen as an insult to the President Mary Robinson immediately before England's Grand Slam triumph at Lansdowne Road just weeks earlier, ran out at the head of the Leicester team, the scene was set for a raw, tribal battle with a dozen subplots.

Leicester didn't have to wait long for Munster's anticipated early bombardment. With Paul O'Connell and Donnacha O'Callaghan disrupting the champions' line-out, the visitors led for most of the game and even when a fundamental error costing seven points allowed the English team to slip into the lead, O'Gara immediately responded in kind. Before the end, Mike Mullins and Alan Quinlan combined to send Peter Stringer racing in behind the posts for the try which finally released pent-up tension, and for only the third time in six years Leicester were consigned to the losers' dressing room at Welford Road on a 20–7 scoreline.

Almost inevitably, Munster found themselves on a flight to France for a semi-final tie appointment with Toulouse which was designed to intimidate all but the bravest. Alas, it proved a journey too far for coach Alan Gaffney and his team. It was as if the achievement of avenging their Heineken Cup defeat by Leicester had consumed all their ambition and Freddy Michalak's finely taken try proved the decisive score in a 13–12 victory for the bluebloods of French rugby. Not for the first or last time, Munster were made to endure the lonely feeling of losing by a single point on the flight back to Limerick.

Tribulation on this scale was by now presenting players and management with a huge examination of character. Galvanic personalities like Mick Galwey and Peter Clohessy had reached the end of their playing careers without experiencing the fulfilment of success at European level and the suspicion was that, unless they acquired the know-how to survive tense finishes at the business end of the competition, men like Anthony

Foley and Ronan O'Gara would also depart disillusioned.

Nor did the plot of the 2004 competition do anything to improve matters. After playing some impressive rugby on occasions in the pool games, their luck appeared to be changing when, for once, they enjoyed the bonus of playing a semi-final tie in Ireland. Lansdowne Road was the venue for their meeting with Wasps and all was going to plan on another carnival occasion as some 40,000 supporters saw them lead by ten points late in the second half. At that point, O'Gara had been replaced because of a hamstring injury but there was still a sufficiently broad seam of experience in the team – or so it seemed – to protect that advantage.

Alarmingly, the reverse proved the case. When the Londoners increased the pressure on the home defence in the last, tense phase of the game, yawning gaps began to appear and helped by a controversial try from Trevor Leota, the visitors scrambled through against all expectations. Of all the setbacks suffered in European competition, this was the most disturbing from a Munster perspective and now, having lost two finals and three semi-finals, even some of their most steadfast admirers were beginning to ask pertinent questions.

The European campaign of 2005 ended in equally disappointing fashion. After recurring doubts about the quality of their back three, the acquisition of the multi-honoured All Black, Christian Cullen, was being hailed as one of Munster's more astute moves. For all their power up front, they were viewed by many as lacking the finishing skills to complement that asset and the arrival of New Zealand's record try-scorer was designed to redress that apparent weakness. Unfortunately, it didn't work out quite as planned, primarily because the Kiwi spent much of his time with the Irish province recovering from injury.

That was a bitter blow in what was always going to be a difficult campaign after their inexplicable collapse against Wasps the previous season. Their pack was as intimidating as ever to the opposition, the more so after Denis Leamy had celebrated his promotion as an established member of the back row with some typically opportunist tries. Shorn of genuine pace behind the scrum, however, they failed to impress in their qualifying pool and it made for a situation in which they travelled to Twickenham needing to win with a bonus point against Harlequins to secure a home tie in the quarter-finals of the competition.

Victory was duly secured but alas, not with the four tries required to avoid the hazards implicit in the journey to Spain to meet Biarritz in San Sebastian for a place in the last four in the competition. A daunting challenge was made all the more treacherous by the absence through injury of Ronan O'Gara, and while David Wallace's try kept them competitive for a spell, they eventually fell to a 19–10 defeat. In his three years in charge of the team, Alan Gaffney had delivered two titles but sadly, not the European accolade coveted by their loyal fans. Now he was returning to Australia to take on a new role with the national team and after a period of reflection, Declan Kidney was appointed to succeed him in Limerick.

Kidney was credited with laying the foundation blocks for Munster's smooth transition to professional rugby during his first term in charge of the team and in the wake of Gaffney's exit, he was now viewed as the one most likely to lead them to the biggest prize of all. And it was against that background that the team's supporters sought to rationalise consecutive league upsets at the hands of Leinster and Ulster midway through the 2005/06 season.

Whatever about Ulster, defeat by Leinster was always calculated to induce long, painful inquests and it scarcely augured well for the all-consuming goal of bringing the Heineken Cup to the province for the first time. The start of their qualifying programme, away to Sale, was never going to be easy, given that the Lancashire club was at that time riding high in the English Premiership table. Now, like all English clubs, they coveted the scalp of Munster as the prelude to possibly the biggest season in their history.

So worried was the Munster back-room team that they recruited the motivational skills of Roy Keane to help focus minds. Whatever Keane said, it wasn't enough and helped by some of the mistakes which by now were recurring with disturbing frequency for the team in red, Sale won decisively, denying their rivals the consolation of even a bonus point.

For a squad with a sharp competitive edge, that was a major setback but years later, Declan Kidney would recall it as something of a watershed. 'Sale were a very good team but leaving the ground that night, we knew we had let down our supporters. There and then, we resolved to put things right.'

Kidney and his players were as good as their word. After the trauma of losing to Leinster at the RDS on New Year's Eve, they headed to France for a heavyweight collision with Castres. On two previous visits to the Stade Pierre Antoine they had known only the pain of heavy defeats but now the roles were dramatically reversed. Here it was the French who left disillusioned after the visitors had crossed seven times in a 46–9 win that would rank high on their list of European achievements.

They still needed to beat Sale and secure a bonus point in their last pool game at Thomond Park to make it into the last eight – and the likelihood of an intimidating away tie against Toulouse. Months earlier, they had underperformed against the expensively assembled English team and the wounds of that defeat were still raw as they trotted out on to the hallowed Limerick turf. Commentators likened it to the make or break game against Gloucester in 2003 and the mindset of the Munster men showed when, directly from the start, Sale's French lock, Sebastian Chebal, was driven back some twenty-five yards after gathering Ronan O'Gara's towering kick

That established the mood for a captivating display with David Wallace's injury-time try securing the bonus which secured the all-important extra point. To top off the celebrations in Limerick, Leinster, against all the odds, outplayed the tournament favourites Toulouse in France to set up an all-Irish semi-final with the unmistakable trappings of Croke

Park and the All-Ireland Gaelic football championship, on the third Sunday in September. But this was the RDS and what better way to announce their new maturity than with a win over the most enduring of their rivals.

Leinster appeared to have put themselves in pole position with that flamboyant performance, rightly regarded as the best in the competition to that point, to see off the multiple champions in Le Stadium in Toulouse but if this was designed to spread alarm in Munster nobody told Kidney or his players. In a masterclass which is still recalled with relish down south, they dealt with the latent threat of the Leinster team by destroying their pack. And from this base, they ran in three tries, the second from O'Gara being received with adulation by Munster and pained indignation by those in the opposite camp.

A 30–6 scoreline ensured that the Reds were now through to their third final in seven years. This time it was Biarritz who barred the way to the prized silverware and the prospect of witnessing retribution on a grand scale attracted more than 50,000 of the Munster faithful to the Millennium Stadium in Cardiff.

No less than Foley and O'Gara, Peter Stringer had been central to the Munster odyssey on many big occasions. Trevor Halstead, a strongly built Kiwi centre, was by contrast a relatively recent recruit to the cause but in a very real sense, it was his presence which galvanised their midfield formation. Halstead's intercept try had put the gloss on the victory over Leinster and now under the closed roof of the Cardiff stadium, he triggered tidal waves of joy in the stands with the score which lifted Munster from the depths of a horrendous start.

The game had been in progress less than three minutes when a missed tackle in midfield resulted in Sereli Bobo scooting down the touchline for a try which shook Munster and their supporters all the way down to their boots. If Halstead's achievement was to restore their belief in breaking two tackles to put the Irishmen in the lead in the seventeenth minute, Stringer's enduring testimonial was to conceive the audacious try which, history recalls, finally took the trophy away from Biarritz.

The tiny scrum-half was in a minority of one as he assessed the options before feeding a scrum wide on the right just inside the Biarritz 22. Only he, it seemed, noticed that Bobo had strayed inside off his wing and that Serge Betsen was likewise missing from his allotted number six duties. And it was through the ensuing gap that Stringer scampered for the decisive try without a finger being laid on him. Biarritz, in the manner of their heritage, didn't go quietly but after closing the gap to a single point, they watched with a deep sense of foreboding as O'Gara kicked the late penalty which finally brought Munster into their kingdom.

Two years later, Ronan O'Gara would claim eleven of Munster's sixteen points as they broke an abrasive Toulouse challenge to lift the trophy for a second time but for him, nothing compared with the deep fulfilment of the win over Biarritz.

'Two thousand and six was the year which changed everything for us,' he said. 'That was the year we threw away our "nearly" tag and convinced the rest of Europe that we were indeed a team of winners.' Long after the tumult and the shouting had died away, Peter Stringer's genius would survive as the badge of a truly remarkable group of players.

– Chapter 28 –

Ireland on Song

Cricket – Ireland v Pakistan, March 2007

It was by no means the sexiest item in the sporting diary they kept at the old *Irish Press* office on Dublin's Burgh Quay, on a beautiful, hot weekend back in the summer of 1954. Established journalists on the paper might have rubbished the notion of presenting themselves at an unfashionable cricket ground in north County Dublin for the final of the Irish Junior Cup.

At this remove in time, I can't even be certain of the clubs involved, but for a teenage hack in search of experience, not to mention the modest fee involved, it was an opportunity that couldn't be spurned. So, on a bicycle which had seen better days, I set out for Balrothery to further my apprenticeship in sports journalism.

The action on the pitch continued late into the evening and when the spoils of victory were eventually apportioned, I was invited with other guests to partake in some light refreshments in the clubhouse. Mobile phones were but a distant dream in those days – come to think of it, even landlines were pretty sparse at the time – and in those circumstances, I was required to get back on the bike and furnish my report, in person, to the people working on the sports desk at the *Irish Press*.

It meant that I didn't arrive there until 10 PM, only to be told to my horror that I had missed the deadline for the first edition of the paper and that my toil in the sun had all been in vain. Not only would my magnum opus not appear in print, but I wouldn't be paid for a long if distinctly enjoyable day in the countryside.

I learned two important lessons that day. In the newspaper industry, deadlines – and the unswerving requirement to meet them – are paramount. I also discovered at first hand that when it comes to cricket in that part of the country, the intensity of the passion on the pitch is matched only by the hospitality and general bonhomie off it.

Many years later, I would come to appreciate the depth of that passion still more and in time it would prove a major component in the chemistry which elevated Irish cricket to a level only a super optimist could have envisaged in the difficult challenges of life in the 1950s. Just as rugby is an integral part of the DNA of the citizenry of Limerick, the sound of leather on willow is the unmistakable aural evidence of people indulging a natural talent in the hamlets of north Dublin.

The first role model I encountered when I began covering cricket on a more regular basis, in the capital, was a true-blue city man, Jimmy Boucher. A quiet, unassuming person, J. C. Boucher was, by any standard, an accomplished practitioner of spin and when his eye was in, he was also a handy man with the bat in the course of a long career with Phoenix and Ireland.

The national team at the time was designated quaintly as the 'Gentlemen of Ireland', a title which said much about the Corinthian ethos of the game. And when Boucher wasn't included in the middle of the order, the team was on occasions composed of ten Protestants and Louis Jacobsen, a distinguished member of the Jewish community in Dublin.

Gradually, however, the net widened with the emergence of the Pembroke opening batsman, Stanley Bergin, a fellow sportswriter, identifying a new breed of Irish cricketer. Bergin, who had been diverted from his first love, Gaelic football, was never the quickest of scorers but in time shared in some fine partnerships.

Gerry Duffy was another Dubliner who excelled with the bat and eventually, the general improvement in the levels of local teams was reflected in the action of several English county clubs taking a greater interest in the young players emerging on the other side of the Irish Sea.

Ed Joyce, who hailed from a celebrated cricketing family in Bray, wasn't the first Irishman to dip his toe in the larger pool, but once he graduated to the England team his name and his place of origin became a constant source of good 'copy' for the media in Britain. Joyce, good enough to open the batting for his adopted county, would in time return to reunite with his Ireland colleagues after failing to deliver on his full potential on a consistent basis.

That could scarcely be said of Eoin Morgan, a gifted left-handed batsman from Rush, County Dublin, who smashed cricket balls across boundary lines with such power that on occasions it appeared irreconcilable with his sparse frame. Joyce, who had been hugely influential in helping Ireland to qualify for the 2007 World Cup Finals in the West Indies, was wearing an England shirt by the time the men in green set off for a four-month build-up programme that would raise the sport in Ireland to a new level in the course of a protracted preparation for cricket's biggest event of the year.

At twenty, however, Morgan was already the gleaming jewel in the squad which Adrian Birrell, the national coach, took to the Caribbean for Ireland's biggest ever appointment on a cricket pitch at a stage when the Rush man was seeing the ball so early that even the quickest of the pace bowlers could expect trouble.

Remarkably, twelve of the fifteen players in that squad were amateurs. When they weren't indulging their sporting instincts at weekends, they were required to earn a living in trades and professions as disparate as teaching, sales, electrical work and in one instance a postman. In that situation, the only opportunity they had of bonding was when they travelled abroad for international assignments. Only four members of the squad, Trent Johnson, Dave Langford-Smith, Jeremy Bray (Australia) and the South African all-rounder, Andre Botha, were born outside the country.

Compared to the well-paid, full-blown professional players they would encounter in the West Indies, they were viewed by some as a raggle-taggle outfit whose presence in the championship finals was merely designed to make up the numbers. It is to the eternal credit of Birrell, in the last year of the five-year contract he had signed with the Irish Cricket Union, that he refined the raw talent he had inherited and by enriching the group with the inclusion of some significant additions, arrived at a point where, trading on merit alone, they could look even the best teams in the eye.

After a build up which began some two years earlier, he embarked on the final phase of the World Cup preparations, a four-month world tour, by bringing his players to his native country and involving them in games with local opposition.

'One of the highlights of my World Cup adventure,' he would say later, 'was inviting the guys to see my home town, Port Elizabeth. It was very important for me to show them who I am and where I come from. I wanted the players to meet my family and friends and that experience, for me, was every bit as memorable as the time we spent in the Caribbean.'

The second segment of the preparations, participation in the World Cricket League catering for countries with associate status in Kenya, was far less satisfactory. Beaten on the last ball of the innings by Scotland in their opening game, they defeated Bermuda next time out only to succumb to Kenya, Canada and the Netherlands in quick succession. Instead of topping the table as hoped, they finished in second-last place, a near disastrous showing which, apart from lost prestige, cost them the chance of participating in the Twenty20 World Cup in South Africa later in the year.

Fortunately, redemption was soon at hand. From Nairobi they travelled directly to Abu Dhabi and an Intercontinental Cup engagement with the UAE. Birrell didn't need to tell the players that they had let themselves down in Kenya – the accompanying press entourage did the job for him. To have any chance of doing well in the Caribbean, they needed a big performance to get the show back on the road – and thanks in the main to Eoin Morgan, they got it.

In an innings of many exquisite shots, Morgan got to a mountainous 203, the highest ever by an Irishman in international competition, and Birrell's men went on to win with a day to spare. Suddenly, the homeward trip to Dublin for a two-week break was a lot happier than anybody dared imagine after the indignities heaped on the team in Kenya. The effect was to lift the expectations of a nation, and people with only a peripheral interest in cricket were now getting involved.

On their arrival in Trinidad for the final part of their preparations, Ireland played warm-up games against South Africa and Canada. Faced by the challenge of bringing down their compatriots, Adrian Birrell and Andre Botha can only have been delighted after the bowling of Dave Langford-Smith and Trent Johnson reduced South Africa to 66 for 7 at one point in their innings. Helped by a swashbuckling 67 from Andrew Hall, they eventually hoisted their total to a match-winning 192, but taken in tandem with a summary win over Canada, that performance would establish the Irish as the most dangerous of the associate teams in the World Cup.

Compared to Scotland, the highest qualified of the second-tier countries in the finals, Ireland were treated kindly in the draw. Whereas the Scots were in with Australia and South Africa, two of the shorter priced teams to lift the trophy, Ireland came out in their preliminary group with Zimbabwe, Pakistan and the West Indies.

The West Indies were now but a shadow of the team which once dominated the sport, and which just two years earlier had lost by ten wickets to the Irish in Belfast. Ireland could also claim a previous win over Zimbabwe and the memories of that achievement were still vivid enough to convince the players that when push came to shove, they could achieve at least one win before packing their bags for home. For better or worse, fate ordained that they open their programme against Zimbabwe – and it would provide a roller coaster of emotion for the supporters of both teams

Kingston, Jamaica was home to the Irish for all their games in Group D of the qualifying programme. Then, on 15 March 2007, the talking finally stopped and after fifteen months of waiting, it was time to match presumption with conviction in the fabled Sabina Park stadium. Zimbabwe might have more opportunities of competing against top teams but if Ireland was to accelerate its upward curve, victory over a team which had recently slumped to a 5–0 series defeat by Bermuda was imperative. The start was anything but impressive for the Irish who, put into bat, lost William Porterfield in the first over.

With Eoin Morgan now joining Jeremy Bray at the wicket, they pushed out the score to 43 for 2 before Morgan edged a deceptive delivery into the slips. After the heroics of Abu Dhabi, that was a shock to the system and it got even worse for the vocal Irish supporters in the crowd as Andre Botha and the O'Brien brothers, Niall and Kevin, all went cheaply. Eventually, it was left to the unflappable Bray to save the innings with a superb century for a total of 221 for 9 off 50 overs, but on a relatively good wicket, the target was still attainable for the Zimbabweans.

Two dropped catches by Niall O'Brien and Eoin Morgan gave the opposition all the encouragement they needed at the start of their innings and when they got to 87 for 1, the alarm bells began to ring for the green hordes. At 129 for 3, the Zimbabweans were cruising until their opener, Vusi Sibanda, unluckily trod on his wicket and was gone for 67.

Thus encouraged, Ireland's hopes of escaping the wages of those early batting blunders were briefly revived. But when Zimbabwe arrived at a situation in which they needed just nine runs off the last two overs to win, it looked as if all the escape routes had been closed off for Trent Johnson and his team. In a crisis demanding nerves of steel, Johnson handed the ball to Kevin O'Brien, who had conceded eight runs in his only previous over and the young Dubliner repaid that trust in buckets by bowling a double wicket maiden.

Now the burning question was who would bowl the last over. Both Dave Langford-Smith and Boyd Rankin had overs to spare but without a moment's hesitation, it seemed, the skipper chose Andrew White to shoulder the responsibility. Once again, his judgement would be vindicated to the hilt.

The first four balls yielded six runs, leaving Stuart Matsikenyeri on strike with just two deliveries remaining. Johnston came close to taking the most crucial catch of his long career as Matsikenyeri, on 73, went after the bowler but unfortunately couldn't hold the ball and prevent the two runs which ensued to tie the match. The Irish captain now encircled the batsman with his entire team as Matsikenyeri searched for the single which would win the match. In the event, he couldn't make contact with Wilson's cunning delivery and the relief of the men in green was almost audible as the game ended in the most thrilling of all ties.

In the sense that the Zimbabwean game appeared to offer the Irish players their best chance of a win, a share of the points was vaguely disappointing. And yet, the manner in which they survived that test of character impressed the international media corps so much that it made the clash with Pakistan just two days later even more appealing.

Fittingly, the game which would define Ireland's sojourn in the Caribbean was played in Kingston on St Patrick's Day. Estimates were that the support for Johnston's men had now increased still further and there may have been up to 2,000 supporters in full voice gathered in Sabina Park for the biggest national sporting occasion since the heady days of Jack Charlton.

Pakistan, the great imponderables of world cricket, were no longer regarded as unbeatable, but at number four in the rankings and buttressed by some of the best players in the game, they still commanded a lot of respect. Undeniably, however, they were still stained by scandal, and the absence of their two outstanding bowlers, Shoaib Akhtar and Mohammad Asif, from the squad was a painful reminder of this.

The official reason for their no-show was injury but others suggested that it was their earlier suspensions and the possibility of those bans being revisited which accounted for their absence. Yet with players of the quality of Younis Khan, Mohammad Yousuf and the team captain, Inzamam-ul-Haq, there appeared to be little justification for the apprehension expressed by their highly respected coach, Bob Woolmer. Having watched the Irish in their warm-up games against South Africa and Canada, Woolmer rated them as the most dangerous of the associate teams in the finals and warned against the danger of underrating them.

That reservation may well have been rooted in the state of the pitch. When the covers had been removed, the amount of grass on the track shocked almost everybody. Seasoned observers called it one of the greenest wickets they had seen at this level and until it had been tested, nobody could be certain of the dimensions of the lottery involved. Put another way, neither team wanted to bat first, and in that scenario the toss of the coin by match referee Chris Broad became critical. To the manifest relief of his colleagues, Johnson called it right and in that instant the Pakistanis, put into bat, may have sensed the worst.

Yet, midway through the first over bowled by Dave Langford-Smith, they had seven runs on the board, thanks in the main to a no ball which Mohammad Hafeez promptly dispatched to the boundary. That was ominous but then, almost immediately, came the first of the successes which would turn this into a joy day beyond the comprehension of even the most upbeat Irish person in the ground. Hafeez edged an outswinger to wicket-keeper Niall O'Brien and suddenly, a cancer of self-doubt swept through the Pakistanis.

Younis Khan was barely strapped up before he was obliged to walk out to the middle and even for one of his daunting experience, it can only have been an ordeal. Just a couple of minutes later, he was on his way back to the pavilion after Boyd Rankin had enticed him into presenting Andre Botha with a comfortable catch in the slips. At 15 for 2, Pakistan were already in deep trouble and it got worse for them after Yousuf, the master craftsman of so many marvellous innings, miscued the square drive to William Porterfield at backward point.

Inzamam-ul-Haq, Imran Nazir and Shoaib Malik, undone by the treachery of the pitch as much as the skill of the bowlers, all went in quick succession as the Blarney Army sang and danced through to the luncheon interval. For all that jubilation, however, they cannot have been unaware that on a pitch as unpredictable as this, it was far from certain that their heroes would make it over the line. Moreover, the cloud cover was beginning to thicken and with the expected onset of showers, interruptions in play could be expected.

Against that background, it was imperative that Ireland make a secure start. The required run rate of 2.66 per over was modest but if conditions worsened and Pakinstan's seamers hit their straps, Johnston's storm troops could yet find themselves in trouble. Alas, those fears were to be substantiated all too painfully in the course of a long, fretful afternoon.

Jeremy Bray, architect of that stirring performance against Zimbabwe, went to the first ball of the fourth over, trapped in front by Mohammad Sami, for three paltry runs and then, even more disturbing, Eoin Morgan was soon gone as well. Morgan's muted display with the bat in the opening game had been tempered only by the reasonable expectation that he would improve next time out. This was his kind of stage, a fertile setting in which his artistry would surely thrive and yet he still fell victim to an identical delivery from Sami for just two runs. With six overs gone, two wickets lost and only 14 on the board, it was suddenly nail biting time for the fans.

Not for the first time in his career, the Northants keeper Niall O'Brien strode into the breach, a relatively small man with a heart as big as a dustbin lid. Unfazed by the pressures welling up around him, he settled in with William Porterfield to form the partnership which would eventually wrestle control back from the favourites. Porterfield contributed just 13 runs from 50 deliveries in moving the score on to 62 before he left, reasonably confident in the knowledge that his team was now on an unstoppable march to victory.

Joined by his brother Kevin late in the afternoon, Niall O'Brien punished anything that approximated a loose ball and while rain forced them off for a brief spell, he was not to be derailed. Eventually, he was stumped by Kamran Akmal for 72 after jumping down the pitch in the expectation of hitting Shoaib Malik out of the ground, but the crescendo of cheering which accompanied him on his way back to the pavilion confirmed the good news that Ireland were now on the brink of a win of epic proportions.

Appropriately, it was the captain who secured the winning runs, picking up a slow delivery from Azhar Mahmood to lift the ball over midwicket and into the stand for the second six of the day. Pakistan, one of the most celebrated if eccentric powers in international cricket, had been beaten by three wickets and the party which marked their elimination from the championship would last until breakfast.

'All credit to the Irish for taking their chance but we made it easier for them by batting abysmally,' said the Pakistan coach, Bob Woolmer. 'Three years' work had gone into the preparation for the World Cup and to fall like this is very disappointing. My contract runs out soon and while I'm reluctant to continue in international cricket, I'll sleep on my future in the sport.'

Before daybreak the following morning, Bob Woolmer, born in India, a Test player with England and a coach in South Africa before accepting the challenge of mending Pakistan's many problems, would be dead, found in a pool of vomit in his hotel bedroom. And as the shock news spread around the world, so too the speculation that his death was in some way linked with match-fixing – a crime not unknown in sport – and the massive upset in Sabina Park just hours earlier.

The initial judgement was that he had died of natural causes but it did nothing to appease the cynics. And when Jamaica's deputy commissioner of police, Mark Shields – on secondment from Scotland Yard – was called in to oversee the investigations, the stench of scandal began to intensify. The entire Pakistan tour party, players and officials, were fingerprinted, and soon afterwards the police announced that Woolmer had in fact died of manual strangulation and in support of that conclusion, it was stated that a bone in his neck had been broken in the struggle.

Fortunately, that conclusion was proved to be grossly wrong and some three months later, it was disclosed that he had indeed, died of natural causes. A man with a record of distinguished service to the game deserved a more dignified farewell, but in the sense that the earlier scaremongering was shown to be wholly false, it was a relatively decent ending to a tragic story.

Thanks to the victory over Pakistan, Ireland went through to the finals of the Super Eights against all the odds – a splendid achievement for a largely amateur squad. Victory in Bridgeton over a Bangladesh team which had earlier seen off India and South Africa was the highlight of their Super Eights programme, ensuring, as it did, full one-day international status. A sell-out crowd in the Kensington Oval enjoyed a great game but local organisers were quick to state that the match had sold out months in advance in the expectation that it would feature two of the earlier casualties, India and Pakistan.

Four years on, Ireland would show that their victory over Pakistan was no mere flash in the pan when beating England in the 2011 World Cup Finals. That match will forever be remembered for the swagger of Kevin O'Brien and his astonishing innings of 116, the fastest ever in the competition to that point. That was a significant stage post on Ireland's journey to full international Test status, but when one reflects on the carnival in Jamaica and the chemistry of skill, stamina, bravery and not least crowd support which put Ireland at the centre of world cricket for at least twenty-four hours, the success over Pakistan had to take precedence.

'There is no doubt in my mind,' Andrew White wrote later, 'that the crowd drove us on to the tie in the first game and subsequent win over Pakistan. They took the West Indian people along with them and really captured their imagination. Unquestionably, they had a special impact on the tournament.' Old Jimmy Boucher, I suspect, would have tipped his cap to that.

– Chapter 29 –

O'Driscoll Rainmaker

Rugby – The Golden Double, March to May 2009

Before Brian O'Driscoll emerged from Blackrock College to impose himself on international sport at the highest level at the start of the millennium, two Ulstermen, Jack Kyle and Mike Gibson, were generally held to be the brightest stars in the pantheon of Ireland rugby players.

The measure of O'Driscoll's progress is that some thirteen years on, the Dubliner is viewed as not just an exceptionally gifted rugby player but probably the finest talent that Ireland has produced in any team discipline since the cult of individualism became fashionable in the renaissance of sport in the 1950s.

When Richie McCaw, the celebrated New Zealand flanker, was named in a poll as the outstanding player in international rugby in the first decade of the twenty-first century, the dissenters were many and loud. Of McCaw's athleticism and leadership qualities, there is universal approval. And yet, the great majority of those who supported O'Driscoll's claim to that title, were far removed from Ireland's shores.

Many reasons have been adduced for the Irishman's popularity as the complete rugby player, but Paul O'Connell, captain of the Lions squad in South Africa in 2009, was probably as close as anybody to the answer when, commenting on the loss of O'Driscoll for an important game he said, 'When you lose a player whom you regard as your best defender as well being your best attacker, that loss is incalculable.'

The point was well made. Even at times when he was primarily responsible for creating and finishing in the top third of the pitch, the Leinster man was regarded as the team's most effective forager in ruck situations, a centre three-quarter who discharged the duties of a number seven on the floor so successfully that he was singled out for special attention in this facet of the game by opposing coaches.

Remarkably, it was not until his final year at Blackrock that he was acknowledged for the abnormal talent that he was, but after making his senior international debut against Australia at Brisbane in June 1999, he announced himself in the grand manner on the international stage with a hat trick of tries in Paris on his eleventh appearance in the team. That represented Ireland's first away win over France in twenty-four years and the effect was to change the whole psyche of the national team.

From a situation in which ten-man rugby was seen as the most expedient way forward for those controlling the destiny of the side, O'Driscoll's tour de force in front of 80,000 appreciative spectators in the Stade de France encouraged the belief that Ireland now possessed a cutting edge to complement traditional qualities of power and purpose up front. And in the wake of Keith Wood's retirement after the 2003 World Cup championship in Australia, Eddie O'Sullivan bought into that philosophy with the announcement that O'Driscoll would henceforth assume the responsibility for captaining the team.

O'Sullivan had succeeded Warren Gatland as national team coach in somewhat controversial circumstances in November 2001 and quickly identified the need to achieve a greater degree of consistency if they were to enhance the image of Irish rugby at a time when it was about to undergo major change. In the mood, they were capable of beating any team, with the notable exception of the All Blacks, on home terrain but the fact that they had not secured a Triple Crown success since 1985 or even more unlikely, a Grand Slam since 1948, testified to their brittleness away from Lansdowne Road.

With Declan Kidney installed as his number two, O'Sullivan soon began to make significant progress and with O'Driscoll calling the shots on the pitch, they claimed victories over Scotland, Italy, France and Wales – the latter on a 25–24 scoreline in Cardiff. Suddenly, the prospect of ending that sixty-three-year wait for a clean sweep became a national talking point. The last game in the 2003 series was against England at Lansdowne Road and in the light of their enviable home record, success seemed eminently achievable.

Alas, the huge build up to the game merely served to heighten the impact of the fall that followed. Lawrence Dallaglio's third-minute try after the Ireland back row had failed to control the ball from Peter Stringer's put in, established the pattern of a miserable day for the home supporters and with Jonny Wilkinson at the top of his game, it was England who completed the Slam on the way to the biggest prize of all in the World Cup Final in Australia some seven months later.

Ironically, Ireland would be the first team to beat the world champions at Twickenham six months later when Girvan Dempsey's try at the end of a flowing movement secured the first of four consecutive victories over the 'Auld Enemy'. The consequence of Dempsey's score was a first Triple Crown success in twenty-two years and having made the breakthrough in the home of English rugby, they would repeat that achievement on no fewer than three occasions in the ensuing six years.

The bigger prize would prove considerably more elusive. After O'Driscoll's heroics in 2000, Paris would again unnerve visiting teams and on those occasions when French teams found themselves under pressure in Dublin, they still managed to compete abrasively. Typical was the experience at Croke Park in 2007 when, with just two minutes remaining, Ronan O'Gara kicked a penalty to turn a slender one-point advantage into a seemingly match-winning lead. That was until Paul O'Connell, in a rare lapse of concentration, dropped the restart and after working the ball across the width of the pitch, the visitors got in for the try which broke Irish hearts.

Hardship merely had the effect of steeling Ireland's resolve, and buoyed by the consistency of the Irish teams in the knockout stages of the Heineken Cup, Declan Kidney and his management team sensed that the gap between frustration and fulfilment had dwindled to almost nothing as the nations prepared for the 2009 staging of the Six Nations championship. This, the cognoscenti reckoned, represented the best chance in seventy years of tracking down the precious silverware and with France and England back in town, the optimism seemed well founded.

With another year to run on the GAA's agreement to rent out their pristine stadium, Croke Park provided the perfect backdrop for another collision with France – and this time the gods were smiling on the men in green. In the best rugby played in the all-too-short sojourn of the oval ball game on Jones Road, France made the perfect start courtesy of Imanol Harinoroquy's exquisitely executed try. That didn't figure in any of Kidney's pre-match calculations but in the manner of a team which had grown significantly over the previous year, Ireland did not depart from Plan A and helped by the visitors' indiscipline at the breakdown, they gradually got a foothold in a frenetic contest.

An adverse penalty count of 10–2 didn't endear the Welsh referee Nigel Owen to the French contingent but there were no expedient excuses available to explain their travail after a superb Irish move ended with Jamie Heaslip careering down the centre for the try which lit up the stadium. Gordon D'Arcy, on as a replacement for Paddy Wallace, heightened the Leinster influence by touching down shortly before the end, and the irrepressible Brian O'Driscoll traced a mazy line between Lionel Beauxis and Julien Malzieu to enhance his reputation as a finisher of the highest quality.

Judged even by the loftiest level of expectation, a 30–21 victory was an achievement to reassure in the context of the Grand Slam and O'Driscoll was again among the try scorers as the Irish team grew from an uncertain start to overwhelm Italy 38–9 in Rome. Beating the Italians on the road was one thing but dealing with the threat posed by England was a mission which challenged the character of management and players alike on another day of rich drama at Croke Park.

Two years earlier, Martin Corry's England team had earned the warm admiration of the locals by the manner in which they accepted a heavy defeat. Now, revenge was the raw incentive which drove them to the limits of their potential and were it not for another mountainous contribution by O'Driscoll, they might well have succeeded. The Irish captain, forsaking his natural flair to run the ball, first dropped a rare goal and then, following the withdrawal of England's blind-side flanker, James Haskell, the man with number thirteen on his shirt displayed all the attributes of a natural number seven by burrowing under a forest of bodies for a critical try that would be matched only by his contribution in Cardiff two weeks later.

Before the end, Delon Armitage's converted try reduced the gap to a single point, 14–13, but after what seemed an age the last blast of the referee's whistle sounded and some 82,000 spectators poured out onto the surrounding streets to celebrate a game which had embodied all the classical elements of one of the longest established rivalries in international rugby.

For once, O'Driscoll didn't get his name on the score sheet when the next phase of the championship programme took Ireland to Scotland. Murrayfield tends to yield up victory to visitors only grudgingly. This was no exception but Jamie Heaslip's try following a typical sniping run by Peter Stringer, complemented by seventeen points from the trusty right foot of Ronan O'Gara, eventually carried the Irishmen to a 22–15 success.

The pages of rugby history are illuminated with stories of how favourites came undone on that famous patch of green in downtown Cardiff and memories of previous disasters were all too prevalent as

O'Driscoll led his team onto the pitch for the last, critical assignment on the path to fulfilment. A first half of agonising intensity ended with Wales leading 6–0 and in that situation, Irish eyes looked instinctively to their captain to plot a way back. He was not found wanting, scattering friend and foe alike as he made it across the try line in the middle of a heaving mass of humanity to open Ireland's account early in the second half.

That was the critical moment of an enthralling afternoon and no less than another towering performance from the pack leader, Paul O'Connell, it encouraged the belief that victory could yet be Ireland's. And those fond hopes hardened into conviction when Tommy Bowe, on a flood tide of confidence, took a bouncing ball in full stride to race in under the posts for a 14–6 lead.

Flights of fancy on this scale are never to be entertained in Cardiff. Nothing if not abrasive, Wales hung in and helped by a couple of doubtful calls from the English referee, Wayne Barnes, they rallied so effectively that with little more than four minutes left in the game, a finely dropped goal from Stephen Jones put the home team back in the lead, 15–14.

Suddenly, the hand of history was again touching the shoulders of the men in green. For most of the earlier games, it was Leinster players who worked the magic for Ireland. Now it was the turn of Munster's hardened troops – David Wallace led the charge from a ruck, Peter Stringer fed Ronan O'Gara and the out-half was nerveless as he slotted the drop goal that would exorcise the ghastly memories of sixty-one years.

It was no thing of splendour but in the context of accelerating Ireland's rugby renaissance, the end product was priceless. With the game in its last minute, Paddy Wallace was pinged for fringing at a ruck just inside the Irish half and a nation held its breath as Stephen Jones, the Welsh out-half, addressed the ensuing penalty. Paul O'Connell, immense on the day, couldn't bear to watch after Jones had launched the kick which could have changed everything.

'I thought we had lost it – I feared it would go over,' recounted the

Munster lock. 'When he hit it, I knew it was on target and turned my back. I just saw Geordan (Murphy) getting excited when he realised the ball was falling short. Geordan caught it and the sense of relief was unbelievable. I looked up at the clock and saw it was in the red. It was game over – at last we had reached the Promised Land.'

The celebrations, joyous and raucous in equal measure, were of necessity short lived. Both Leinster and Munster had some unfinished business to attend to in the Heineken Cup and soon Brian O'Driscoll and Paul O'Connell, comrades in arms in Cardiff, were charting vastly different courses. As holders of the trophy, Munster faced a tricky quarter-final tie against Ospreys, a task which was duly accomplished with aplomb.

For Leinster, the challenge was a whole lot different. To reach the last four, they were required to bring down Harlequins, the English Premiership high fliers on their own patch at the Stoop where they had proved unbeatable for much of the season. In the event, the Irishmen prevailed against all the odds but only after a massive display of disciplined defence, best illustrated by the contributions of two of their overseas signings, Rocky Elsom and Felipe Contepomi.

As the name implied, Rocky was the force which turned Leinster's pack from a collection of talented individuals into a coterie of hardened winners. So successful was his Irish sojourn, that he returned to Australia a revitalised player, reclaiming his place in the national team before going on to captain them in their World Cup campaign. Leinster were similarly enriched, acquiring the wherewithal to enable them to indulge their riches behind the scrum and the balance of power in European rugby was about to shift.

Contepomi, signed in the most fortuitous circumstances after he was facilitated in his determination to finish his medical studies in Dublin, remained on board for a much longer period and, like Elsom, was a superb competitor in difficult surroundings. As the playmaker in chief, he would solve a persistent problem at number ten as well as bringing his kicking skills to bear in the most pressurised situations. That facet of the Argentine's makeup served Leinster well against Harlequins, kicking two penalties in the first half before standing tall in an attritional second period, to restrict the Londoners to a solitary score for an epic 6–5 victory.

The reward was a semi-final tie against Munster at Croke Park which, for a variety of reasons, is recalled as one of the great dramas of Irish and European rugby. For one thing, it attracted a mammoth crowd of 82,000 and played against the background of a long-established and occasionally acrimonious rivalry of the two provinces, it also captured the imagination of the public to the point where the biggest stadium in the country wasn't nearly sufficient to accommodate all those wishing to witness the head-on collision.

The stigma of Leinster's horror show at the same stage of the competition in 2006 was still raw enough to evoke dark thoughts of retribution among players and supporters alike. On that occasion, they were overpowered by the Munster pack. Now, with Elsom leading the charge, the roles were likely to be reversed and the local public couldn't wait for it to happen.

First up, tackles by Elsom and Contepomi on Ronan O'Gara defined Leinster's strategy within minutes of the start and from this statement of intent grew the conviction that the reigning European champions would, on this occasion, end up in the losers' dressing room. And that probability came more sharply into focus when in the wake of the loss of Contepomi with a knee injury, Isa Nacewa nailed Keith Earls close to the line and Elsom, on the opposite wing, stunned Ian Dowling with an equally ferocious tackle, taken directly from the Munster manual.

Gordon D'Arcy's thirty-first-minute try, at the end of a patient, skilful build up, heightened the sense of impending doom for Munster and from an interval deficit of 6–11, it would get even worse for the men in red. A subtle sway of the hips took Luke Fitzgerald inside Paul Warwick's tackle for the second try early in the second half and Leinster's conquest was total when Brian O'Driscoll, intercepting O'Gara's laboured pass to Paul

O'Connell, sprinted seventy yards to score under the posts and apply the gloss to an unforgettable day for Michael Cheika's squad.

Leinster supporters, chanting for the gates to be closed on rival fans seeking to depart early, merely served to emphasise the tension underpinning the fixture but victory on a 25–6 scoreline was comprehensive enough to forewarn Leicester, another of the enduring powers of European rugby, of choppy waters ahead as the scene was set for the final at Murrayfield on the fourth Saturday in May.

It was a pairing with a number of precedents and while Leicester held a slight edge overall, the Irish team could reflect that in the past they had gone to Welford Road and triumphed on a ground which had little respect for the reputation of visiting teams. Now the big prize would be won or lost in the Scottish capital and the English champions, prized from their feared fortress, could expect little support from Ireland's Celtic cousins.

The other factor Leinster had going for them was the presence of Leo Cullen and Shane Jennings in the pack. Cullen had emerged as a key man in the new-look team assembled by Cheika, taking over the captaincy after Brian O'Driscoll stepped down because of an overload of commitments.

Cullen, hard and competitive, had been signed by Leicester as the replacement for their legendary lock, Martin Johnson. Now, after a satisfactory stint in the England Premiership, he returned with Jennings to his alma mater, providing his Leinster teammates with an insider's knowledge of Leicester's game plans and the players who implemented them. Geordan Murphy was still playing well at full-back for the English champions but the more obvious challenge was to restrict the influence of big-game players such as Alesana Tuilagi, Dan Hipkiss and up front, Ben Kay and Tom Croft.

As it happened, Murphy departed early with a hip injury but in the manner of their climb to a position of pre-eminence in Europe, Leicester were ruthless as they sought to impose themselves on an ultra-physical battle for forward supremacy. In other times, Leinster might have wilted, but not now. Meeting power with power, they took on the opposition in some heavyweight hits that posed urgent questions of character. And having made their point in this war of wills, they then sought to bring their perceived advantage in creativity into play.

Drop goals from Brian O'Driscoll and Jonathan Sexton, supplemented by Sexton's penalty, had the Irishmen 9–3 in front heading towards half-time, but then came the feared riposte. With Leinster prop Stanley Wright in the sin bin, Julian Dupuy landed a thirty-fourth-minute penalty to be followed almost immediately by the first try of the game. A cleverly constructed build up enabled Leicester to exploit their numerical advantage and to the delight of the English supporters, flanker Ben Woods got over for the try which established them in a 13–9 interval lead.

For the thousands of supporters who had travelled to Edinburgh in support of Leinster's cause, that was a shock to the system. Having succeeded in the first segment of their survival plan by containing Leicester's early surge, the concession of a seven-pointer at a stage when the referee's half-time whistle was expected at any moment, was a significant setback for the Irish team. The consensus was that they needed to put their name on the next score to stay competitive and with Wright by now back on the pitch, they delivered within five minutes of the restart.

Fittingly, it was a try conceived of rare vision and finished in a manner which bespoke the philosophy of Leinster rugby. After Rocky Elsom, his bloodied face reflecting the physicality of it all, won a line-out cleanly, the ball was zealously protected in phase after phase before sufficient space was contrived to allow them to inject an added element of pace in the Leicester 22. Then, with Shane Jennings in support, Jamie Heaslip slipped between Ben Kay and Craig Newby for the score which effectively marked the official declaration of a new epoch in European rugby on a 19–16 scoreline.

Twice in the ensuing three years, the squad once derided as antiquated in the changed and changing world of professional rugby, would scale the summit of the game in the northern hemisphere. And a golden generation of players, identified by Brian O'Driscoll's ageless skills, at last enjoyed the brand of popularity which was once the exclusive preserve of their arch rivals from down south.

– Chapter 30 –

Henry the Ninth

Hurling – All-Ireland Final, September 2012

Ever since he celebrated his arrival in Croke Park on hurling's biggest day of the year with a convincing performance for Kilkenny in the All-Ireland minor championship final against Cork on the first Sunday in September 1971, Brian Cody was destined to stand tall in a county of hurling giants.

For all Cody's brilliance, the Leinster champions couldn't prevent Cork returning home with the Irish Press Cup that evening. But when he captained Kilkenny to victory in the return meeting of the counties twelve months later, he was on the way to establishing himself as, perhaps, the most prolific of all winners in a region renowned for its sporting warriors.

He would go on to secure four All-Ireland senior championship medals in the pivotal position of centre half-back, captaining the team in the 1983 success over arch rivals Cork. Yet his biggest contribution by far to the history of hurling was his unique record in coaching and managing teams garbed in the famous black and amber stripes.

In a managerial career extending over fifteen years, he lost just seven of the sixty championship games in which he took charge of the team up to 2012, guiding them to nine All-Ireland titles in twelve years at the start of the new millennium, statistics which are likely to be recalled in awe as long as the ancient game continues to flourish.

So it was that when Kilkenny embarked on their defence of the

Leinster and All-Ireland titles in 2012, few were prepared to back against the Liam McCarthy Cup leaving Noreside any time soon. True, the Cats had come up short for a record five-in-a-row success in 2010 when Tipperary, dismissed as relative lightweights by the sporting press, produced the biggest shock of the millennium by pulling the rug of comfort from beneath the feet of the champions.

That huge upset was down to the champions' inability to deal with the threat of Lar Corbett on a day when the ace in Tipp's pack made great defenders look leaden footed in plundering a hat trick of goals. In the manner of their heritage, Kilkenny made no excuses but deep down, the winners knew they had been fortunate to see the back of Henry Shefflin, the scourge of so many of their teams in previous years, just thirteen minutes into the game.

With the great man's damaged knee long since repaired, it was a vastly different team that faced Tipp in a repeat of that final in 2011. Now, Shefflin was back and thriving and by the time referee Brian Gavin of Offaly spread his arms wide to indicate the end of the rematch, the prince of Kilkenny hurling had joined two more of the game's immortals, Christy Ring and John Doyle, among the elite players to win eight All-Ireland medals.

The effect was to establish Brian Cody and his star pupil at a new level in hurling folklore. Twelve months on from one of the bleakest days of his career, it was once more business as usual for the manager. And Shefflin, reborn, performed with a panache which gave the lie to the theory that his ageing limbs were no longer capable of sustaining the pressures of championship competition.

For Kilkenny, the critics told us, that was no more than the hand of destiny at work. After the indignity of losing their National League title to Dublin earlier in the year, they were back at the summit once more and with Cody and Shefflin still in situ, all was set fair for another tilt at history in the summer of 2012.

Over in the west of the country, it was a different scenario for Galway manager Anthony Cunningham. Not for him the luxury of being spoiled for choice and having to explain the rationale of good players being left out of his starting line up. Over the years, the county had produced some marvellous hurlers but seldom in sufficient numbers to loosen the stronghold of Leinster and Munster on the major prizes in the game.

The exception was in the glory-glory days of the 1980s when gifted athletes of the quality of Sylvie Linnane, Conor Hayes and, not least, Joe Connolly, stayed around long enough to create a whole new power base for hurling. But it was now almost twenty-five years since the last of their three All-Ireland titles and their decline was so precipitous that the GAA policymakers, in their wisdom, saw fit to redraft the structure of the provincial championships to enable them to play in the Leinster competition.

That bold decision stood tradition on its head but on the premise that Galway were blatantly disadvantaged by their lack of competitive hurling when taking on the champions of Leinster or Munster in the All-Ireland series, it was decreed that in this instance, change could only be for the better. Brian Cody concurred with that logic and he knew for certain that Galway were no longer the Cinderella men of the game after the final of the 2012 Leinster championship.

On two previous occasions in Cody's time in charge of the Cats, they had been caught out by the finesse as much as the fire of the western battalion. Haunted by those memories, the pragmatic schoolteacher cannot have been unaware of the threat posed by the outsiders as they made ready for their ritual trip to Croke Park to defend their Leinster title. And yet, for all his apprehension, he can only have been astonished as the plot of the game unfolded.

Galway's opening flourish was more hurricane than hurling, a seismic force which took the champions off their feet and magnified the self doubts of having to disguise the absence of stalwarts such as J. J. Delaney,

Michael Fennelly and Michael Rice. Spurred by Joe Canning's early goal, Galway would prove unstoppable, matching the champions in raw power as well as outsmarting them when it came to economy in the top third of the pitch. For all the genius of Henry Shefflin, Kilkenny were undeniably second best and as he prepared to take his team on a scenic tour to the final, Cody was acutely aware of the pitfalls along the way.

'What we have seen today was a practical demonstration of the hidden skills of a fine Galway team,' he mused in a shell-shocked dressing room. 'None of us was unaware of the threat they posed but we were still found wanting when they came at us in that opening quarter. Now we must take those lessons on board if we are lucky enough to get a second chance against them in this championship.'

Leaving Dublin that evening without the trophy was a sad if rare experience for Kilkenny supporters who may have regarded it as little more than a joyful jaunt to the capital. But for Cody it served to remind that if they were to keep their All-Ireland title, they would need to have all their big guns firing on the first Sunday in September – that is, if they made it into the final.

In the event, they arrived there without undue fuss. If the cloak of invincibility had been torn from the shoulders of the men regarded as unbeatable by so many for so long, Anthony Cunningham now sensed that Kilkenny's wounded pride would have the effect of making them still more focused on the day it really mattered. And that raised the stakes even higher as both teams made ready for the return match.

The era when Kilkenny relied exclusively on pace complementing exquisite stick work to hustle the opposition into submission had long since gone. Now there was a hard physical edge to their game which rankled with many. And Cody, seldom less than diplomatic in his dealings with the media, was stung by the criticism.

'To suggest that we have to stray outside the rules to stay competitive is clearly dishonest,' he told one newsman. 'Sport is constantly evolving and in that, hurling is no different than any other field game. But to imply that the priorities of our game have changed to the point where we set out to win matches at any cost, is nonsense.'

The effect of that riposte was to heighten the hype in the countdown to one of the most eagerly awaited finals of modern years. For all their relative inexperience on big match days, Galway were unlikely to be found wanting if it descended into a test of physicality but Cunningham was still insisting that the evidence of the Leinster final was conclusive enough to indicate that they were capable of winning, irrespective of how Kilkenny set out their stall.

Yet, in his heart of hearts, he knew that to confirm their superiority they would be required to lift their performance still higher. For one thing, Delaney and Michael Fennelly were now sufficiently recovered from injury to return for the Cats' defence of the title. And chastened by the lessons of the Leinster final, Kilkenny were certain to hit the ground running in the hope of avoiding the early mistakes which proved so expensive in the July meeting of the teams.

Just as was the case in the Leinster game, the names of the rival sharpshooters, Joe Canning and Henry Shefflin, dominated the discussions as a crowd of 81,932 descended on the stadium. Shefflin, seeking that ninth winners' medal which would enable him to move clear of Ring and Doyle as hurling's most successful player, had by now distanced himself from the injury worries which clouded his career in the recent past.

Canning, by contrast, had no fitness problems. Driven by the prospect of sharing in a success which had motivated him from day one of his inter-county career, he was central to the Tribesmen's strategy of undoing Kilkenny's vastly experienced defence. Thriving on the novelty of playing in his first ever Leinster final, he had led the early charge which saw the underdogs open up a huge gap within twenty minutes of the start. And joyously for the hordes sporting maroon and white colours, he proved that lightning could indeed, strike twice.

In spite of what happened in the Leinster final, or perhaps because of it, Kilkenny's defence was all over the place in the first quarter, with the opposing forwards rampaging through wide-open spaces in front of David Herity's goal. And Canning, revelling in the chaos, swept in for the opening goal after just ten minutes. That was food and drink for one of the game's great predators and instantly Kilkenny sensed that their title defence was in dire trouble.

At that point, Iarla Tannian and Andy Smith were winning nearly all the breaking ball in midfield, Niall Burke was extracting more from his duel with Brian Hogan than he could have expected at centre half-forward and with Delaney unable or unwilling to travel outfield to curtail the wandering Canning, the champions were in real trouble. But surrender was never a word in Brian Cody's vocabulary and out of the debris of their early collapse, they fashioned a recovery of remarkable dimensions. After spurning at least two likely chances, Shefflin eventually got his radar in working order and for all their problems, Kilkenny were only five points adrift, 1-9 to 0-7 at the break.

That was nine points fewer than the lead Galway enjoyed at the halfway stage in the Leinster final and even then, it seemed, the fear of a backlash was beginning to dominate Galway's mindset. Whatever the reason, the plot was starkly reversed in the second half when with the Connacht men enchained by a fixation to protect their advantage rather than seek to extend it, Kilkenny were allowed to recover to a point where they were now dominant throughout the field.

Niall Burke's goal in the sixtieth minute, the product of good fortune as much as skill, arrested Galway's slide temporarily. Then, after restoring his team's slender advantage, the ubiquitous Shefflin was cast centre-stage once more. With just three minutes remaining and the scores level, Kilkenny were awarded a penalty after Eoin Larkin had been brought down by goalkeeper James Skehill, and the crowd held its breath as the Kilkenny talisman sauntered across to lift and shoot.

In normal circumstances, the best striker in the game might have gone for broke and backed himself to crash the ball past the three defenders standing on the line. But this was different. First, he consulted with referee Barry Kelly about the time remaining and then glanced across at the Kilkenny mentors on the sideline for an indication of what they wished him to do. No response was forthcoming and having plumped for the certainty of a point rather than the gamble of going for goal, he risked the possibility of being accused of making the wrong decision if Galway got lucky in the dying seconds of a mighty battle.

The only consolation for Shefflin when Canning equalised from a controversial free with the last stroke of the game was that it might have been worse for him. Cody, going where he had never gone before, remonstrated unwisely with Anthony Cunningham about the validity of that late free but the dice had been rolled and for the first time in fifty-nine years, the All-Ireland senior hurling championship final was headed for a replay.

An additional three weeks' work at the end of their most demanding programme in years represented possibly the severest test Cody had faced since taking command some thirteen years earlier. In two fiercely contested games against the western team, Kilkenny had failed to win. Conversely, Galway's self-belief had grown enormously in the course of those matches, even if it required that disputed refereeing decision to facilitate Canning's late equaliser.

Unlike other, more mature teams who had sought in vain to invade Kilkenny's domain, they devised a game plan which enabled them to make even a side of the champions' quality look less than unbeatable. Hooking and blocking in a manner taken directly from the Kilkenny manual, and willing to look them in the eye in any situation, they refused to concede in the psychological warfare which preceded the replay. Come hell or high water, they were ready to deliver in the crusade to take the Liam McCarthy Cup across the Shannon.

Back in Nowlan Park where Cody was seeking to induce one last supreme effort from his ageing players, the emphasis was different. For all his initial disappointment concerning Barry Kelly's decision to award Galway that crucial late free in the drawn game, the manager felt that Kilkenny had been the authors of their own misfortune on a day when they simply didn't perform to pedigree. And he resolved to change his starting line up in the hope of refreshing tired limbs.

Midfield in particular had been a source of recurring problems. Michael Rice's absence through injury was proving more expensive than originally anticipated and with the manager committed to replacing him yet again, the announcement of his team selection was awaited with more interest than usual. Michael Fennelly, tall and elegant, would of course retain the number eight shirt but having watched his partner Richie Hogan struggle for a foothold in the game, Cody now decided to utilise him much closer to goal.

Instead, he would assign the challenge of disguising the loss of Rice to Cillian Buckley, a highly rated young player who was still only at the periphery of big-time hurling when they embarked on the road to Croke Park some three months earlier. As it transpired, Buckley would fill a key role in the drama which followed in the pivotal battle for midfield control, complementing Fennelly so effectively that the coach must have wondered how he managed to leave him out of the drawn game.

Yet the biggest talking point of all was his gamble in naming Walter Walsh for his championship debut up front. Walsh, not long out of minor ranks, was chosen at number thirteen to play alongside Richie Hogan and Richie Power in the full-forward line and nobody, not even Cody, could be certain if he would convert his raw, natural skills into the kind of per-formance needed to get the better of Johnny Coen, a key defender for Galway in the first game.

Central to all, of course, was Shefflin's ability to dredge up another inspired display from a frame which had shipped a lot of damage since his first senior appearance in 1999. Two cruciate injuries in quick succession had earlier threatened to truncate one of the finest careers in history at a stage when Kilkenny were still in full flood. Now, at thirty-three, he was ready to go to the well once more, hoping that on this occasion, he would enjoy better support from his front line colleagues than was the case first time out.

Joe Canning, Galway's leader, would probably have empathised with Shefflin in those feelings. Here, too, was a man who had often carried his team through turbulent waters to make port safely. The question awaiting answer now was whether he could cajole a more sustained performance from an attack which, apart from Niall Burke, got little joy out of Kilkenny's embattled defence after the champions had regained their composure in the inconclusive meeting of the teams.

Within minutes of referee James McGrath throwing in the ball, the pride of Portumna had put down a marker, wheeling away from Tommy Walsh before drawing the free which took the blank look off the scoreboard. That was what Galway fans had come to witness, but if the roar which greeted that score was impressive, it was as nothing compared to the volume of noise in the stadium after David Burke struck twice in as many minutes to send them into ecstasy.

The first of his goals in the fifteenth minute followed a long delivery from Iarla Tannian with Burke making the vital contact which took the ball past goalkeeper David Herity into the net. For a man who had toiled without much reward in the original game, that was more than he or those cheering him could have hoped for and then, joyously, it got even better. Damien Hayes, racing through a startled defence, spotted Burke in splendid isolation in front of goal and the hapless Herity was soon bending his back once more to retrieve the ball from his net.

Within seconds of the first of those goals, T. J. Reid had hit back with a point for Kilkenny but the reaction to Burke's second score was even more significant. Galway's supporters had scarcely settled back in their seats when Power pounced on the rebound after goalkeeper James Skehill had done well to block a powerful shot from Eoin Larkin, and the champions were recharged instantly by the sight of the sliothar in the netting. Skehill, who took a damaged shoulder into the game, was replaced by Fergal Flannery by the time the teams returned for the second half but at that stage, the challengers were already in trouble after Kilkenny's recovery had enabled them to lead by four points.

Kilkenny players would later recall the passion of Cody's half-time message before pushing them out through the door of the dressing room and the manner of the response left no one in any doubt that the old maestro's words had been taken on board. Here indeed was a team intent, it seemed, on exacting retribution for the challengers' defiance in the two earlier meetings of the counties. Galway's refusal to bend the knee had pushed the champions to the limit of their potential and now, with the tide at last beginning to turn, they hankered for the chance to put their supremacy beyond all reasonable doubt.

In this pursuit, they were ultimately successful – but not before cruel luck and a couple of serious errors of judgement had cursed Galway's challenge yet again. Cyril Donnellan, embroiled in a big physical duel with Kilkenny full-back J. J. Delaney, was denied a crucial goal by the referee's refusal to play an advantage shortly after the restart and then Canning was deprived of what would have been an equalising goal in the forty-eighth minute, when his shot struck a post.

In that moment, Anthony Cunningham possibly sensed the worst and barely sixty seconds later, apprehension may have hardened into fatalism in the western camp when, in a moment he is likely to regret for a long time, Donnellan took out his frustration on Delaney and was dismissed by the referee on the advice of a linesman. Delaney retired for temporary repairs and on came the veteran Noel Hickey for the chance of winning a ninth championship medal.

Whatever chance Galway had of wresting back the initiative with fifteen players, there was now little or no light on the horizon. Canning was by this stage playing closer to his own posts than those at the other end of the pitch and with Brian Hogan ensuring no repetition of David Burke's heroics in the first quarter, the traffic was now nearly all one-way. To the obvious delight of the Kilkenny management team, young Walter Walsh was in for a crucial goal in the fifty-eighth minute. Colin Fennelly, a replacement, added another three-pointer soon afterwards and while Jonathan Glynn got one back for Galway before the end, it merely served to put a more respectable look on a final scoreline of 3-22 to 3-11 in favour of the champions.

Down on the sideline, there was little of the rancour which blighted the drawn game. Cunningham wasted no time in walking across to Cody to concede the third and quite the most important of three Titanic meetings of the counties. And the glistening silverware, robed yet again in black and gold, was on its way home for more days and nights of high revelry on Noreside.

It was the big man's ninth All-Ireland triumph in thirteen years in charge of the team and looking across at Henry Shefflin, he said, 'That man has played in every one of the sixty-two championship matches in which I've been privileged to coach the team and I couldn't have asked for a better or more honest hurler to inspire the players around him.' From one serial winner to another, it was the perfect compliment at the end of a competition which enriched the lives of those fortunate enough to have borne witness.